BG

André Kirchner

Stadtrand Berlin
Berlin: The City's Edge
1993/94

Herausgegeben von Thomas Köhler und Ulrich Domröse
Edited by Thomas Köhler and Ulrich Domröse

Hartmann books

André Kirchner: Stadtrand Berlin
Thomas Köhler

André Kirchner und die Berlinische Galerie verbindet eine lange gemeinsame Geschichte. Bereits im Jahr 1989 erwarb Janos Frecot, der damalige Leiter der Fotografischen Sammlung des Museums, mit *Rückbauten* eine umfassende Werkgruppe. Das Interesse am Werk des Künstlers war auch in den folgenden Jahren groß und so konnte schließlich im Jahr 1994 die Sammlung um die Werkgruppe *Stadtrand Berlin* erweitert werden. André Kirchners Fotografien stehen in der Tradition der Stadt- und Architekturfotografie. Die fotografischen Arbeiten sind für ihn Dokument, ohne dokumentarisch zu sein. Im Jahr 1981 nach Berlin übergesiedelt, war die Stadt für den Autodidakten immer auch Material und Ausgangspunkt für seine Werkgruppen, die über einen längeren Zeitraum hinweg von ihm realisiert werden. Er erlebte die Stadt noch in geteiltem Zustand und schließlich den allmählichen Übergang zweier nach unterschiedlichen urbanistischen Prinzipien in den Nachkriegsjahren wiederaufgebauten Stadtteilen hin zu einer als »digital« postulierten Metropole des Informationszeitalters.

In diesem Jahr jährt sich der Mauerfall zum 30. Mal. Gedenkveranstaltungen zu diesem Thema sind häufig mit Pathosformeln überfrachtet, strotzen vor löblichen Bekenntnissen und von zur Schau getragenem Geschichtsbewusstsein. Als Berlinische Galerie fühlen wir uns besonders der Kunstgeschichte verpflichtet: André Kirchners 60-teilige, in den Jahren 1993/94 entstandene Werkserie *Stadtrand Berlin* wird erstmalig in der Berlinischen Galerie gezeigt. Bei Entstehung der Arbeit war bereits einige Zeit seit der Wiedervereinigung vergangen. Spuren der Teilung waren jedoch allenthalben sichtbar. Ausgehend vom Grenzkontrollpunkt Drewitz hat Kirchner einen Zustand der Transition fotografiert. Er zeigt auf geradezu klinisch anmutende Weise ländliche und städtische Situationen, die die Überbleibsel der befestigten Grenzanlagen wie skulpturale Elemente eines Land-Art-Projektes erscheinen lassen. Die Präsentation in der Berlinischen Galerie zeigt alle 60 Fotografien der Serie, umlaufend, einem Fries gleich, an den Wänden des Ausstellungsraumes. Die Arbeit erhält so den Charakter einer Installation und evoziert bei den Betrachter*innen den Eindruck eines Spaziergangs entlang der ehemaligen Grenzbefestigungen.

Herzlich danke ich André Kirchner, der sich bei der Konzeption der Ausstellung gewinnbringend eingebracht hat. Wir sind glücklich, sein Werk in der Sammlung des Museums so umfassend repräsentiert zu sehen.

Ulrich Domröse, dem Leiter der fotografischen Sammlung, ist es zu danken, dass die von seinem Vorgänger erworbenen Werke um *Stadtrand Berlin* erweitert werden konnten. Sein kontinuierliches Interesse am Künstler war schließlich die Grundlage für die Präsentation der Werkgruppe zum Jahrestag des Mauerfalls.

Bei der Vorbereitung der Ausstellung wurde er von Hanna Vogel, der wissenschaftlichen Volontärin der Fotografischen Sammlung, unterstützt, die den Prozess kompetent begleitet hat.

Anja Witte hat für eine exzellente Qualität der Scans für den Ausstellungskatalog gesorgt, die wiederum von der Grafikerin Alexandra Zöller in ein überzeugendes gestalterisches Konzept integriert wurden.

Da Museen in der Regel knapp bei Kasse sind, bedarf es für die Realisierung von Projekten häufig externer Hilfe. Einer der Helfer war in diesem Fall Robert Jarmatz, Geschäftsführer der Firma Pixel Grain, der großzügig die Finanzierung der grafischen Gestaltung des Katalogs übernommen hat.

Mein allergrößter Dank gilt jedoch Waldtraut Braun, einer dem Museum schon lange verbundenen Freundin und Förderin. Nur dank ihrer Unterstützung konnte die vorliegende Publikation überhaupt umgesetzt werden. Es freut mich persönlich sehr, dass so jenseits der großen Ausstellungskataloge ein kleines, feines Druckerzeugnis zu einem wichtigen Konvolut der Sammlung vorgelegt werden kann.

André Kirchner: The City's Edge
Thomas Köhler

André Kirchner and the Berlinische Galerie go back a long way together. In 1989 Janos Frecot, who was then curator of the museum's Photography Collection, purchased *Rückbauten*, a major series of "unbuilt" street corners. Interest in the artist's work remained considerable in the following years, and in 1994 the Collection also acquired the cycle *Stadtrand Berlin* (The City's Edge). André Kirchner's pictures reflect a tradition of urban and architectural photography. He sees his work as documenting without adopting a documentary style. In 1981 Berlin became not only his home but also a source of material and a springboard for several series implemented by the autodidact over lengthy periods. He witnessed the city in its divided state and caught up in gradual transition, as neighborhoods reconstructed in the postwar years pursued separate paths based on divergent principles of urban design, and as the metropolis began to define itself as a "digital" hub in the information era.
This year marks the thirtieth anniversary of the fall of the Berlin Wall. Commemoration events are often highly charged with pathos, oozing laudable declarations and parading historical consciousness. At the Berlinische Galerie our duty is primarily to the history of art: for André Kirchner's sixty-part series *Stadtrand Berlin*, taken in 1993–94, this will be a house début. When he was producing the cycle, some time had already elapsed since German unification, but the traces of division were visible all around. Beginning at the checkpoint in Drewitz, Kirchner captured a state of transition. With a seemingly clinical eye, he depicts rural and urban scenes where the vestiges of fortified frontier installations resemble sculptural features in a display of Land Art. The presentation at the Berlinische Galerie shows all sixty photographs in the series as a running progression, like a frieze, around the walls of the exhibition space. Consequently the series acquires the character of an installation, conveying the impression to visitors that they are walking along the former border strip.

I warmly thank André Kirchner for the fertile interest he took in the conceptual planning for this exhibition. We count ourselves fortunate that his work is so broadly represented in the museum's holdings. Ulrich Domröse, the head of our Photography Collection, takes credit for adding *Stadtrand Berlin* to the works acquired by his predecessor. His consistent interest in the artist ultimately forged the basis for presenting the series during the anniversary of the fall of the Wall.

In preparing for this exhibition, he was assisted by Hanna Vogel, the trainee curator in the Photography Collection, who competently facilitated the process.
Anja Witte took responsibility for the excellent quality of the scans used in the exhibition catalogue, integrated by graphic artist Alexandra Zöller into this compelling design.
As museums are usually short of cash, we often need help from outside to carry out our projects. On this occasion, one of our saviors was Robert Jarmatz, managing director of Pixel Grain, who generously assumed the costs of graphic design for the catalogue.
My biggest debt of thanks, however, goes to Waldtraut Braun, who has long been a friend and benefactor to this museum. Without her support this publication could not have happened.
Personally I am delighted that, alongside our big exhibition catalogues, we are able to present this small, exquisite testimony in print to an important aspect of our collection.

André Kirchner

Stadtrand Berlin
Berlin: The City's Edge
1993/94

01

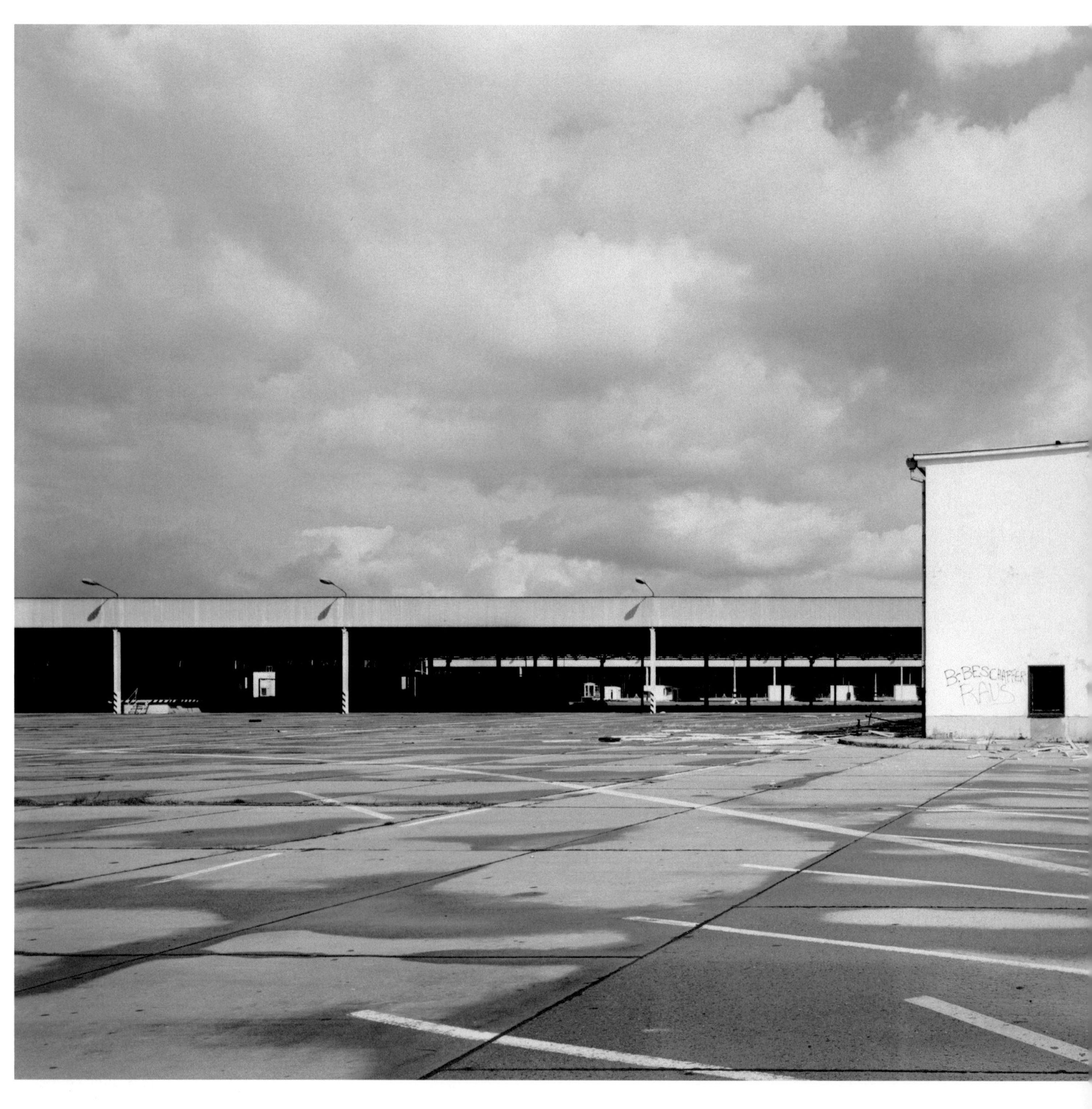

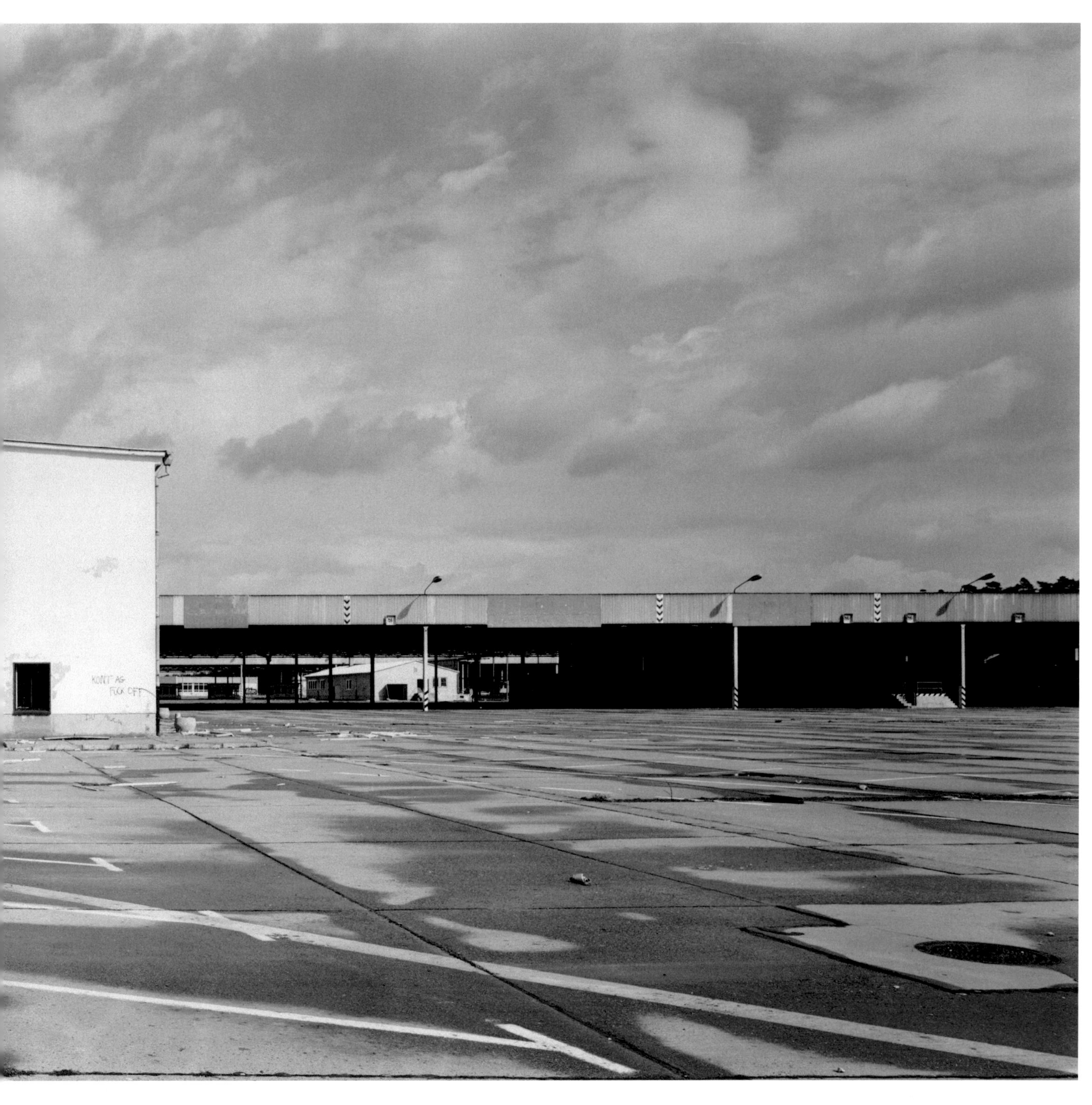
FUCK OFF

02

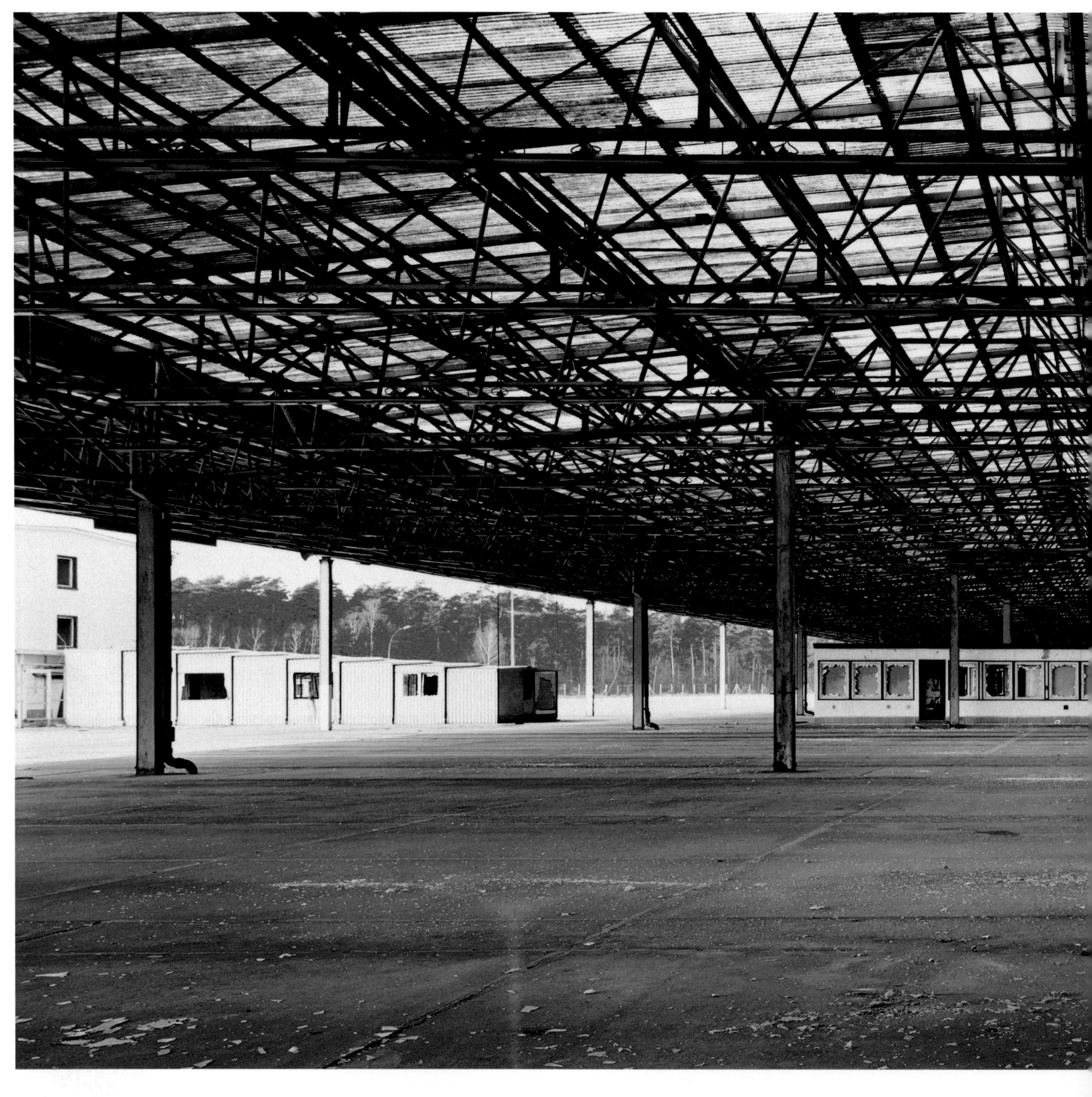

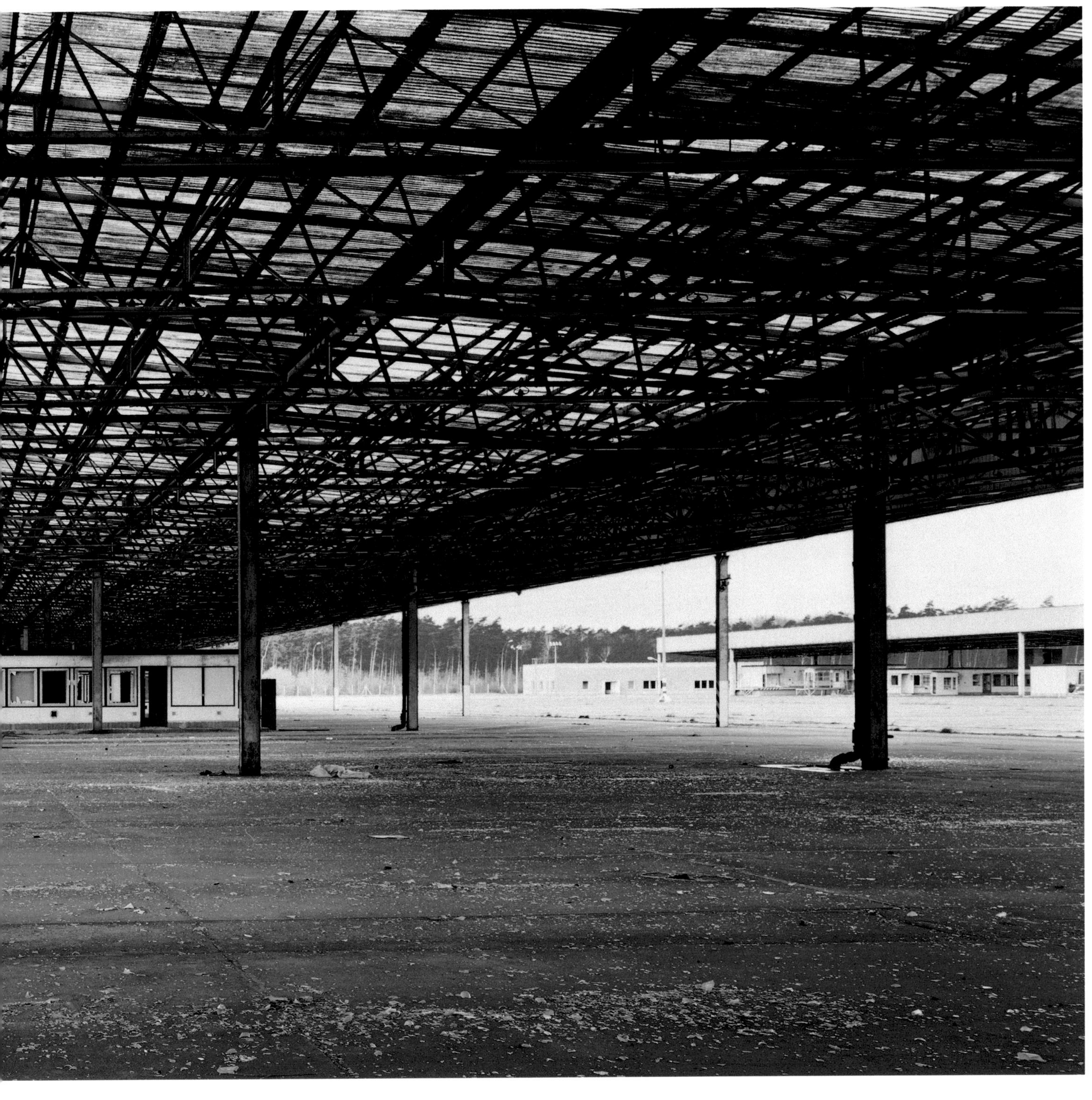

03

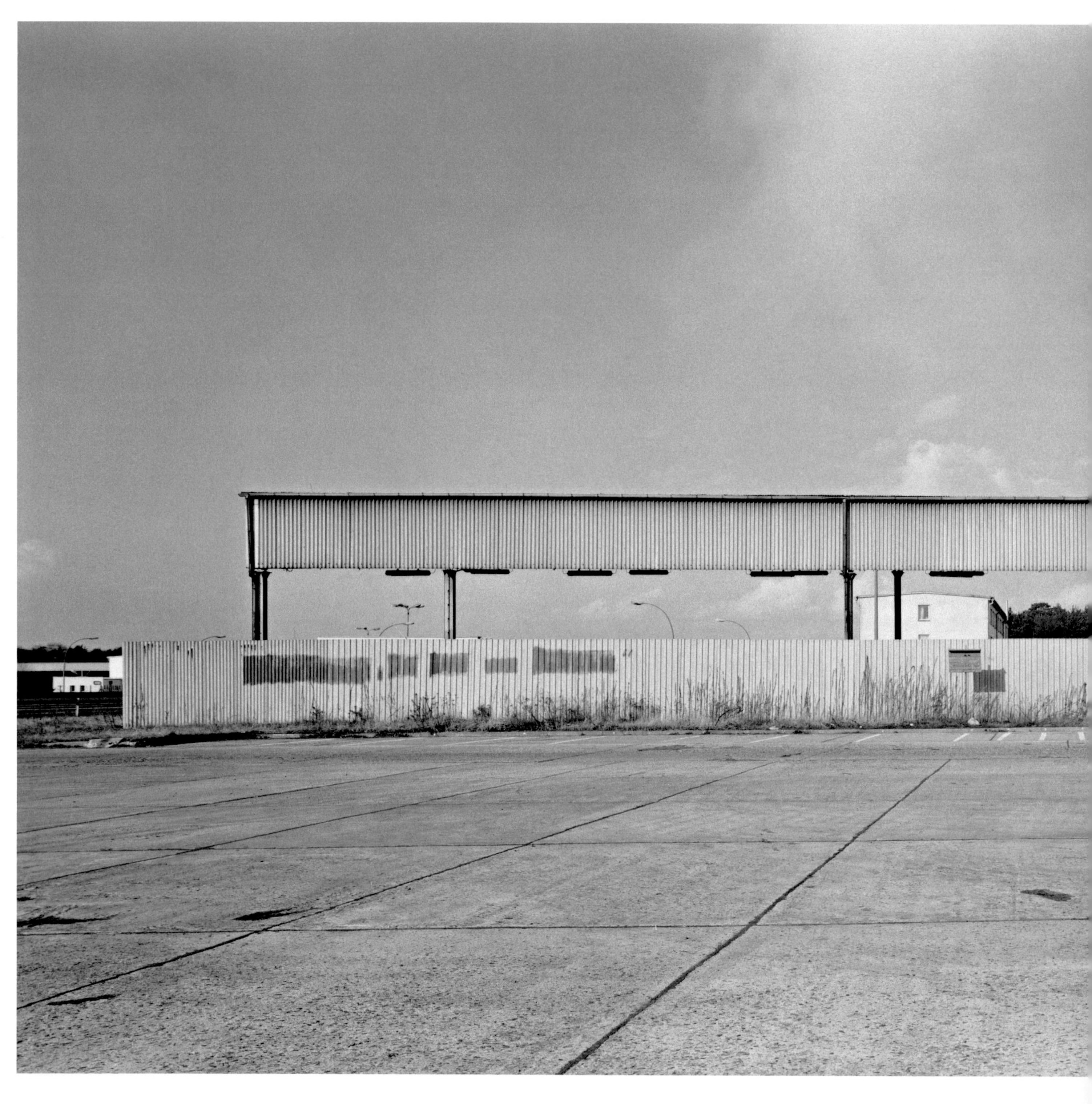

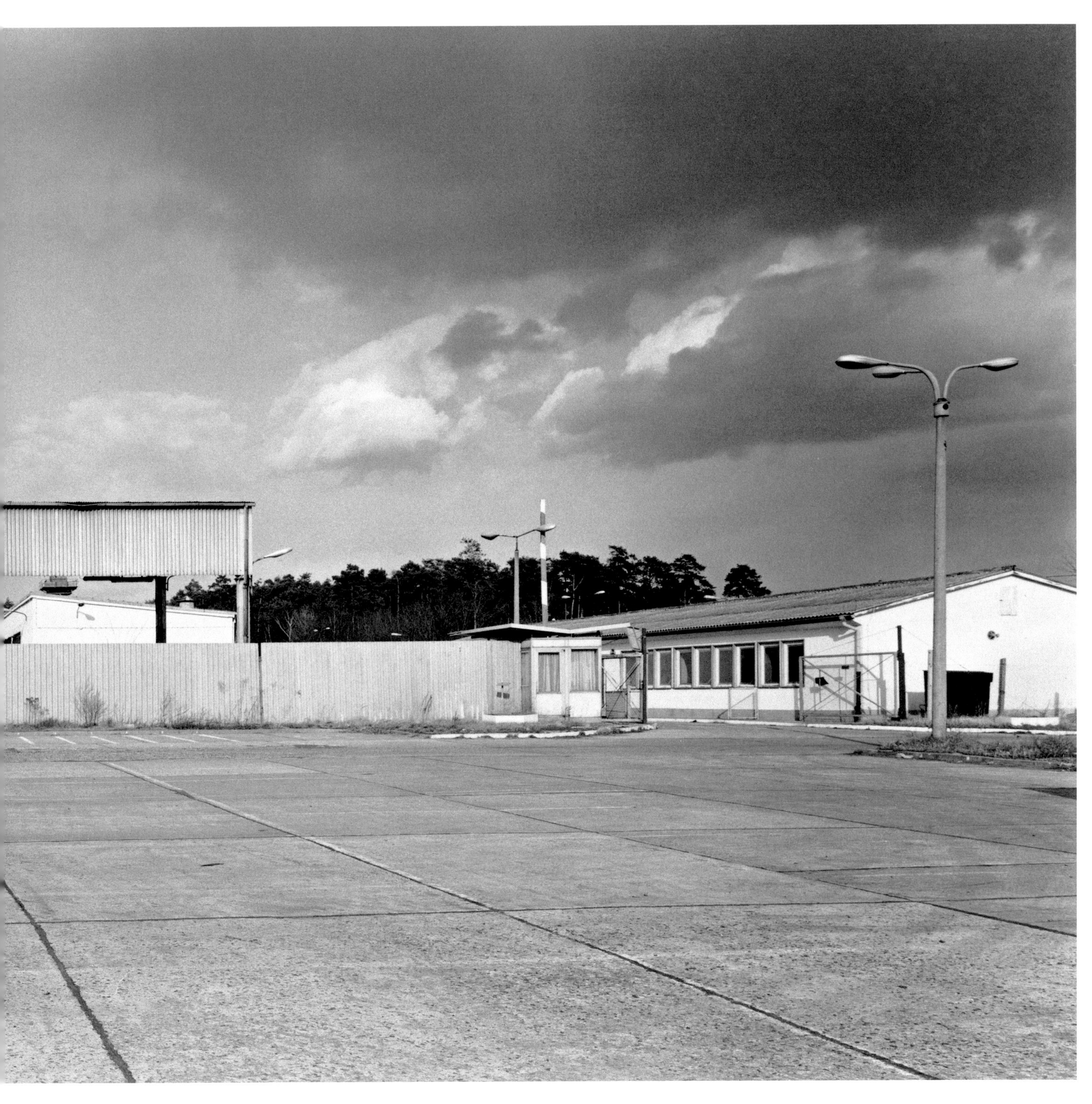

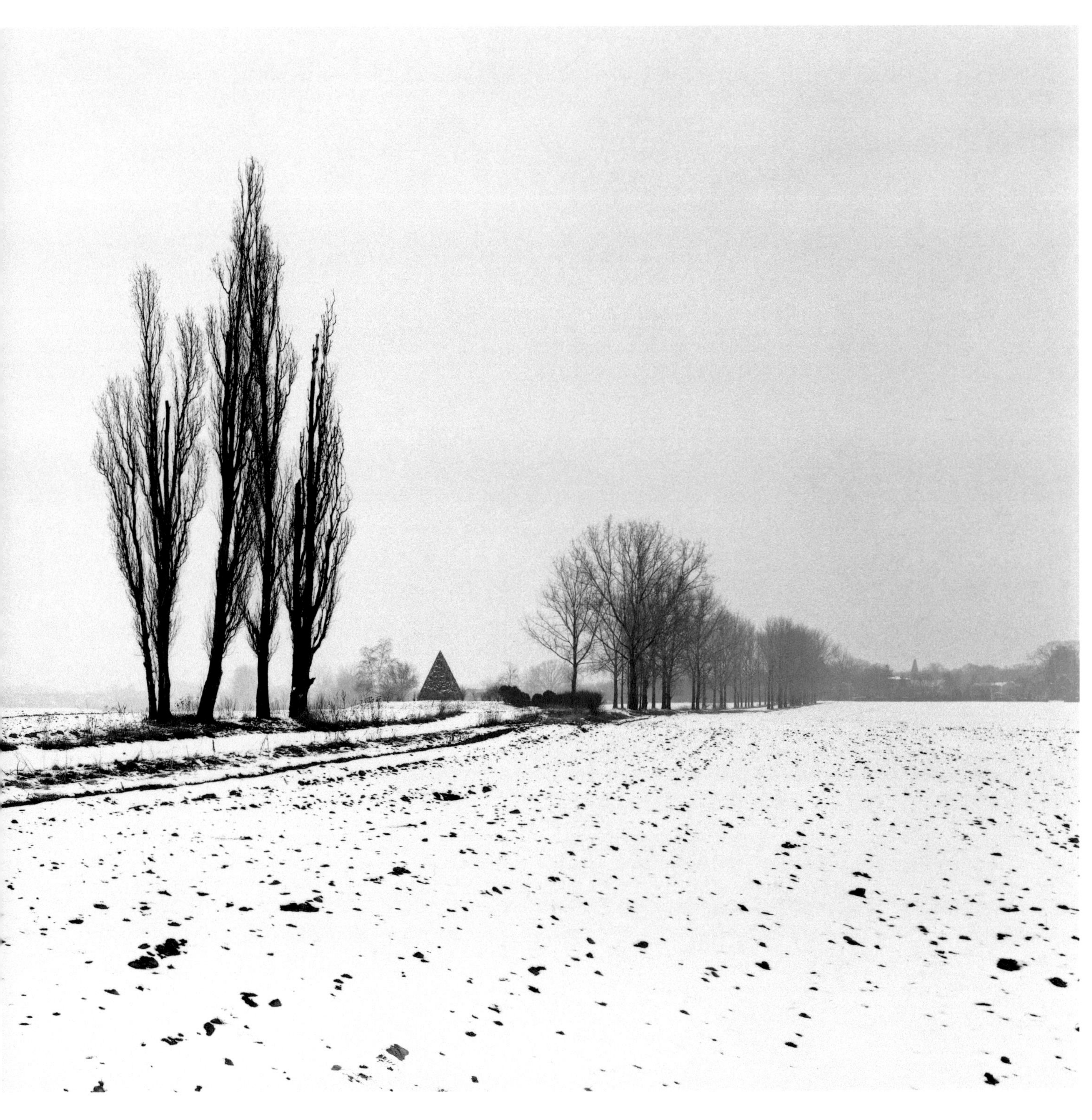

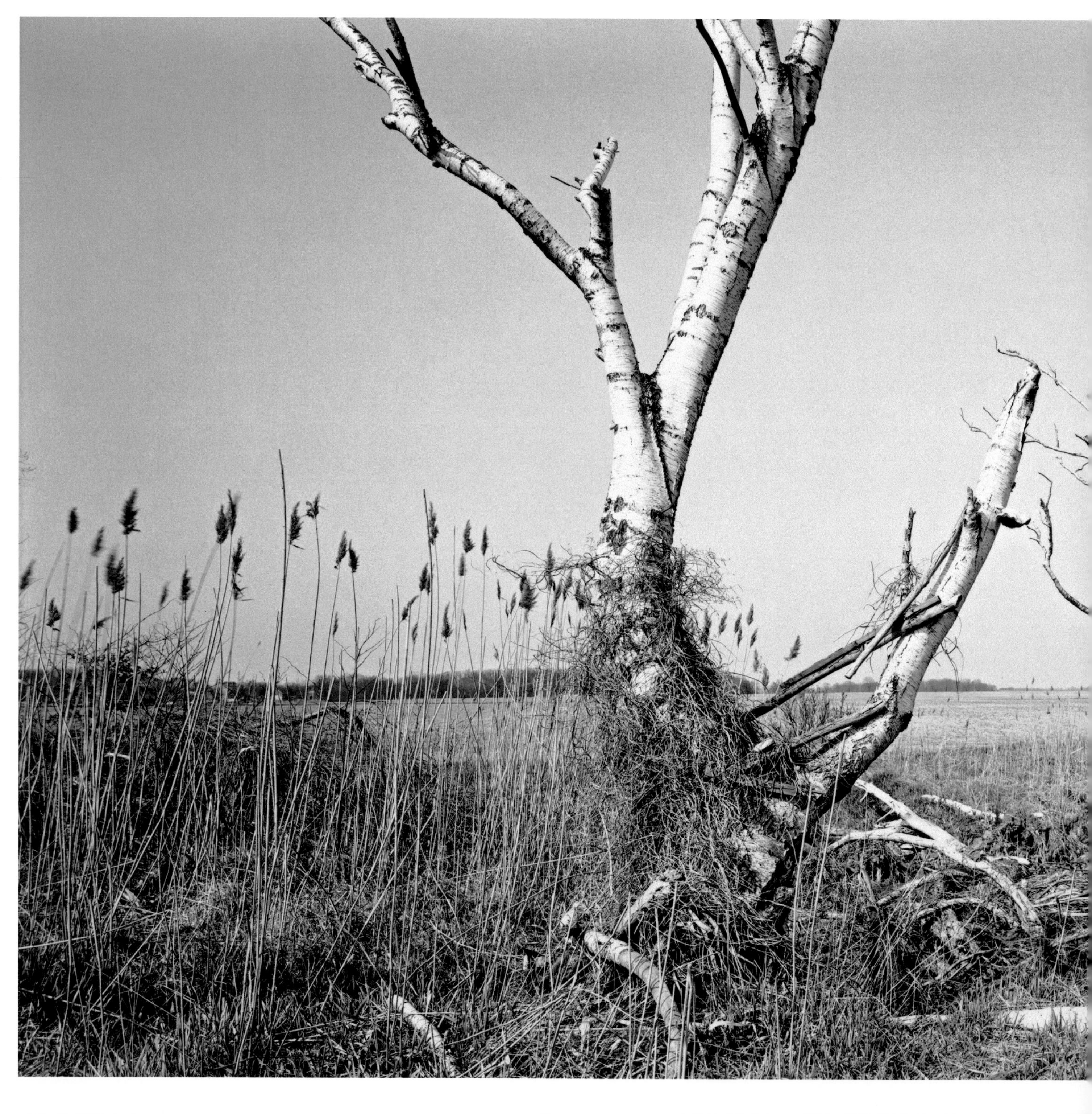

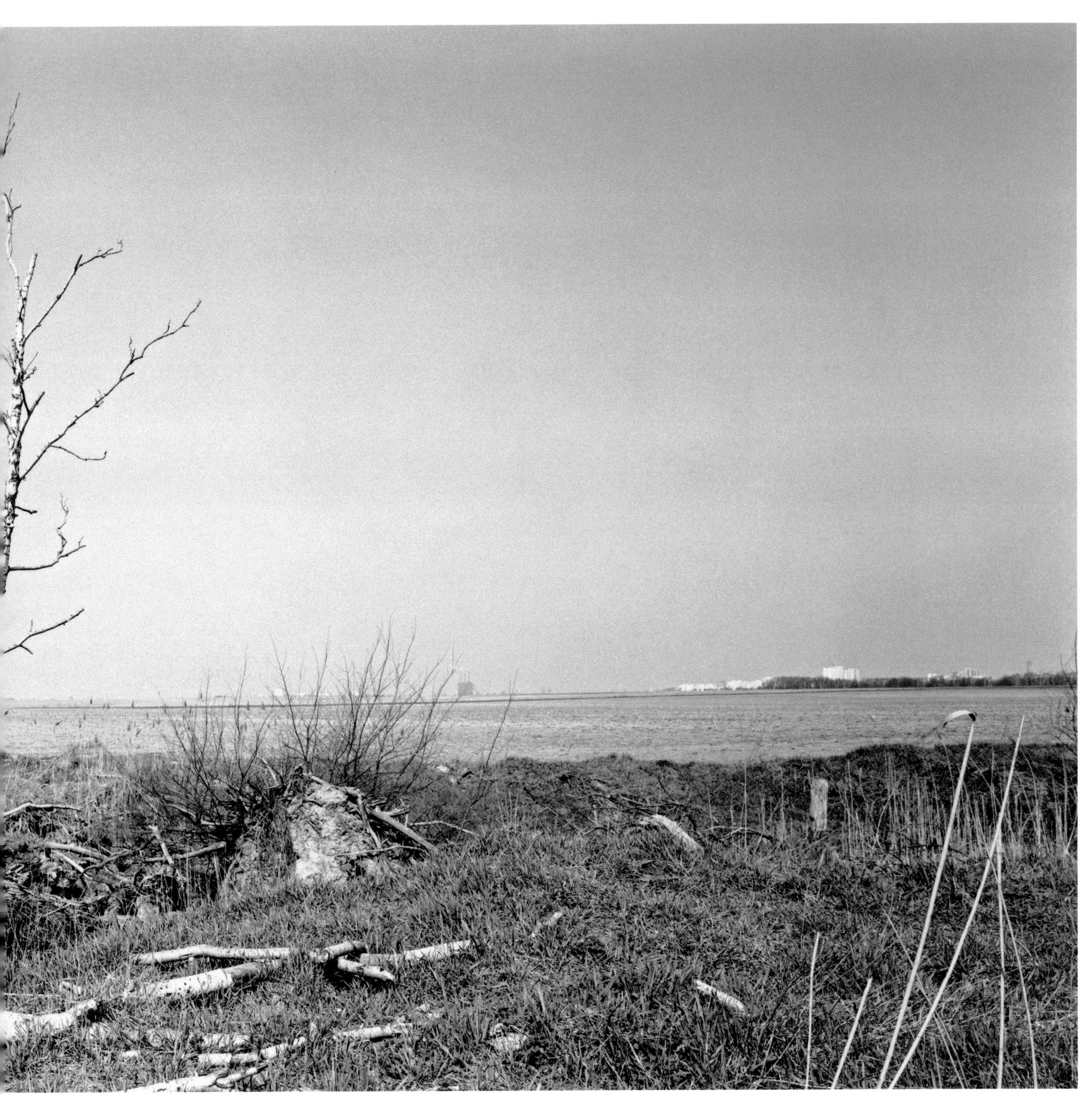

06

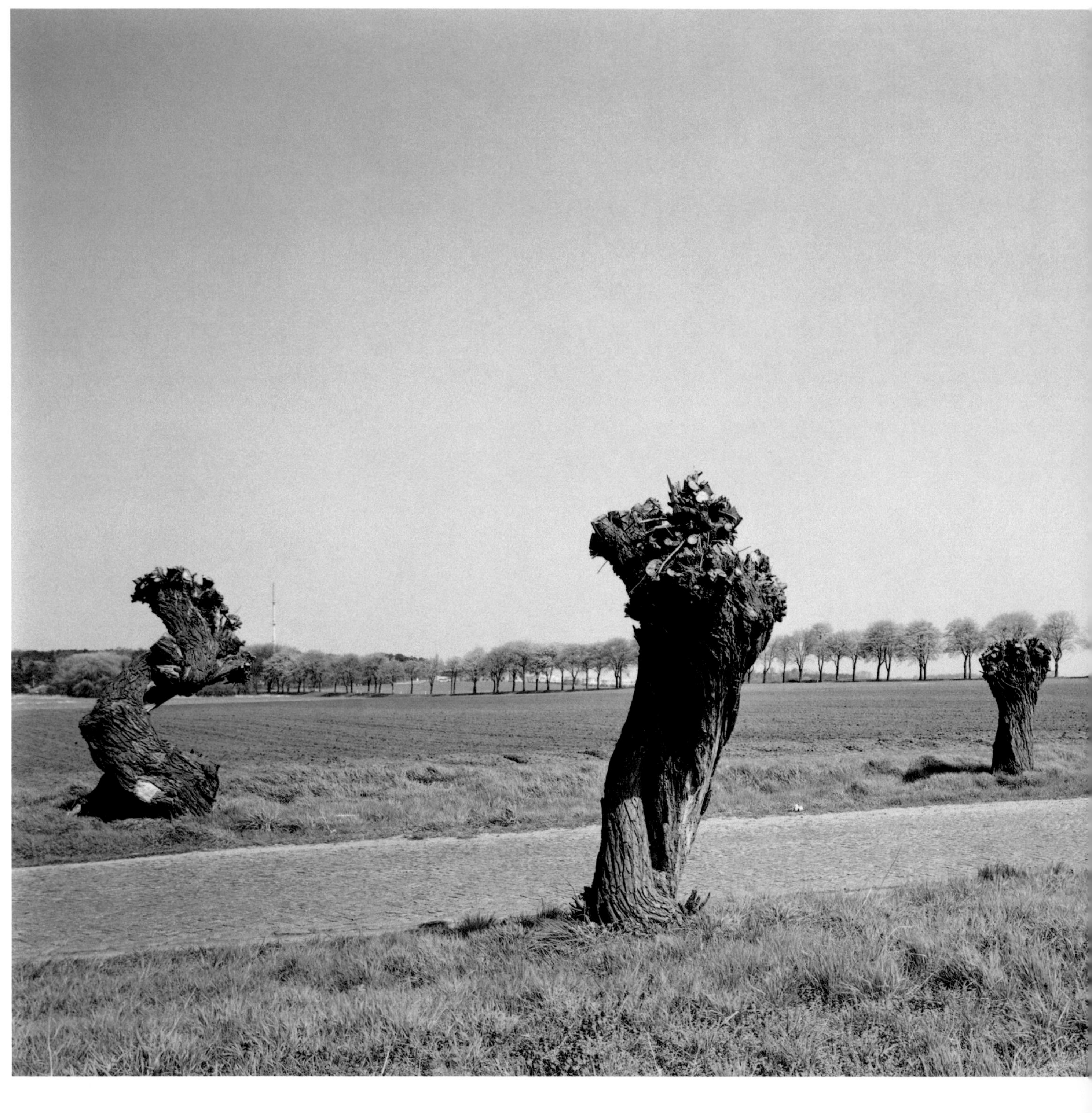

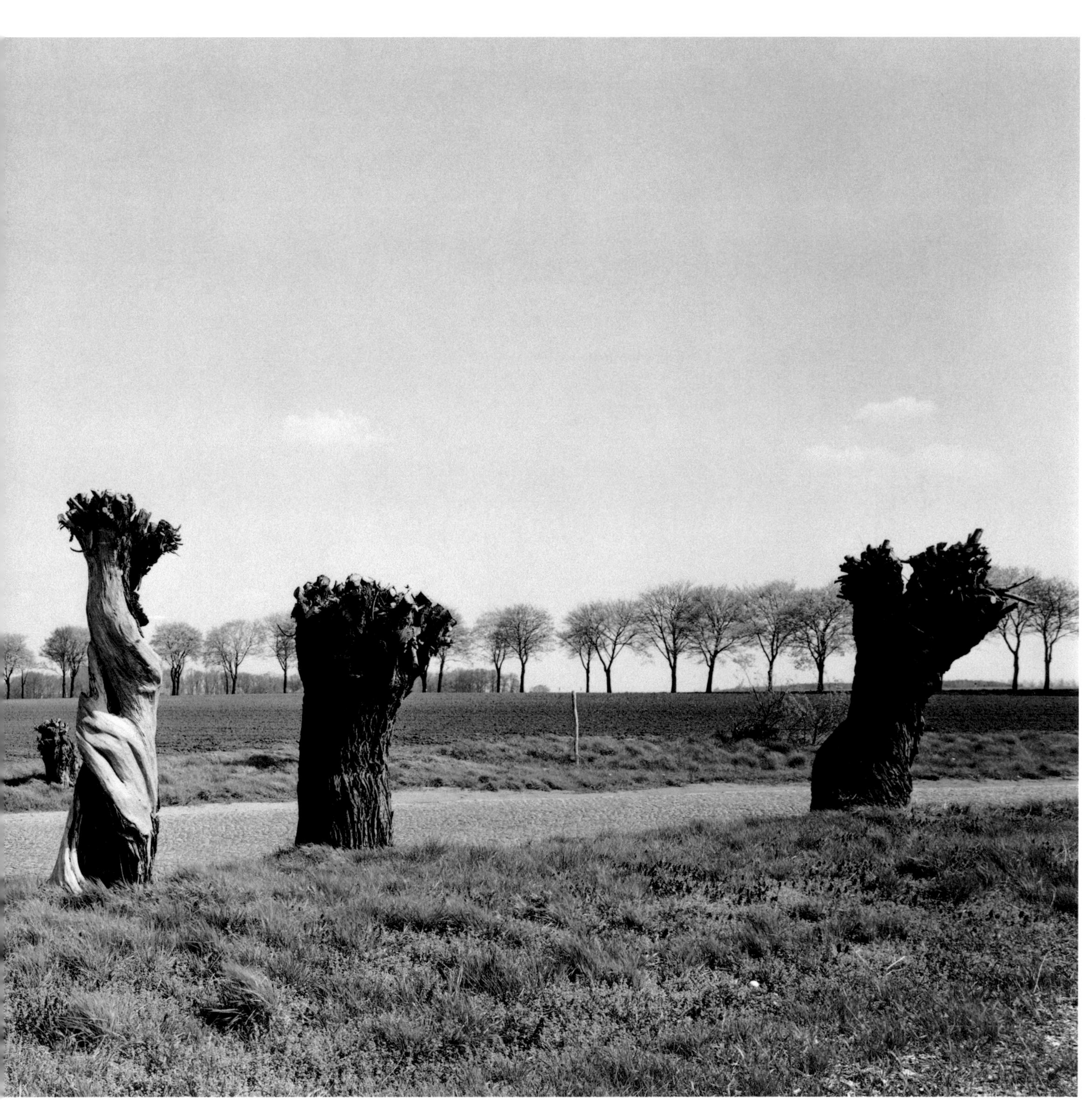

07

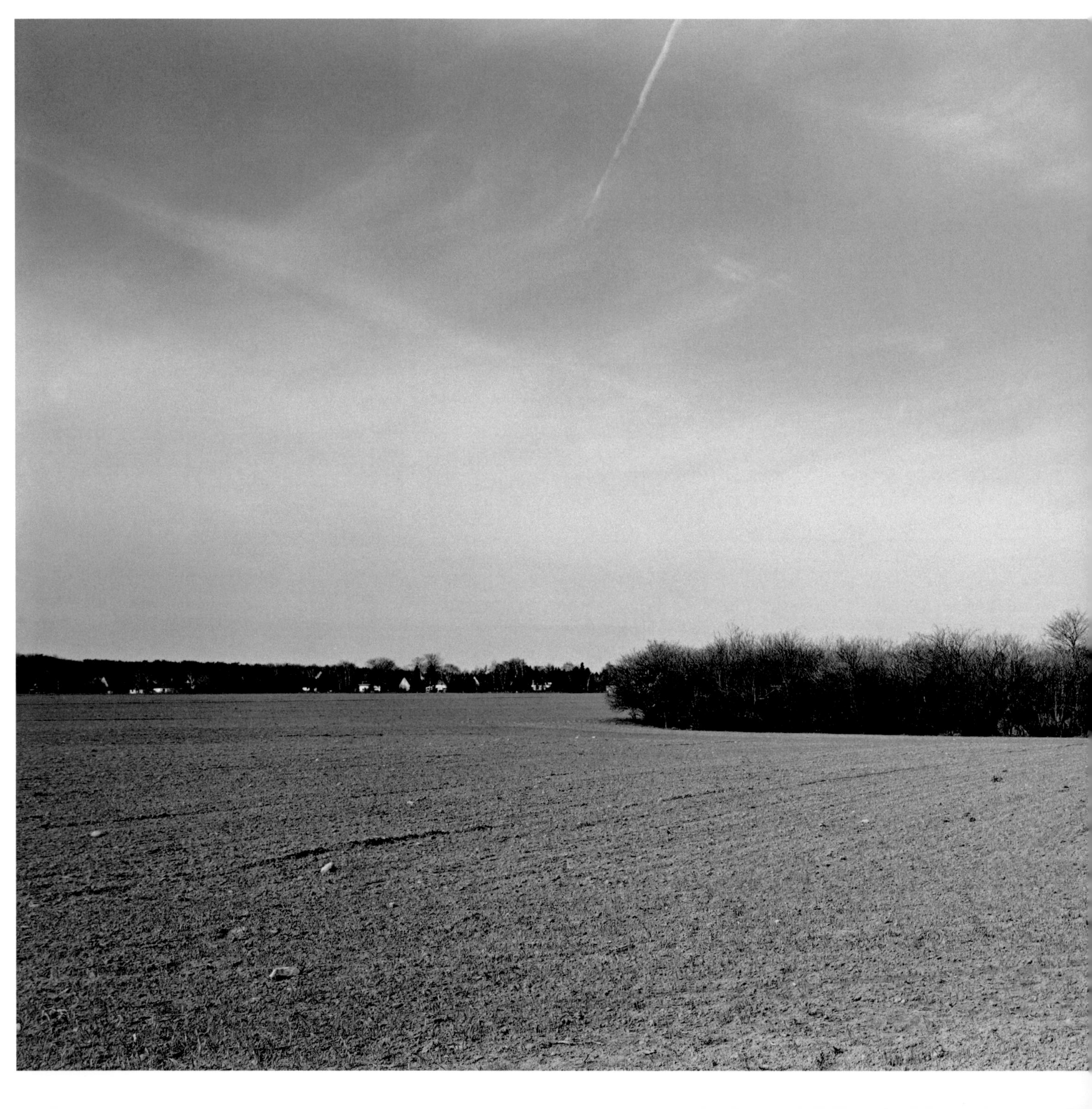

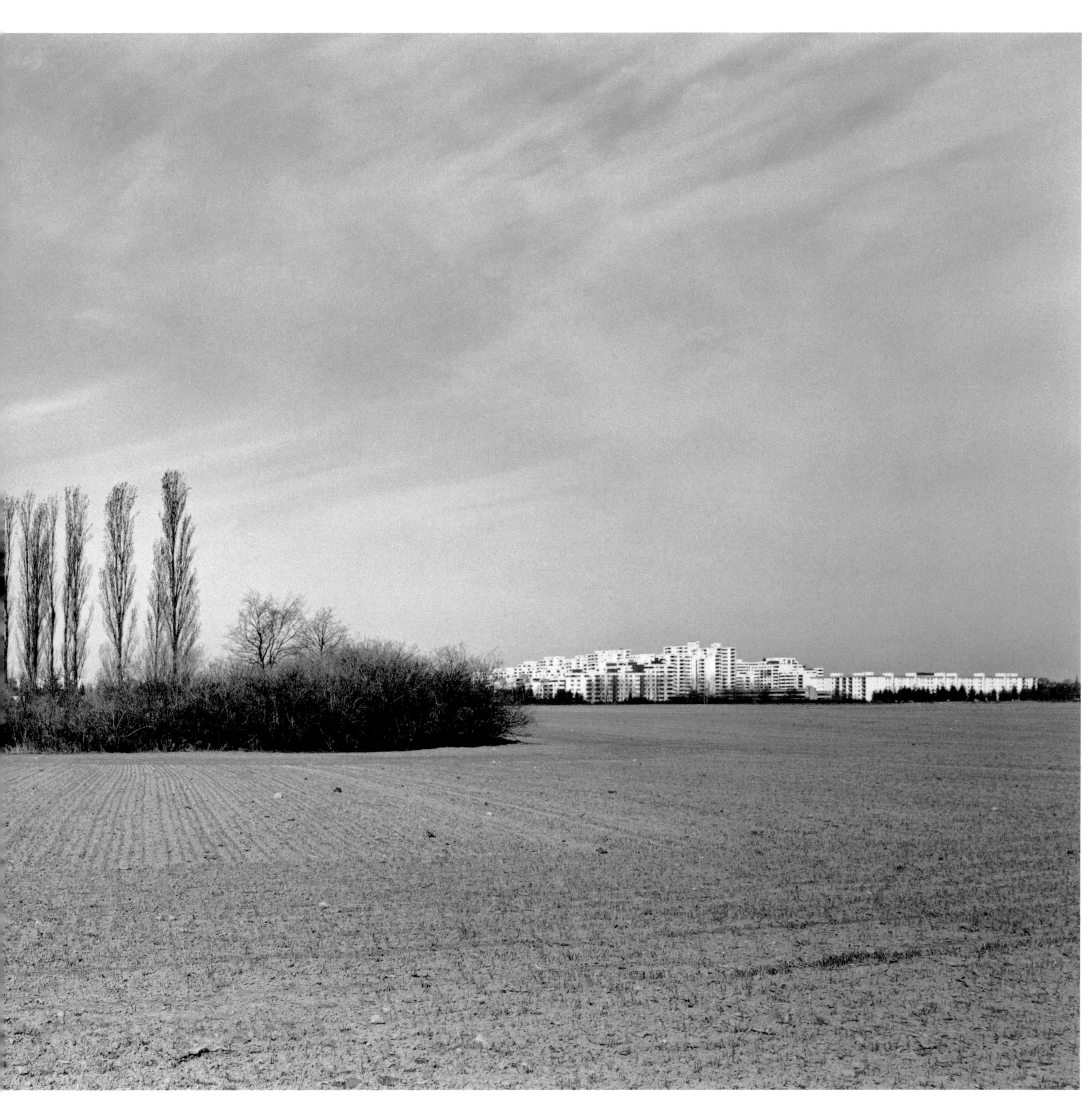

08

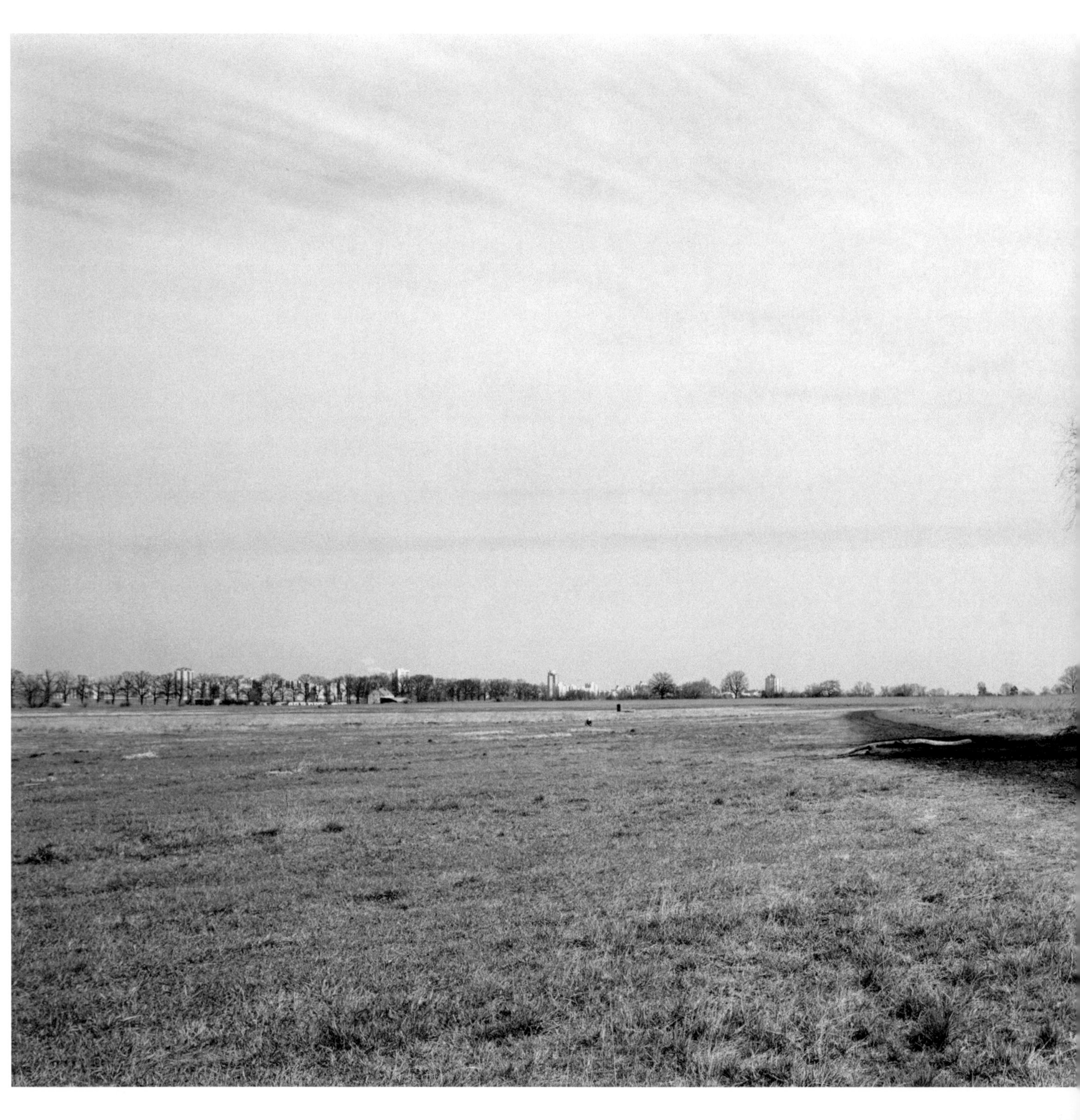

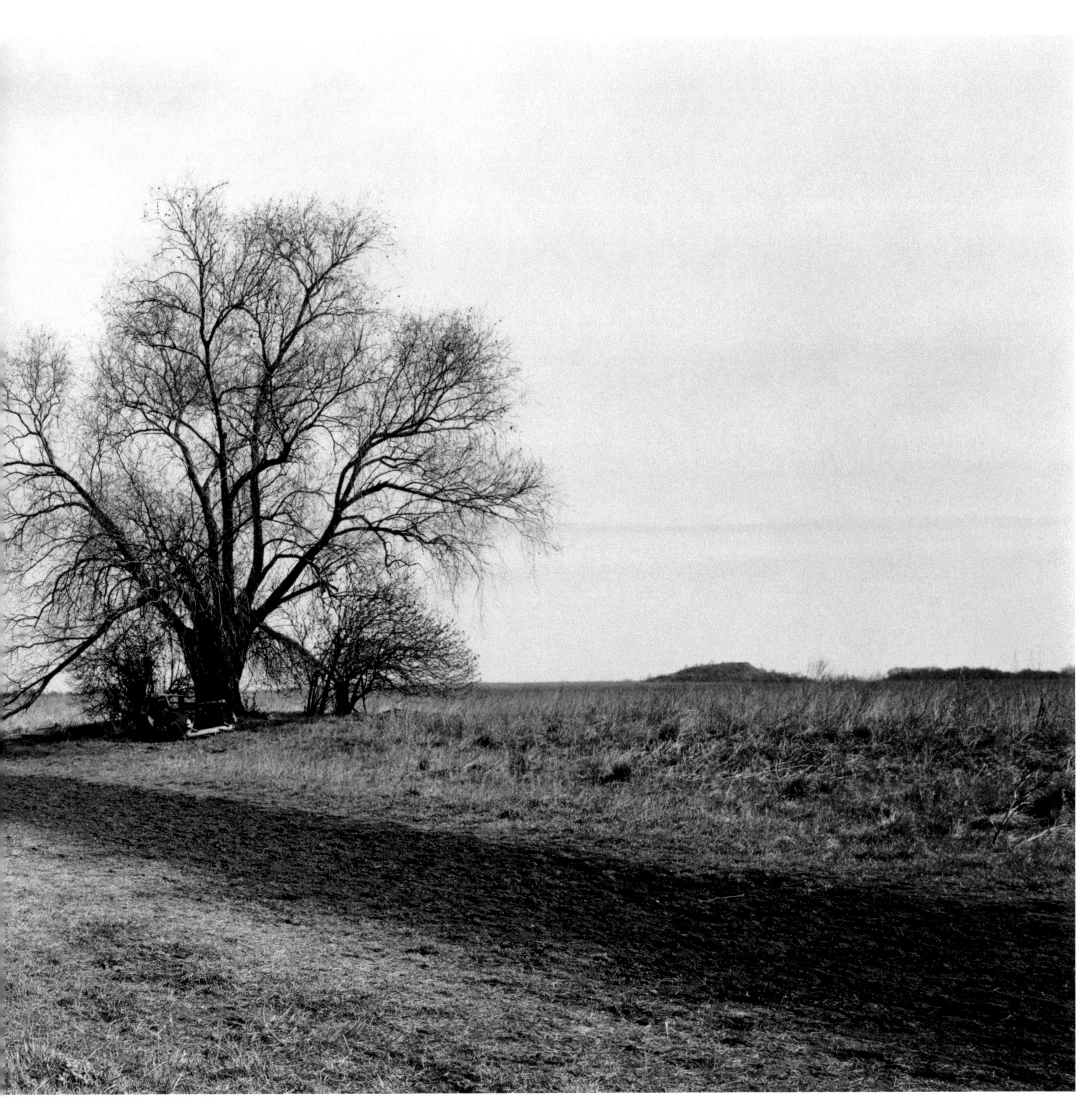

09

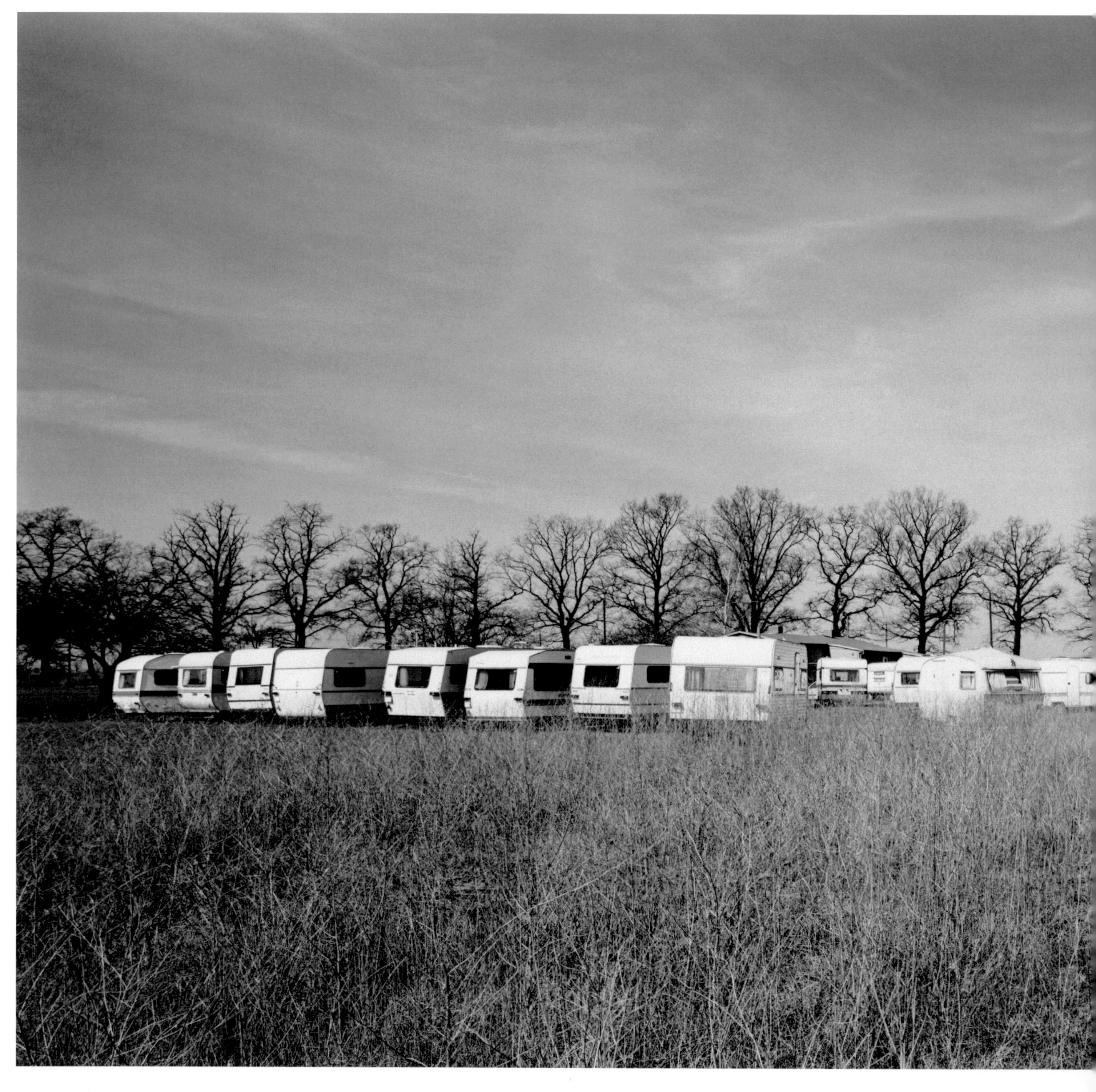

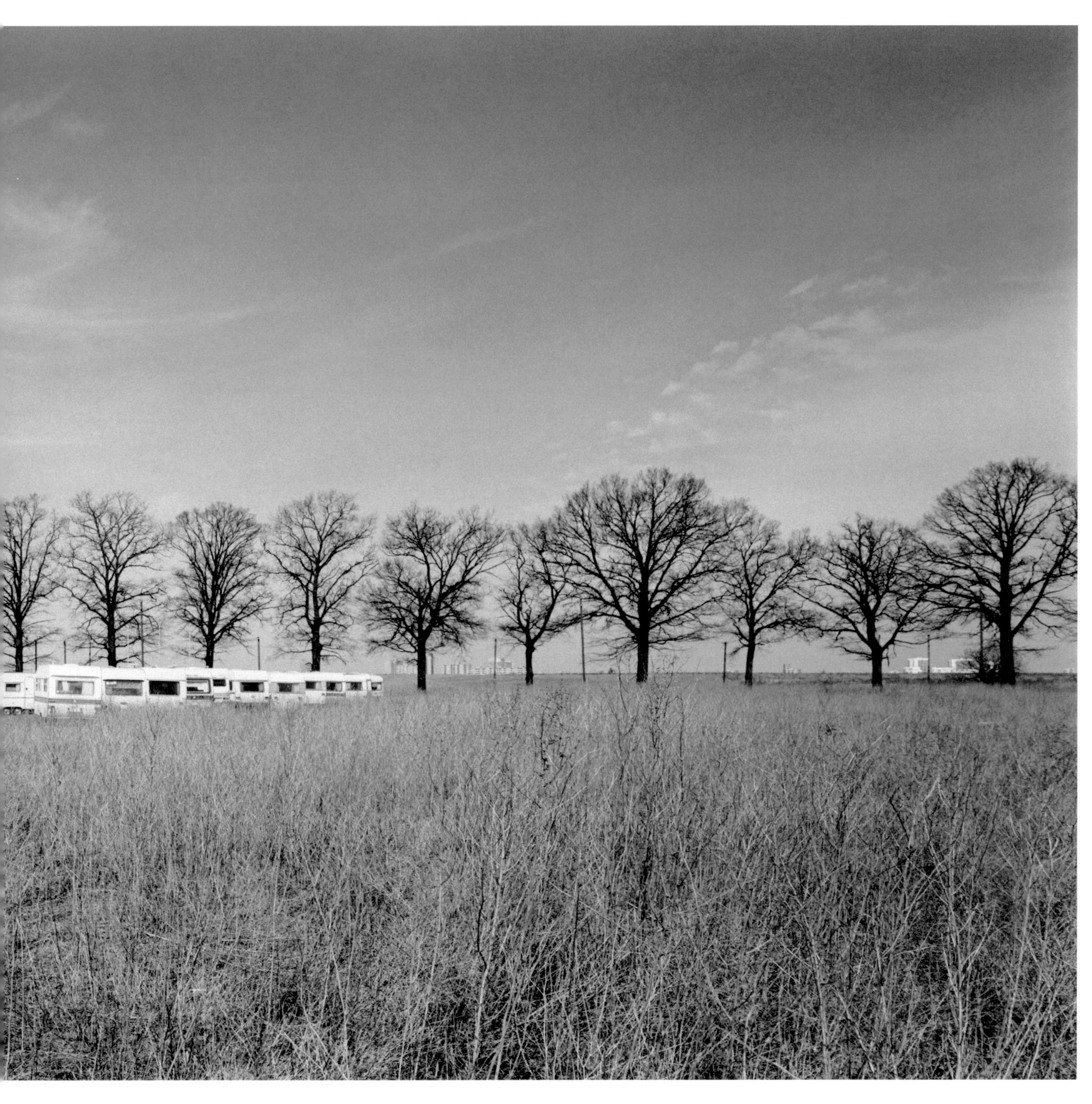

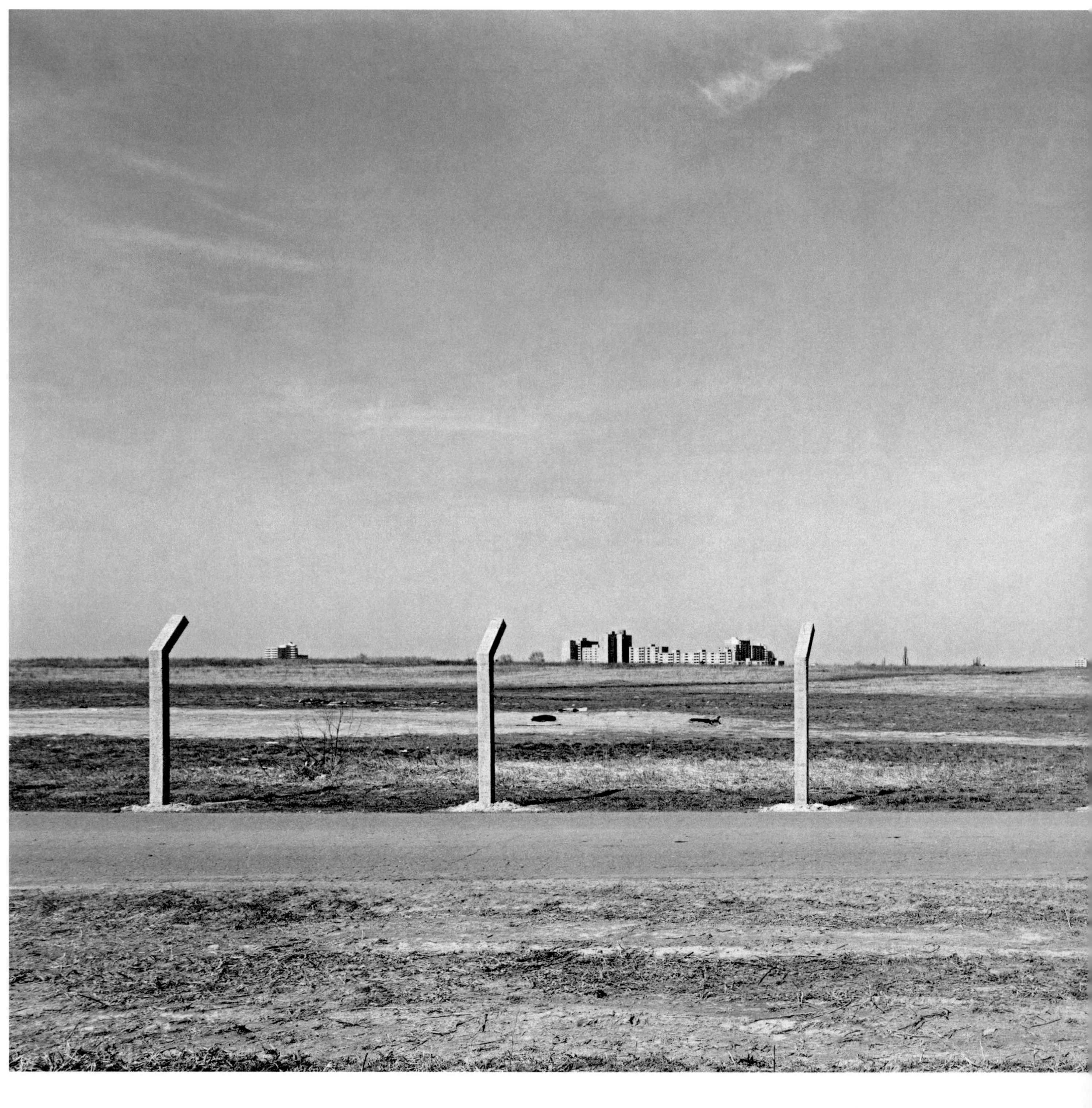

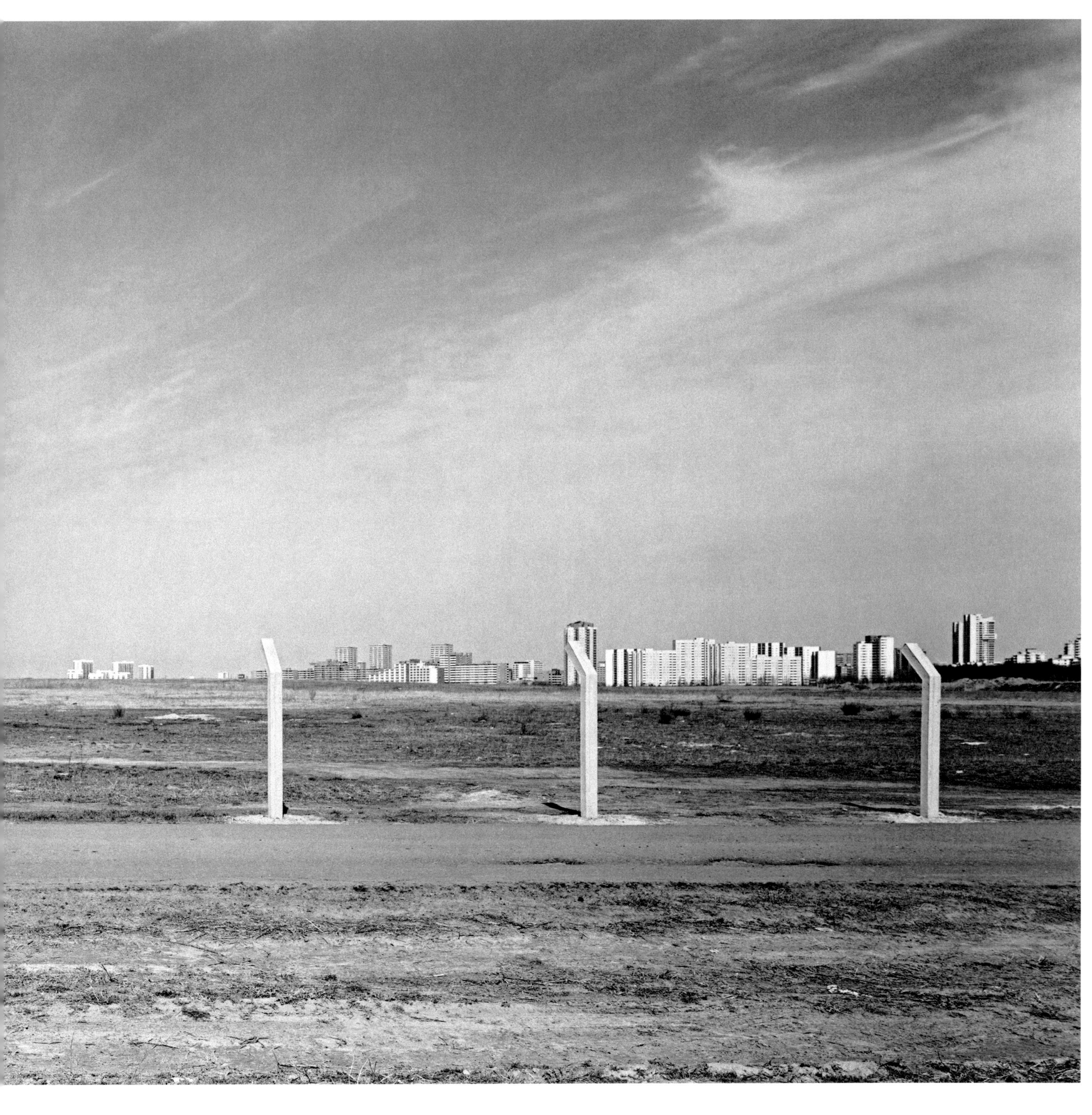

11

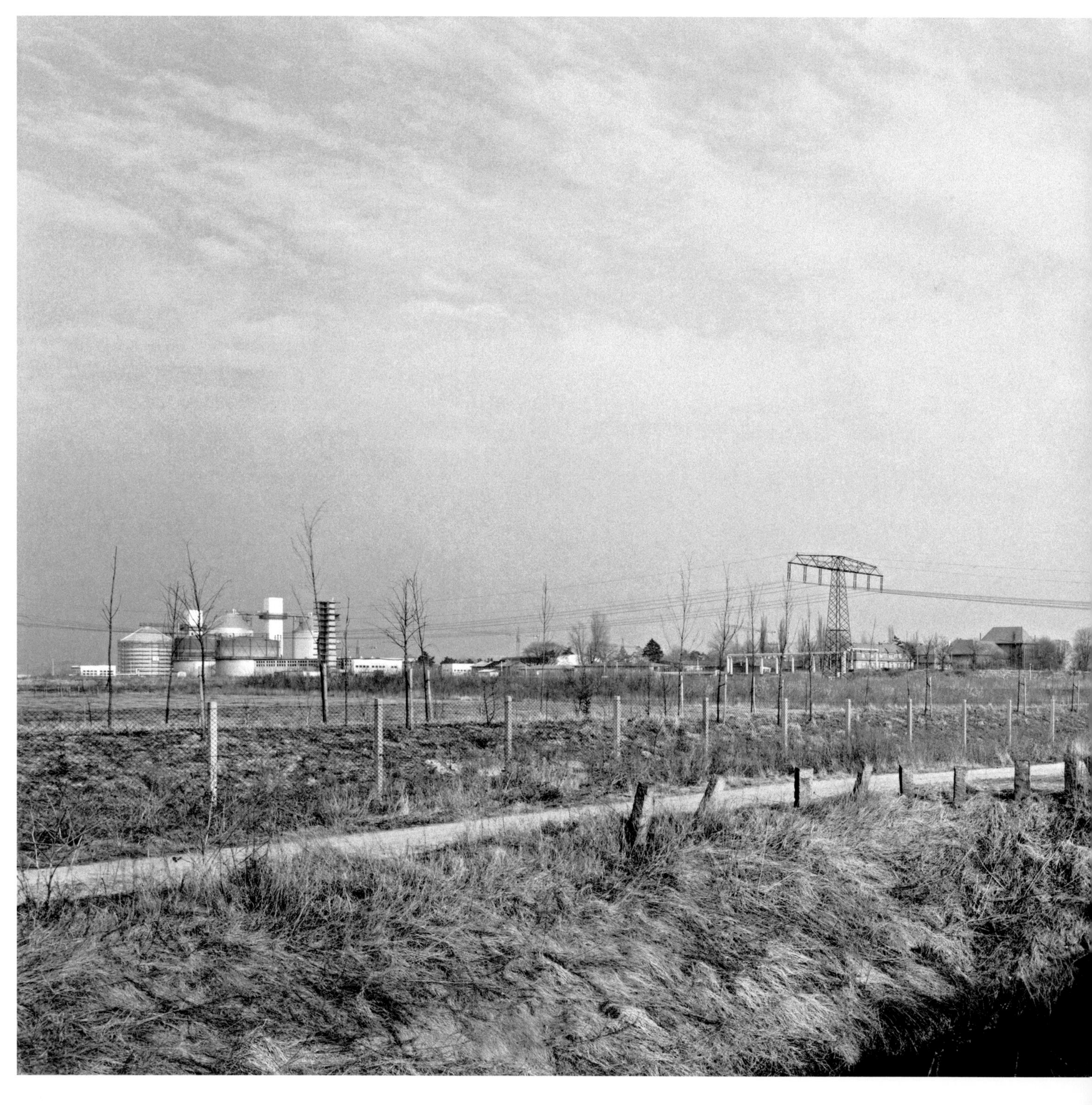

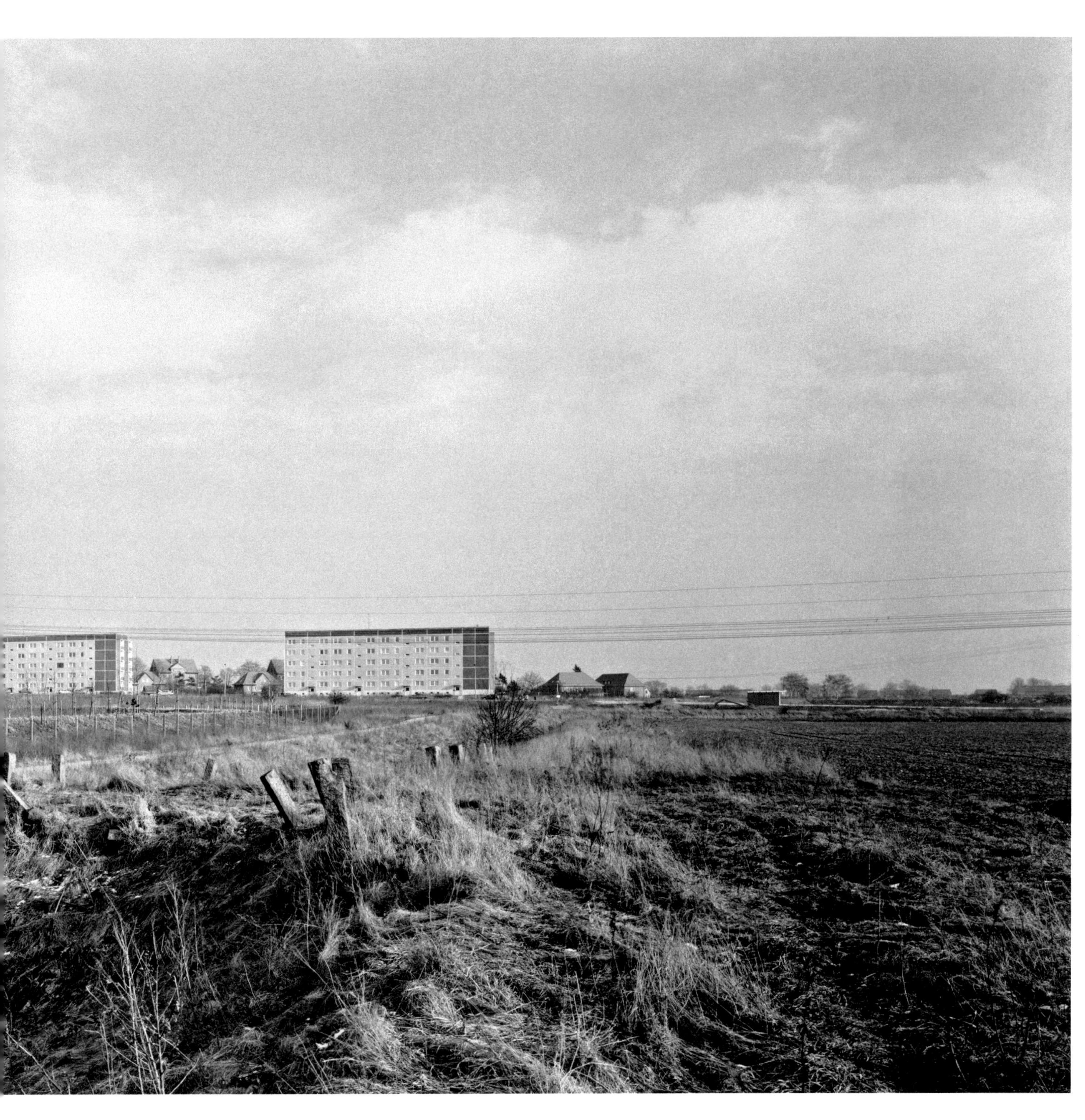

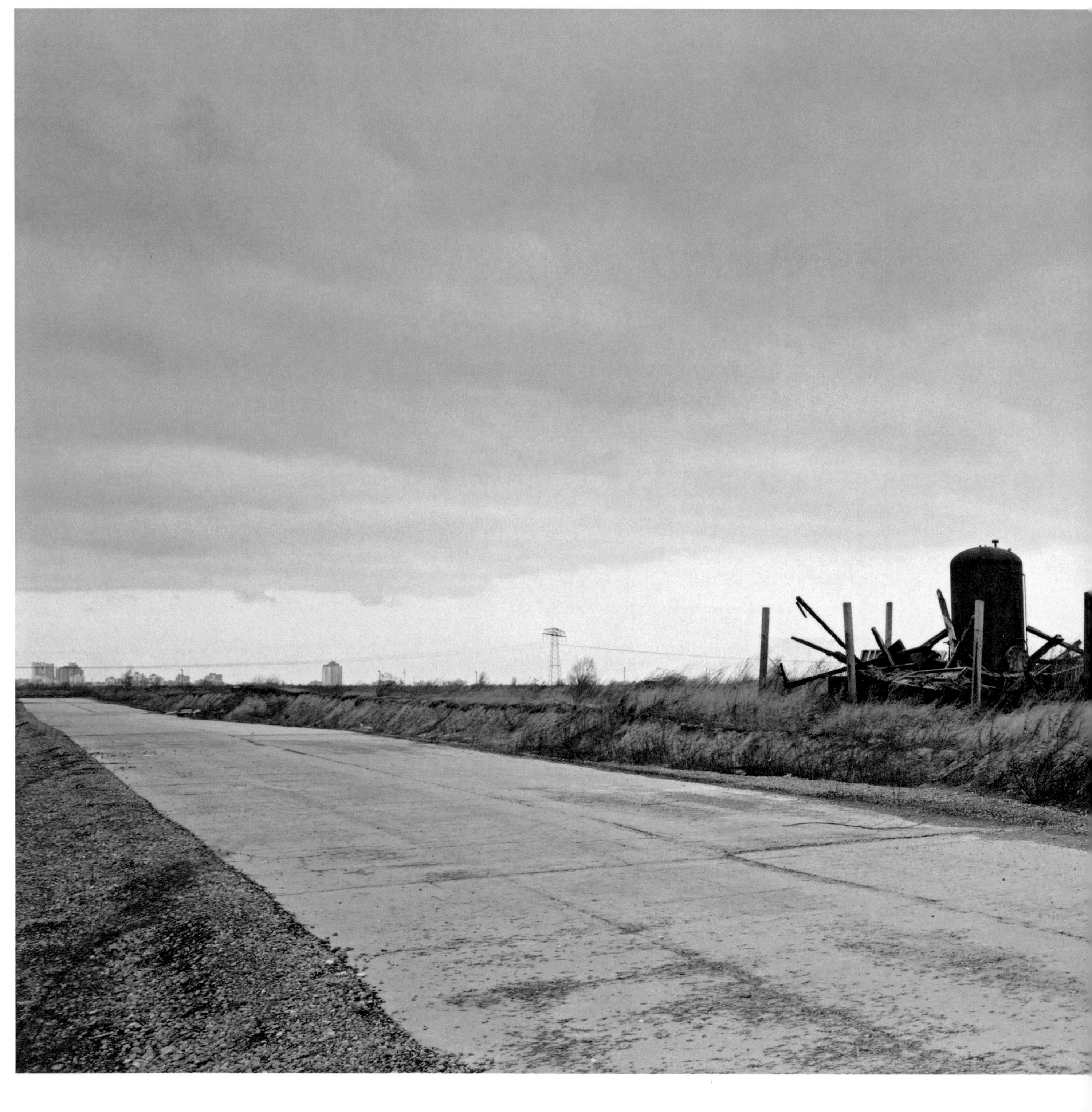

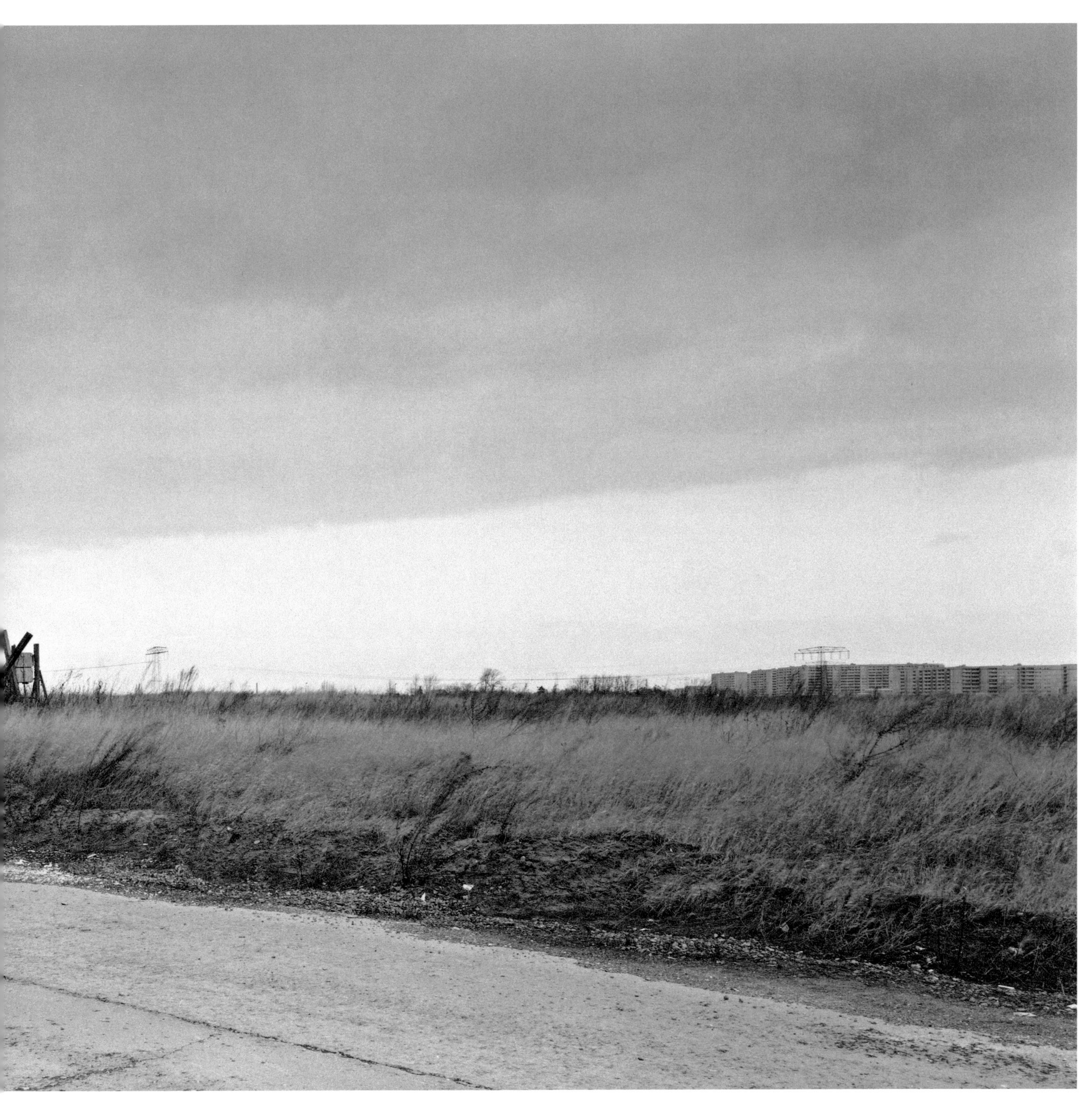

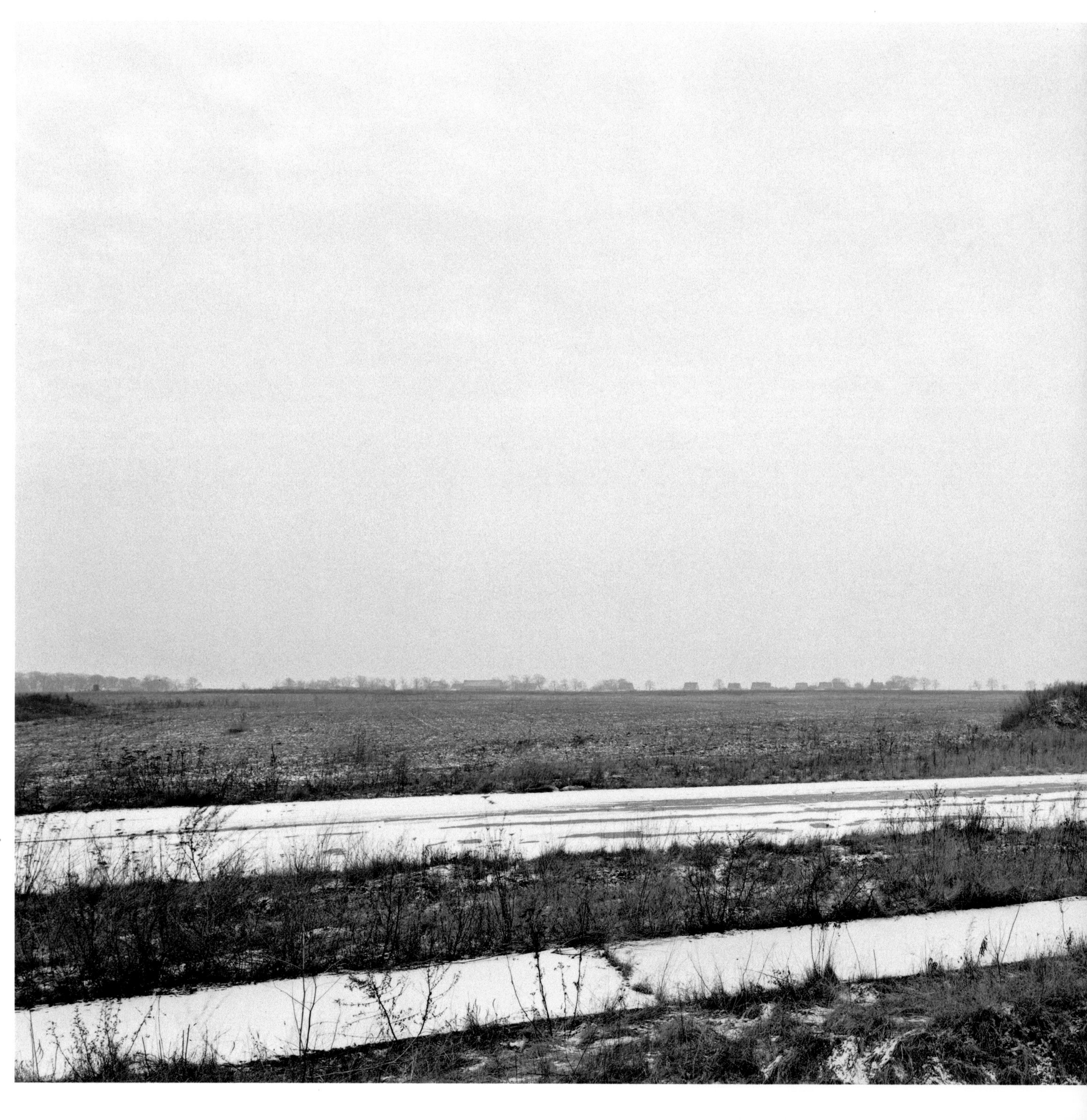

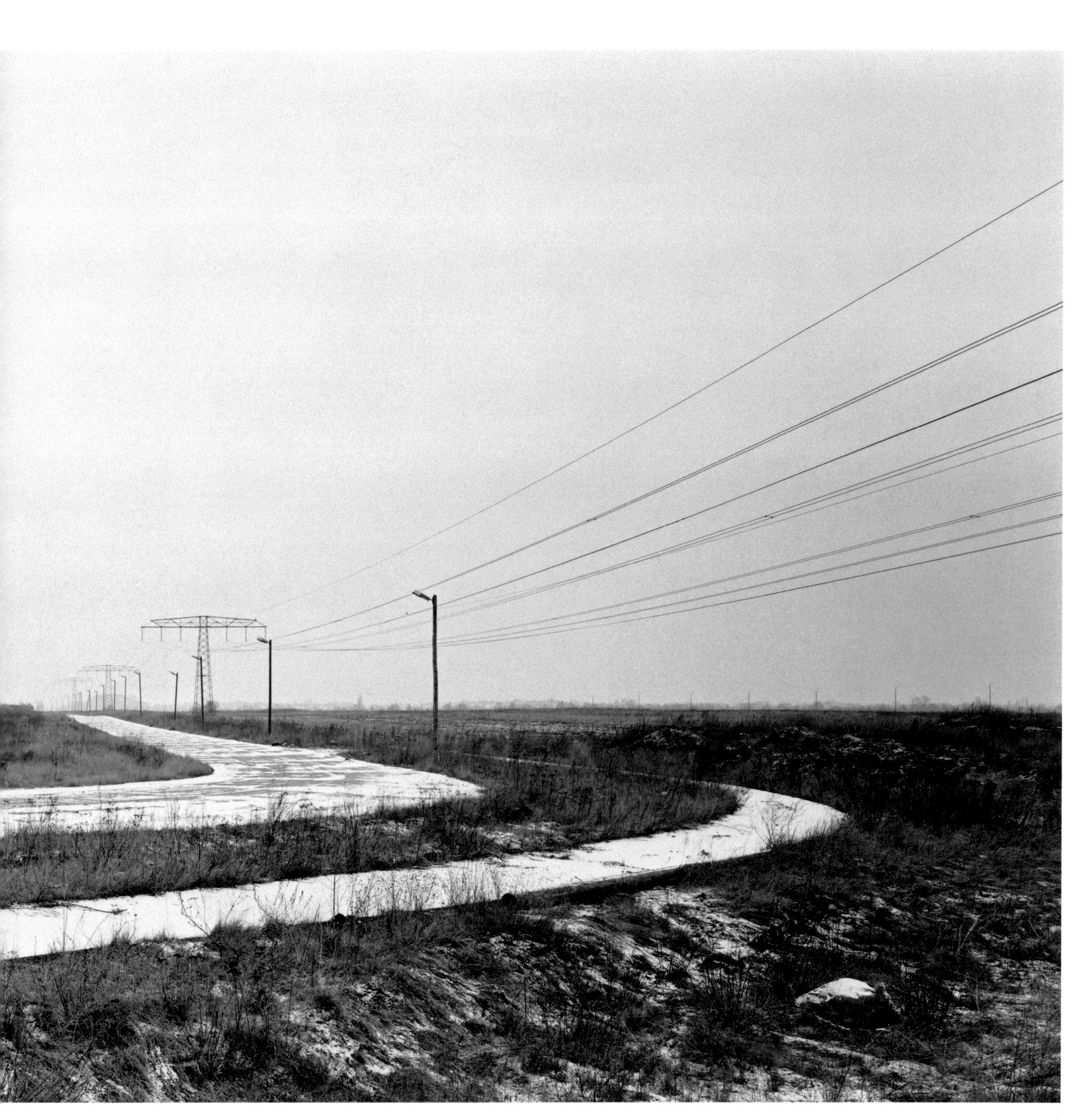

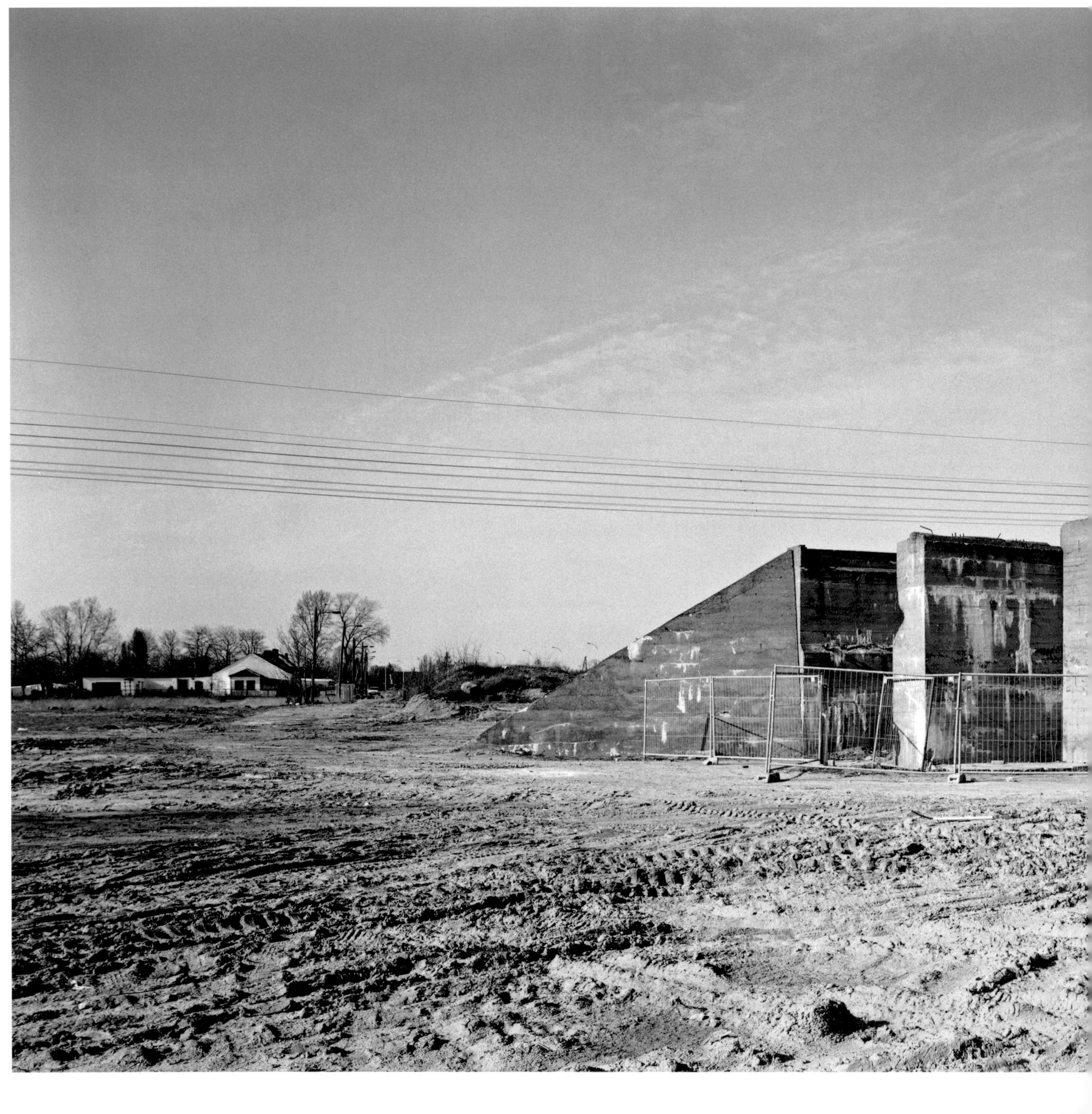

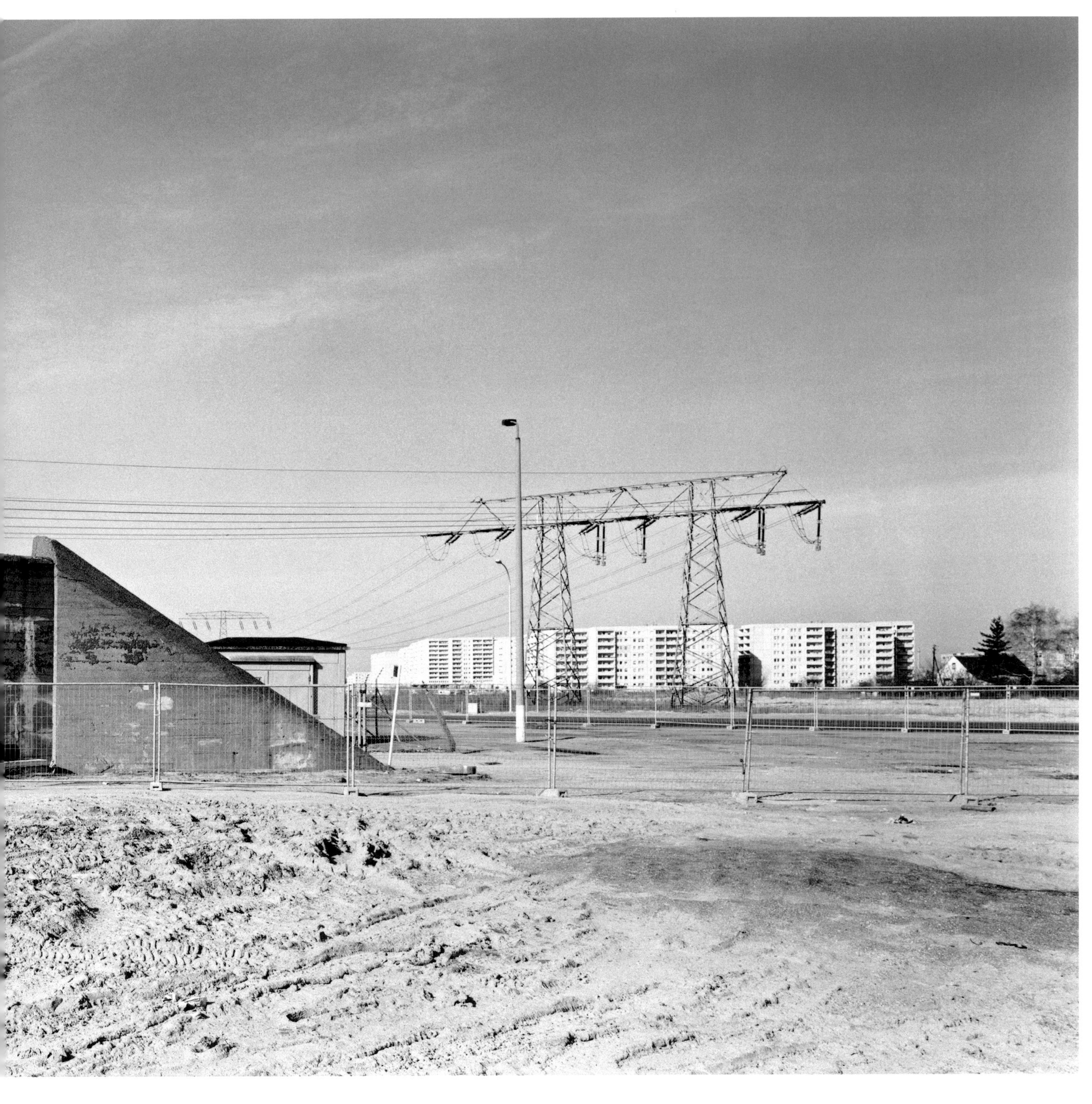

15

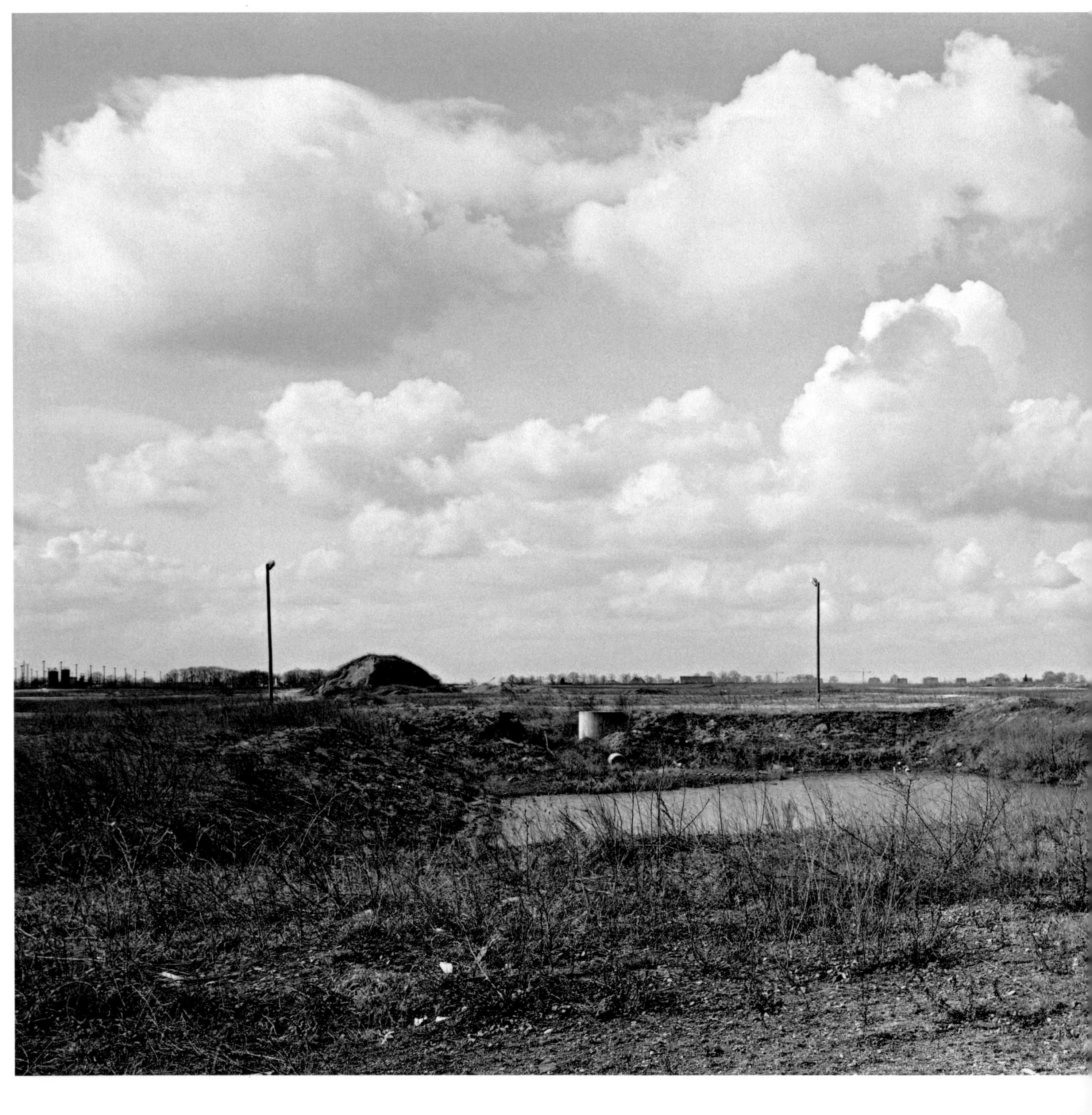

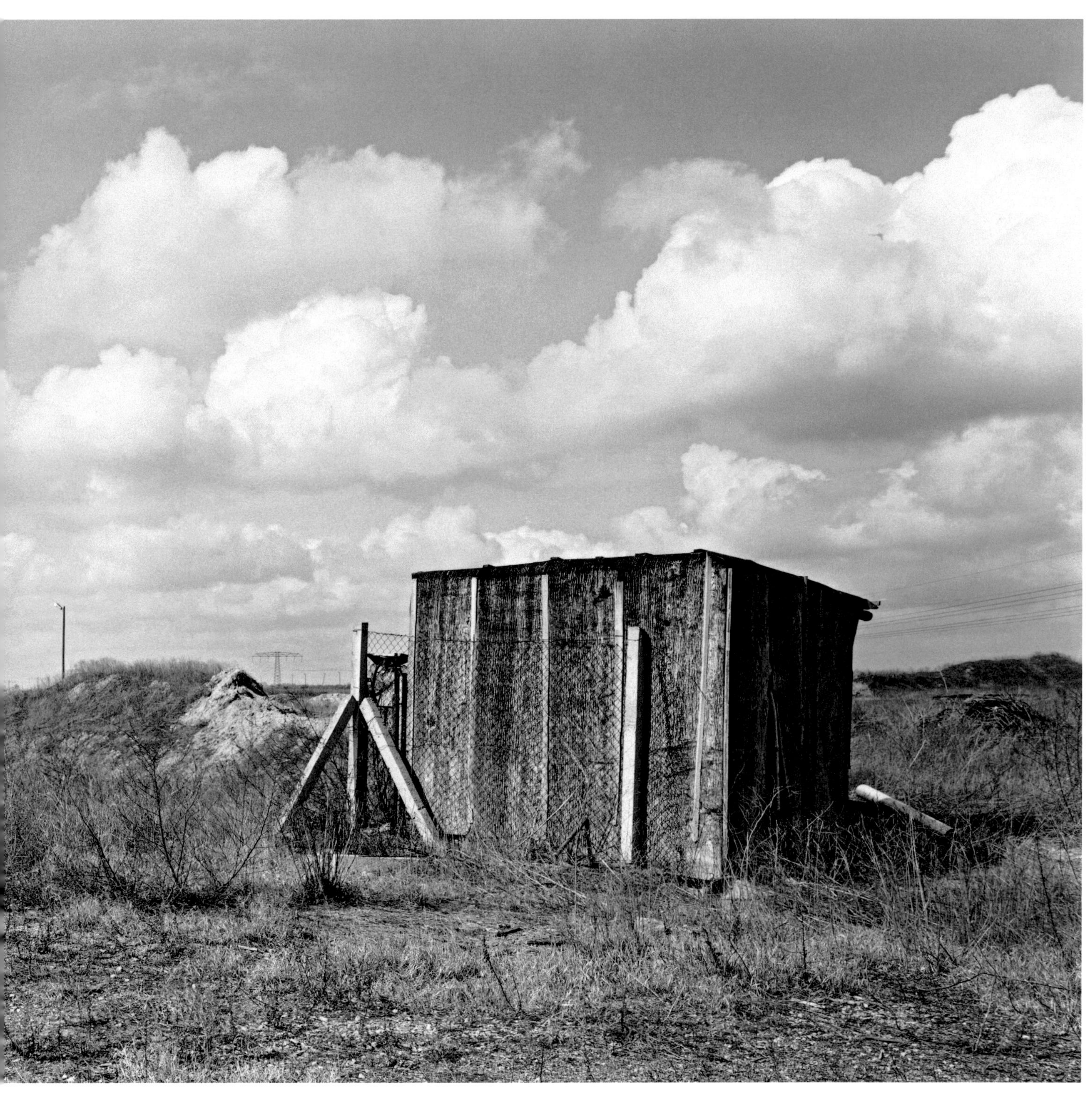

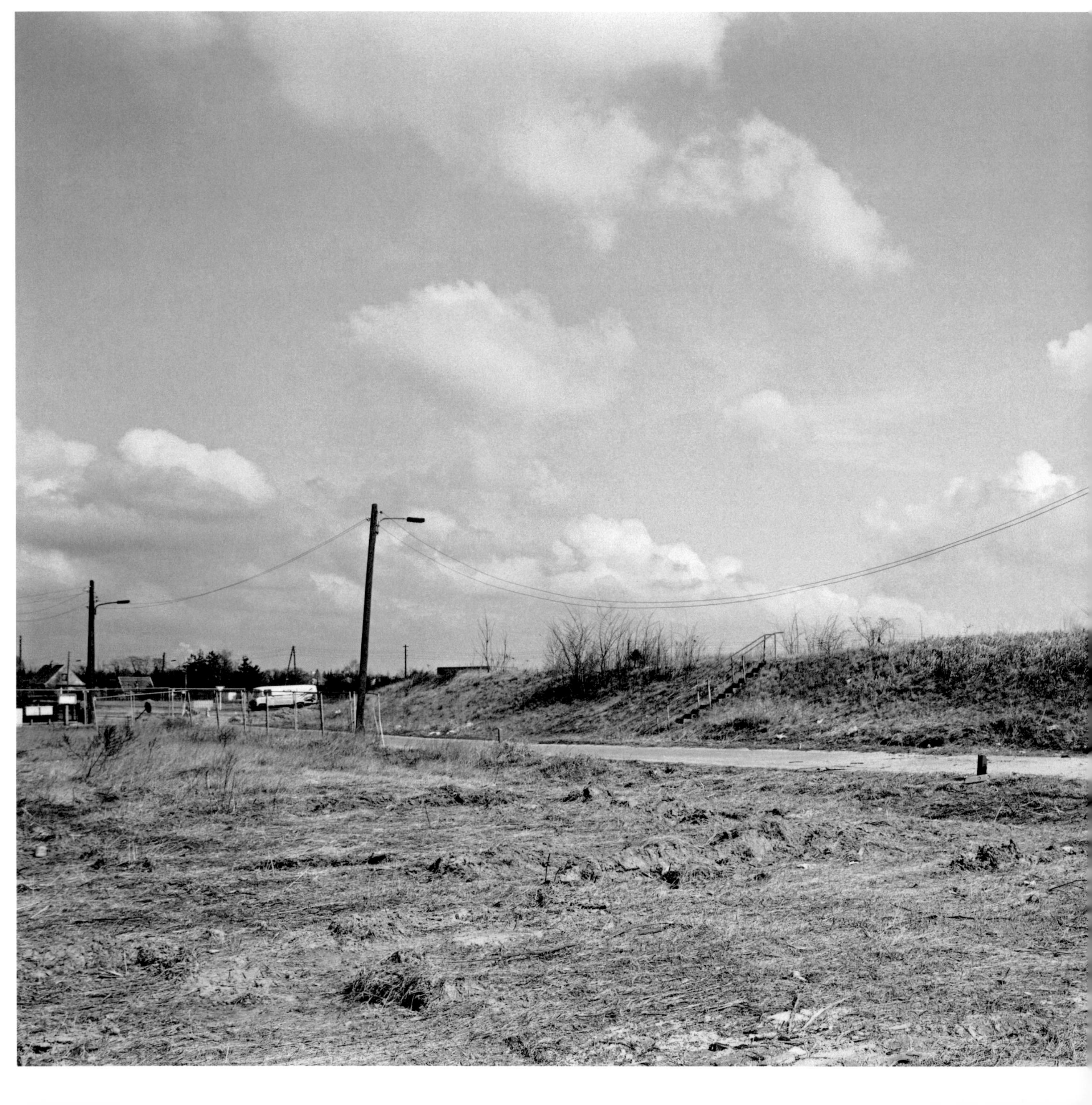

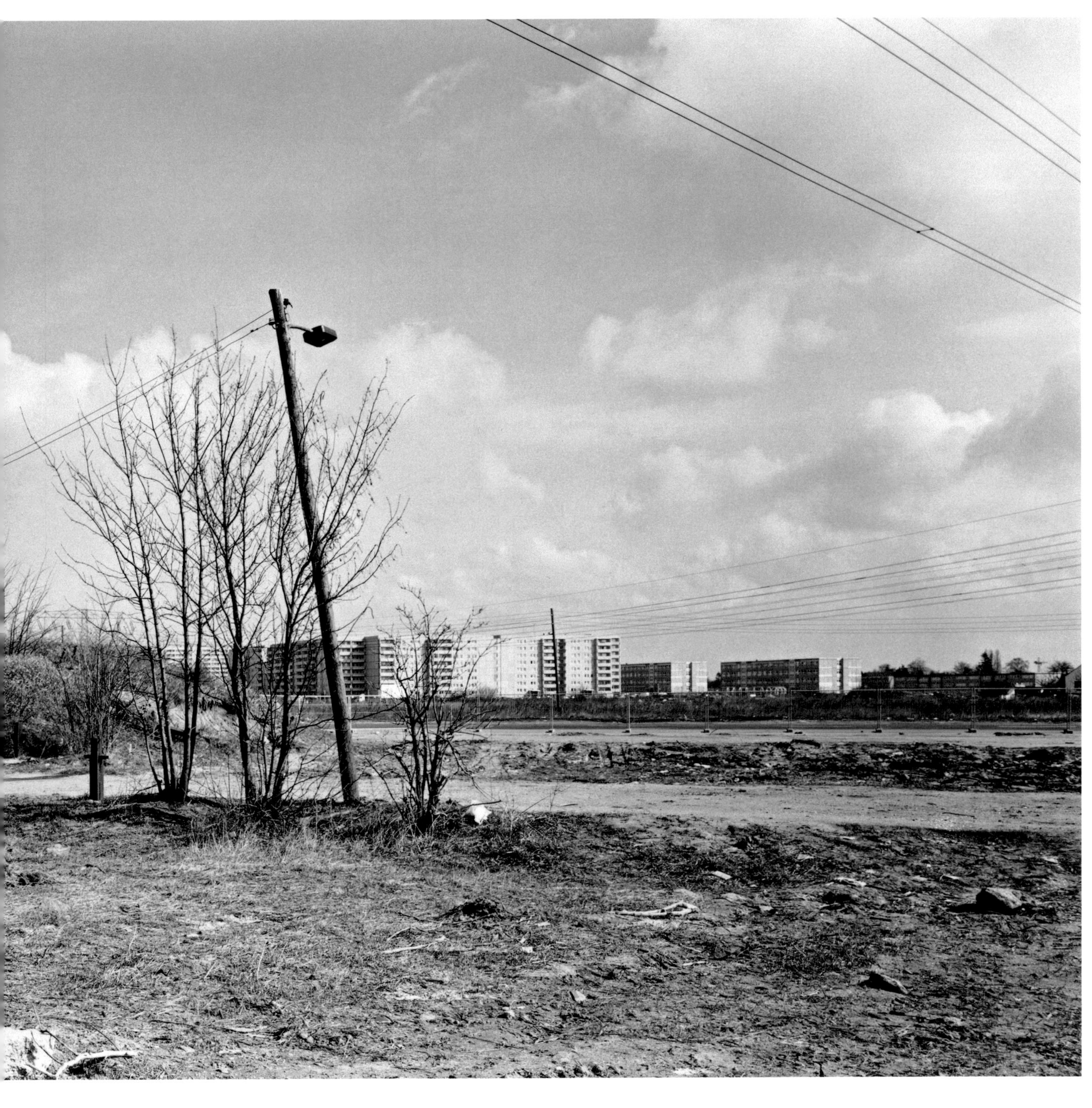

17

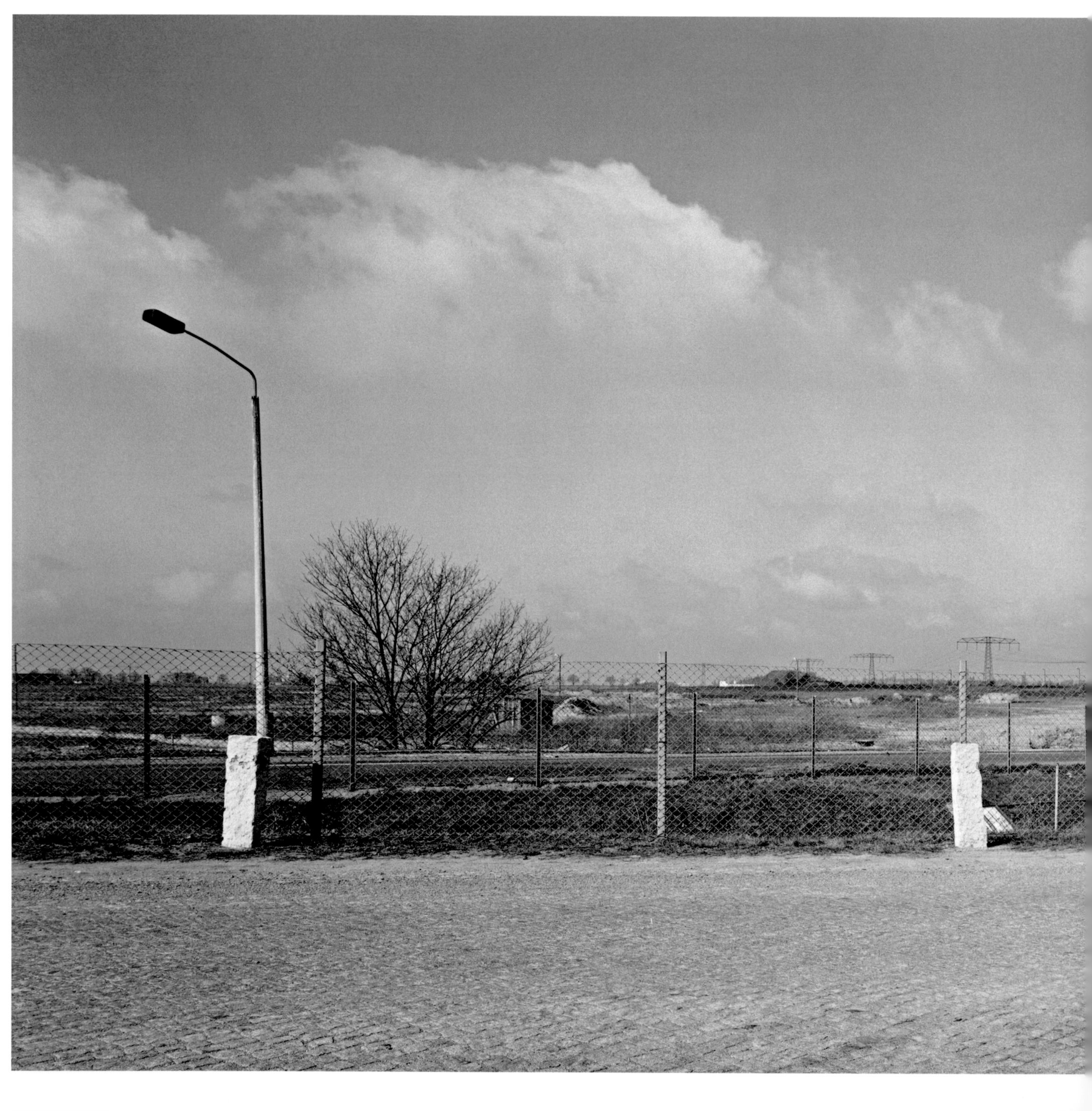

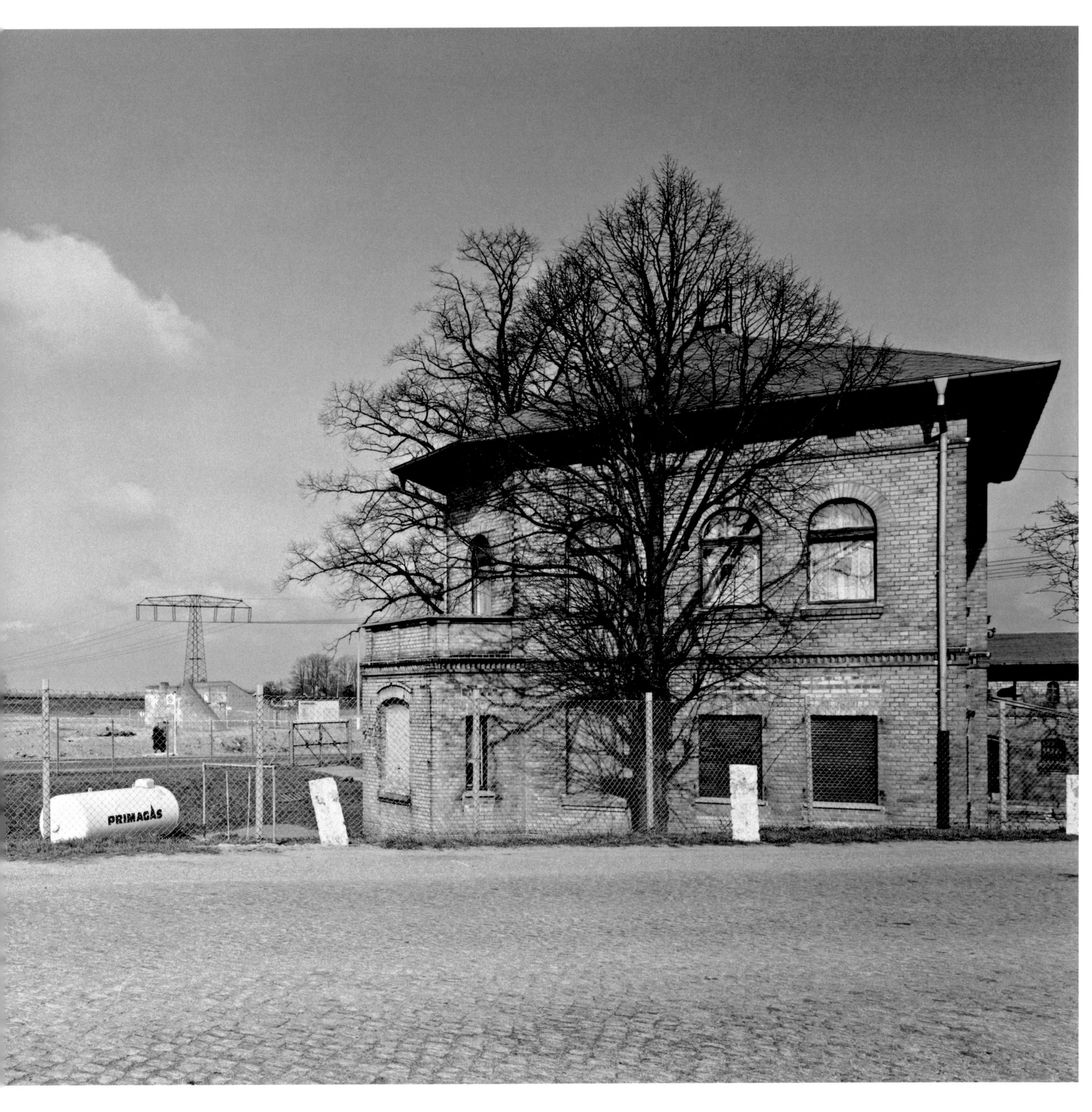
PRIMAGAS

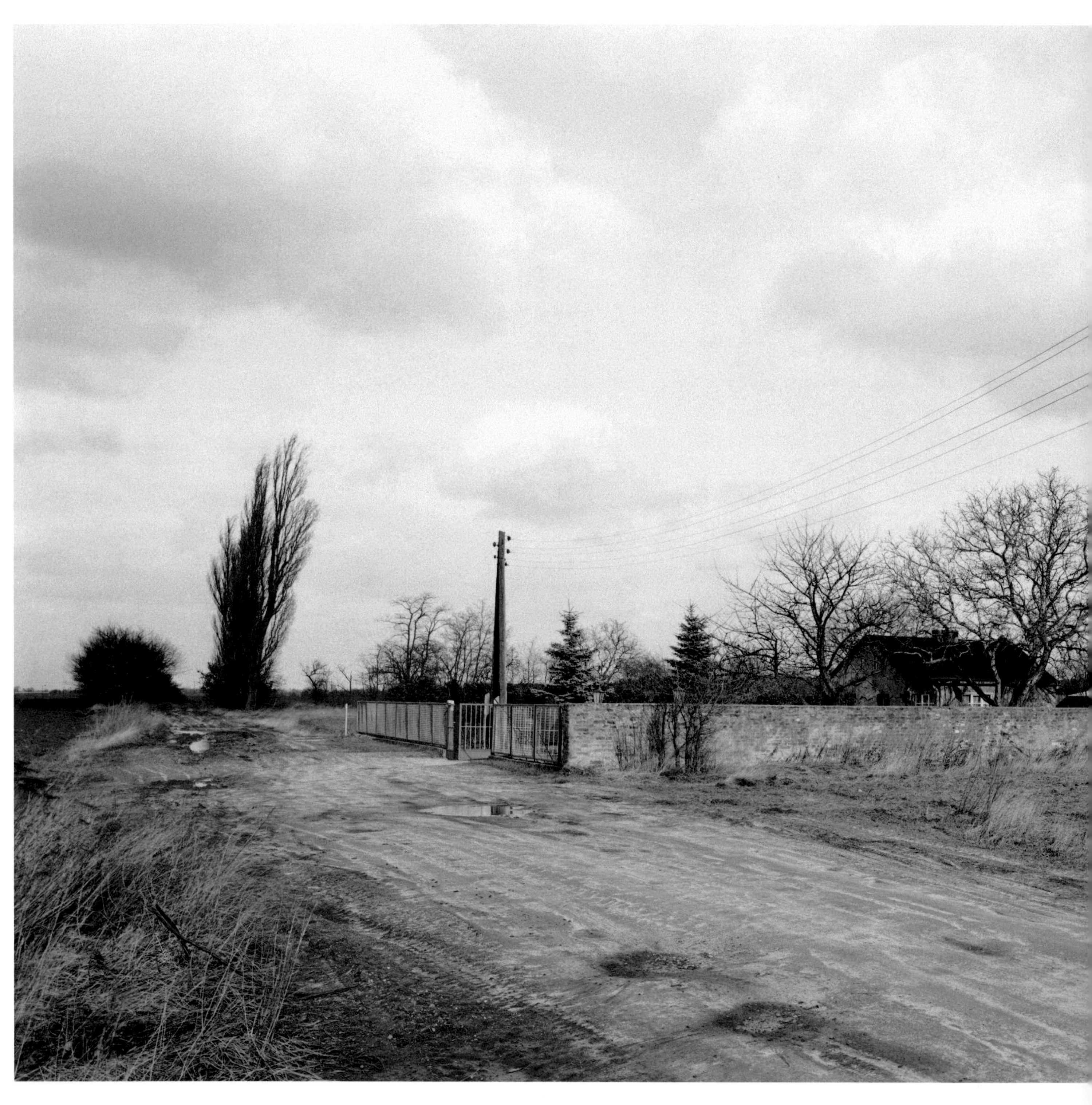

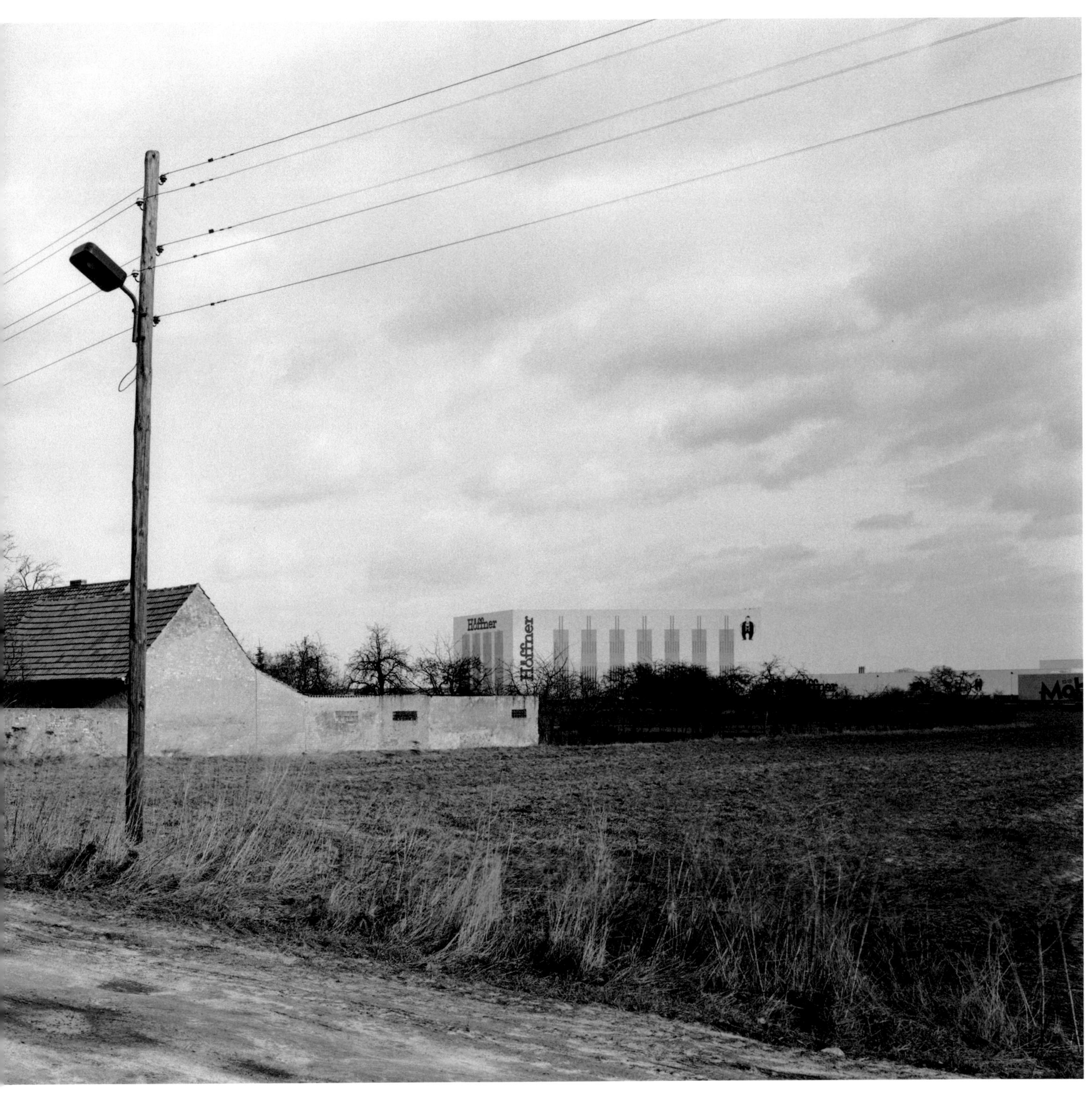
Höffner
Höffner

19

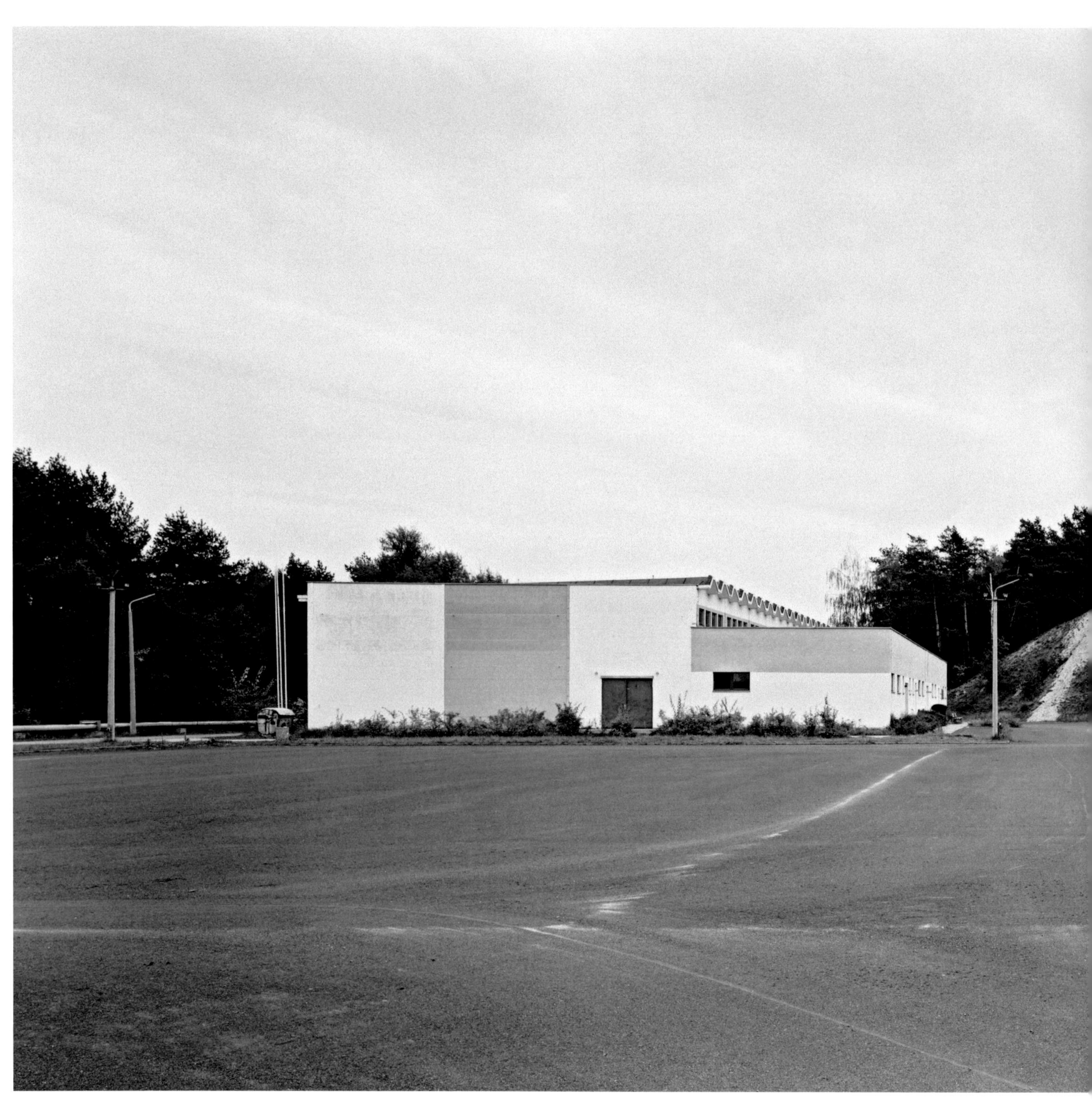

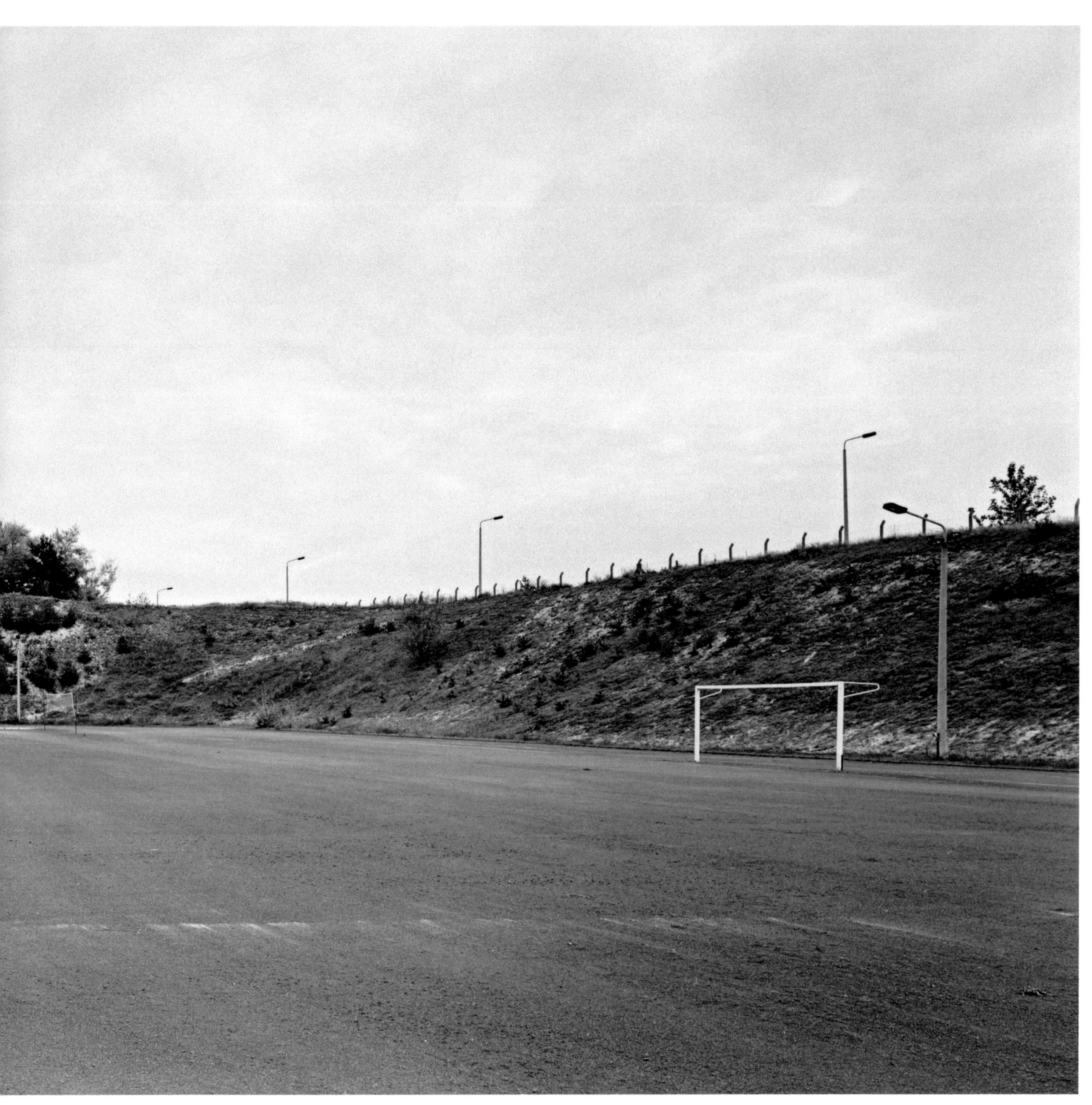

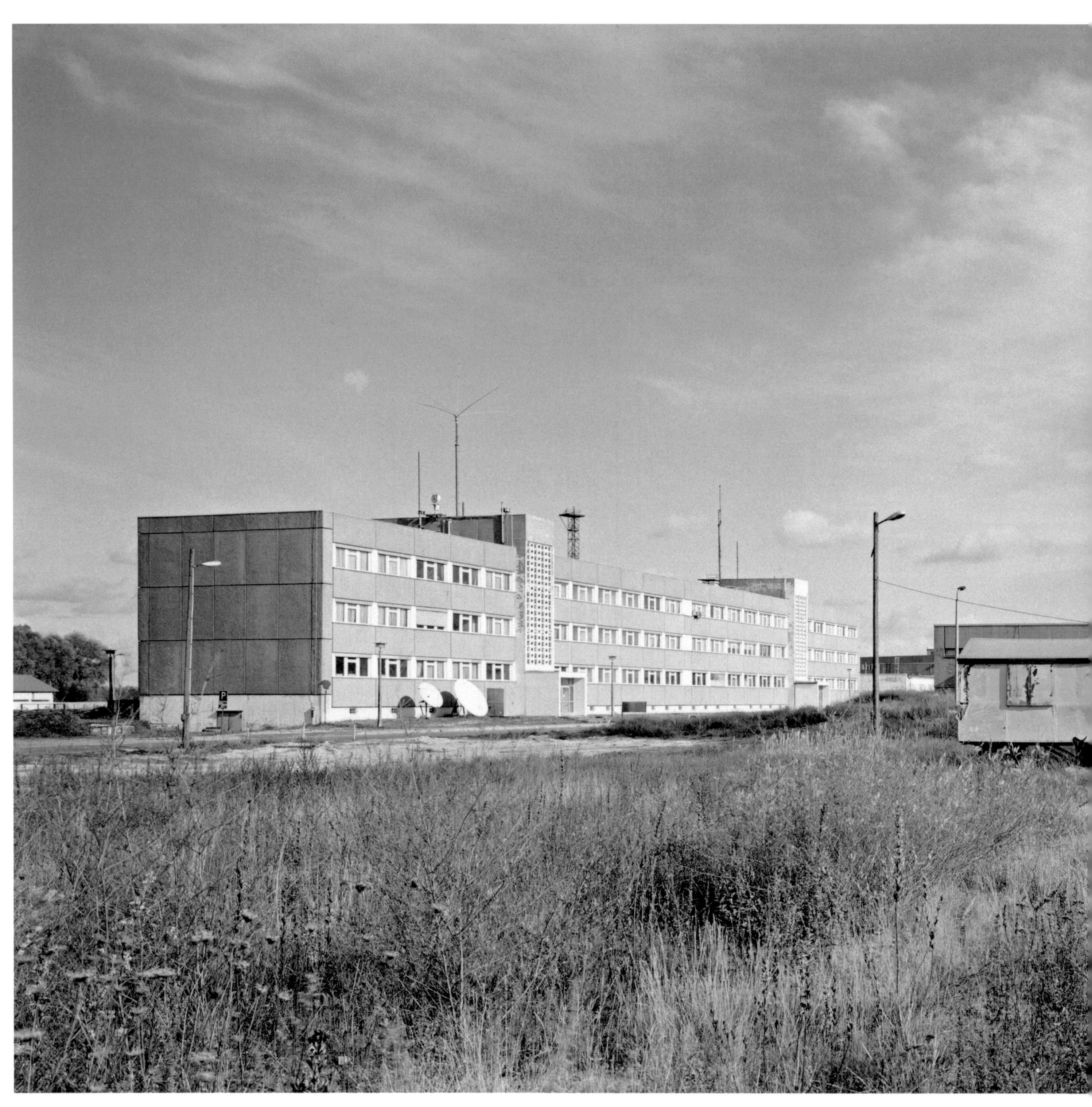

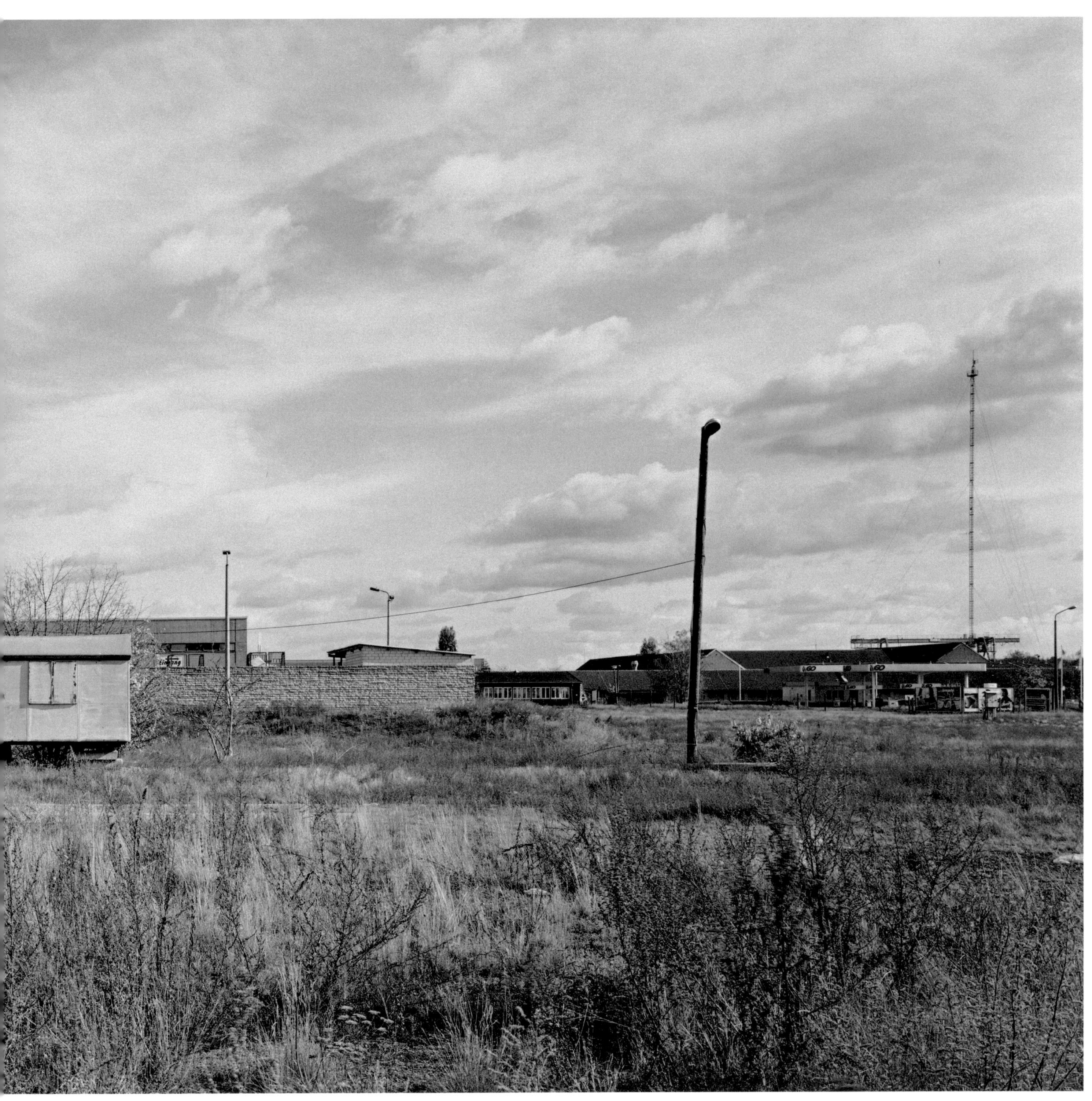

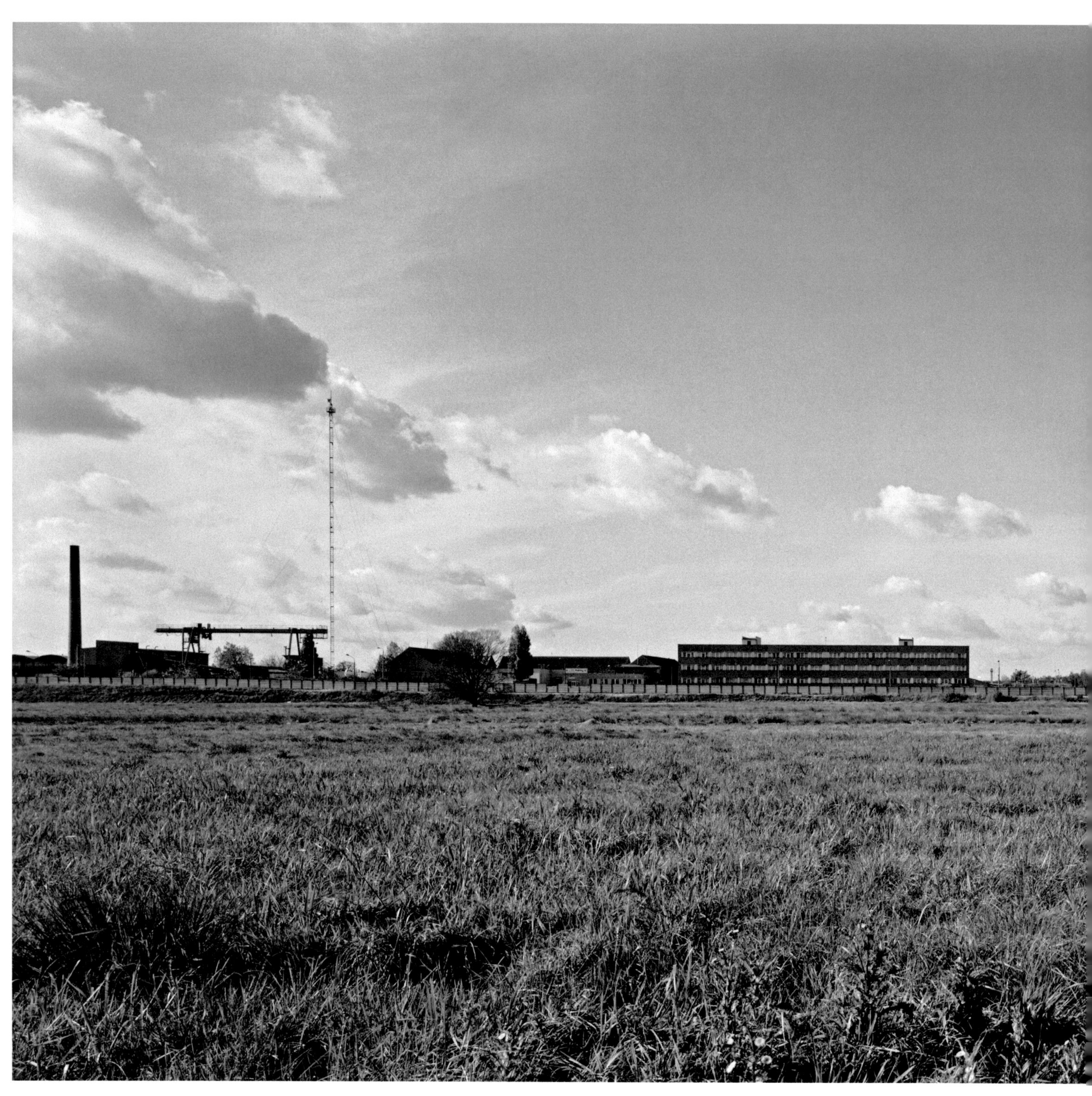

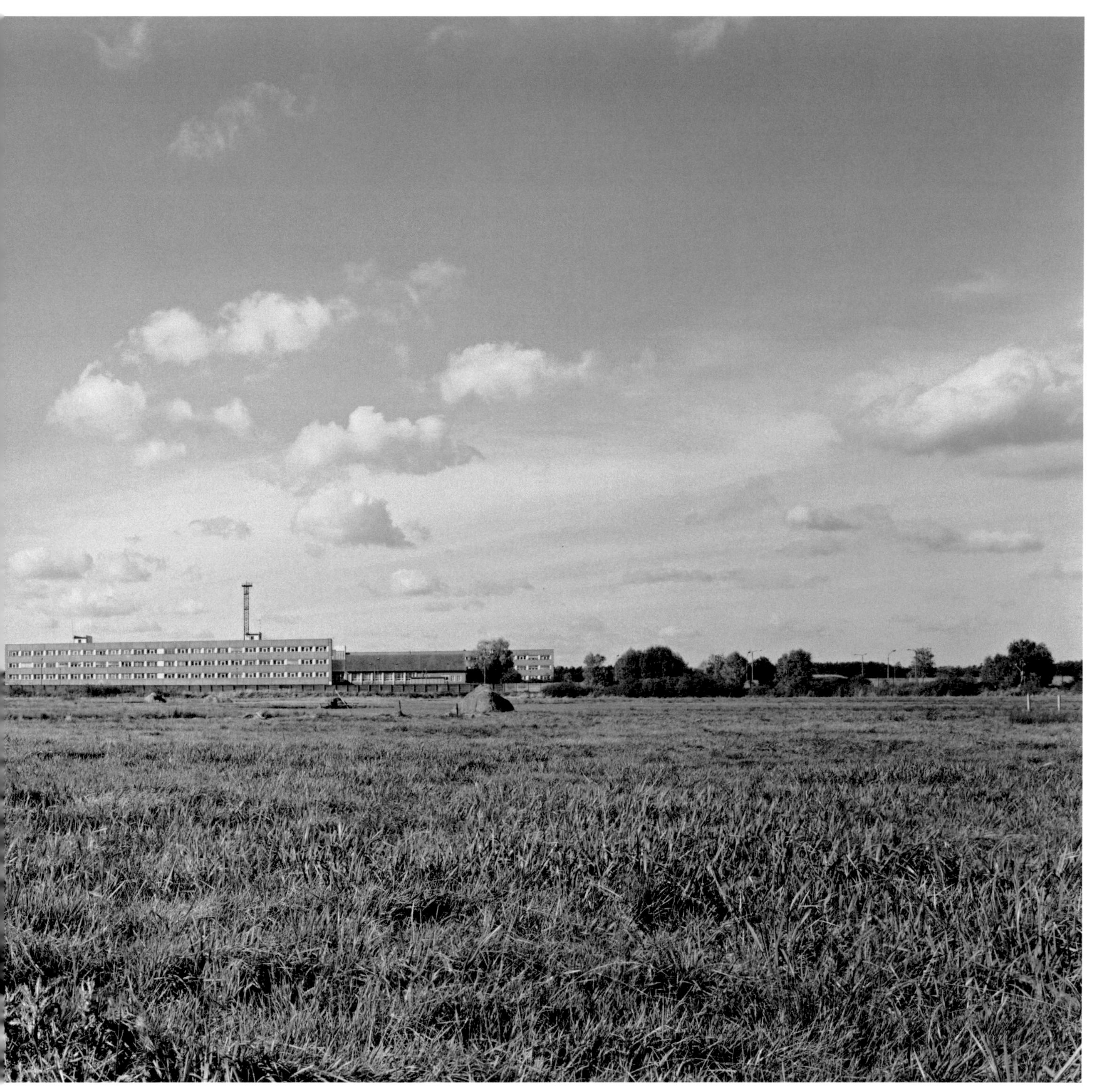

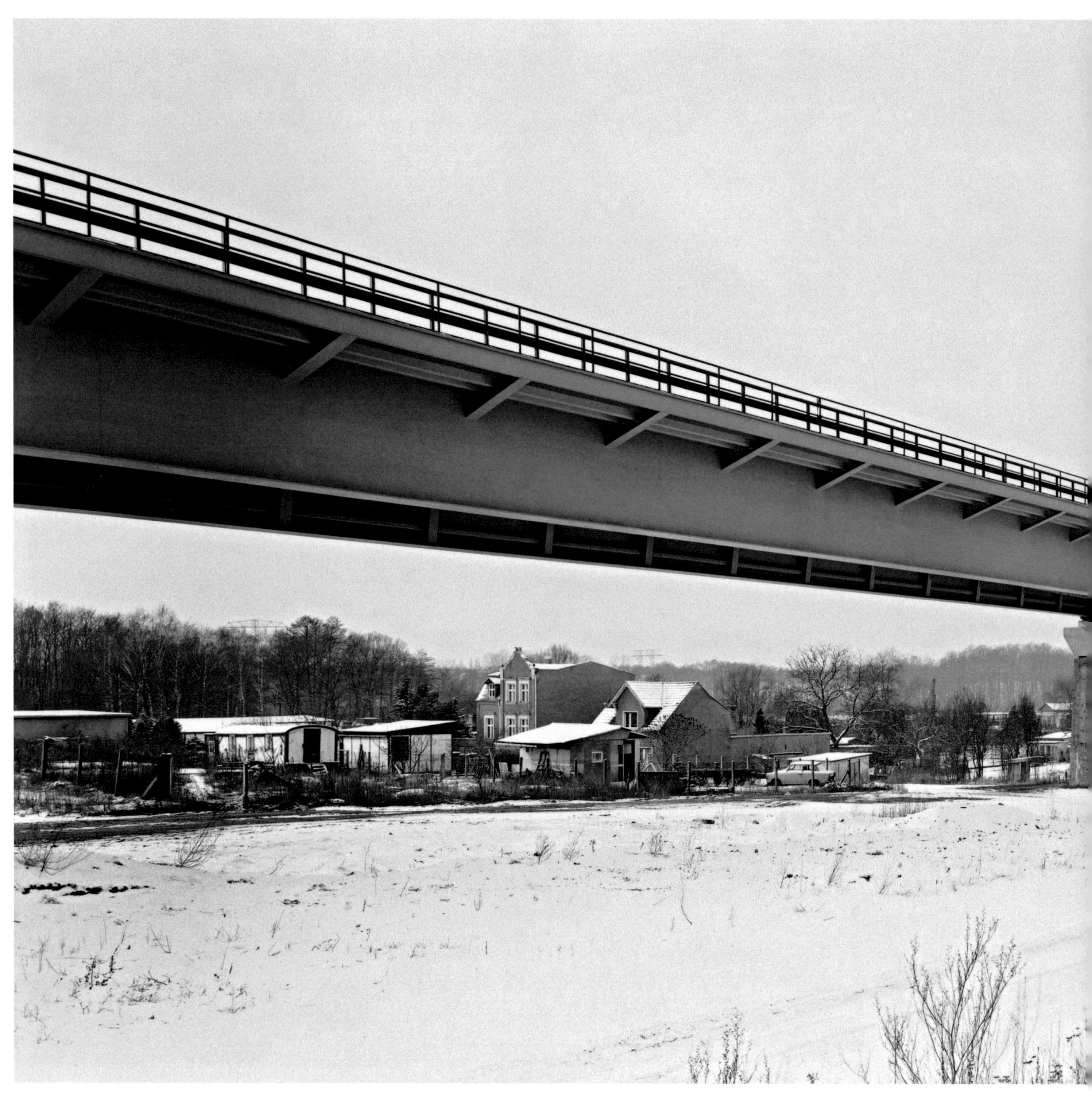

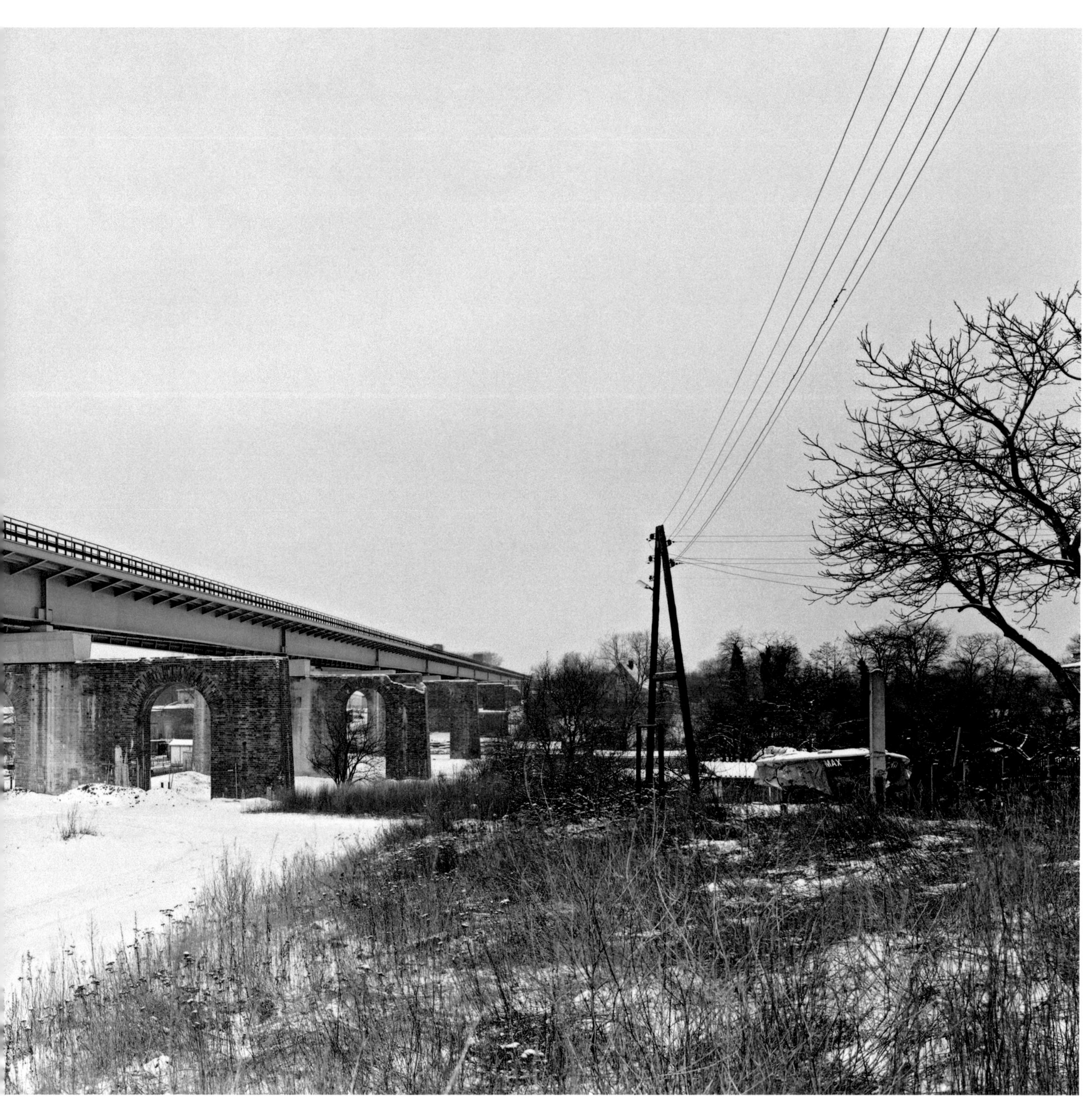
MAX

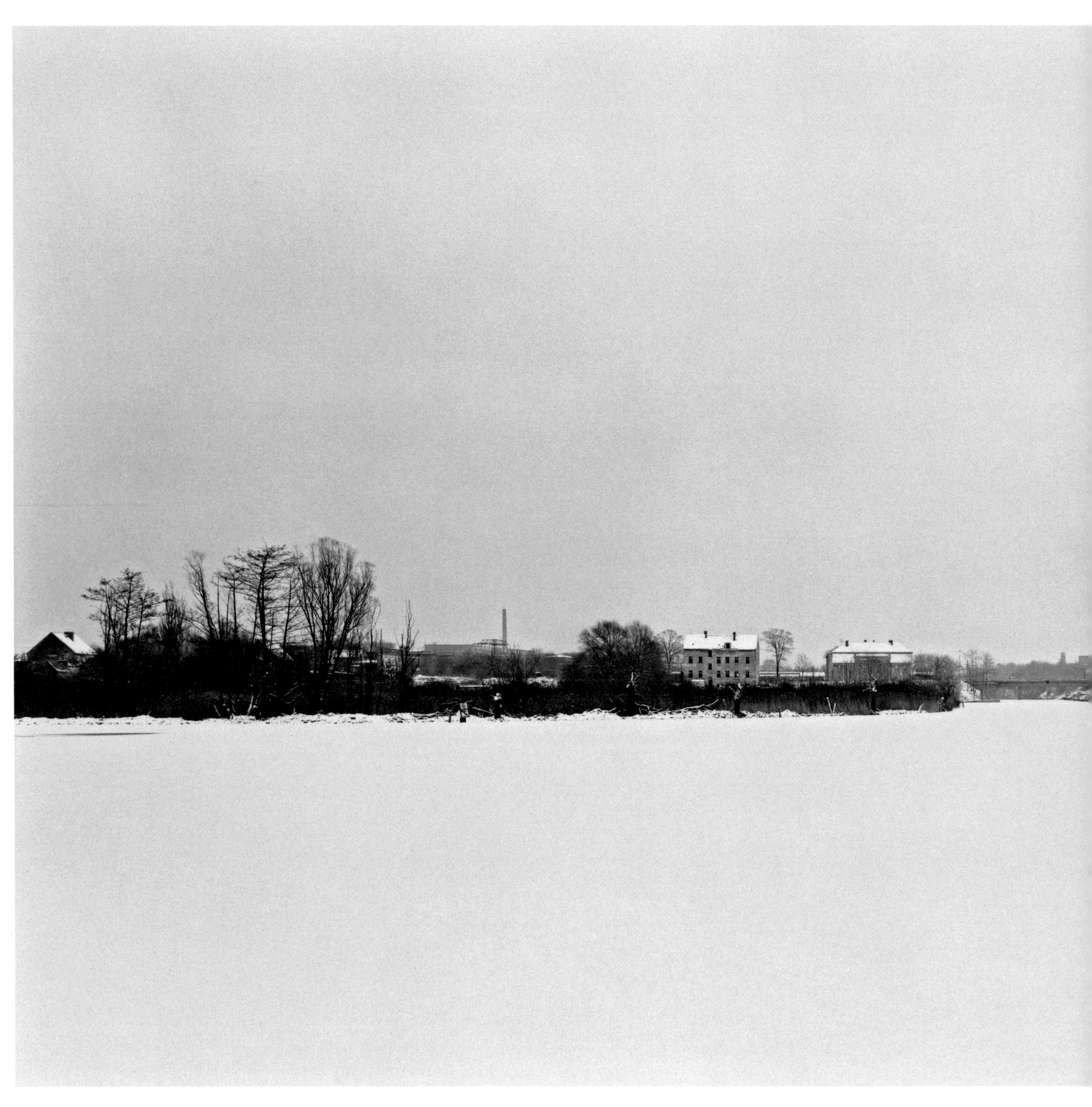

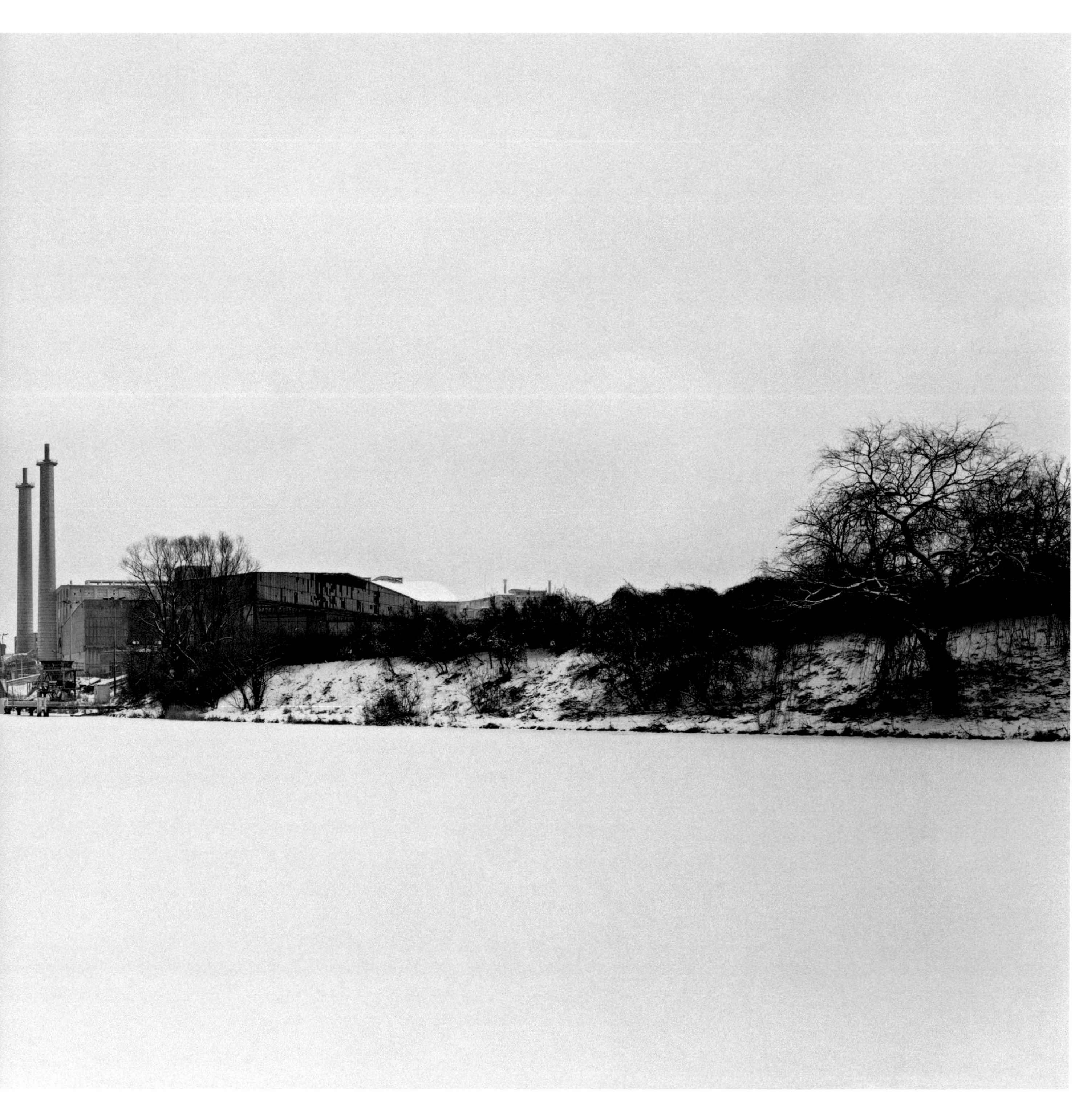

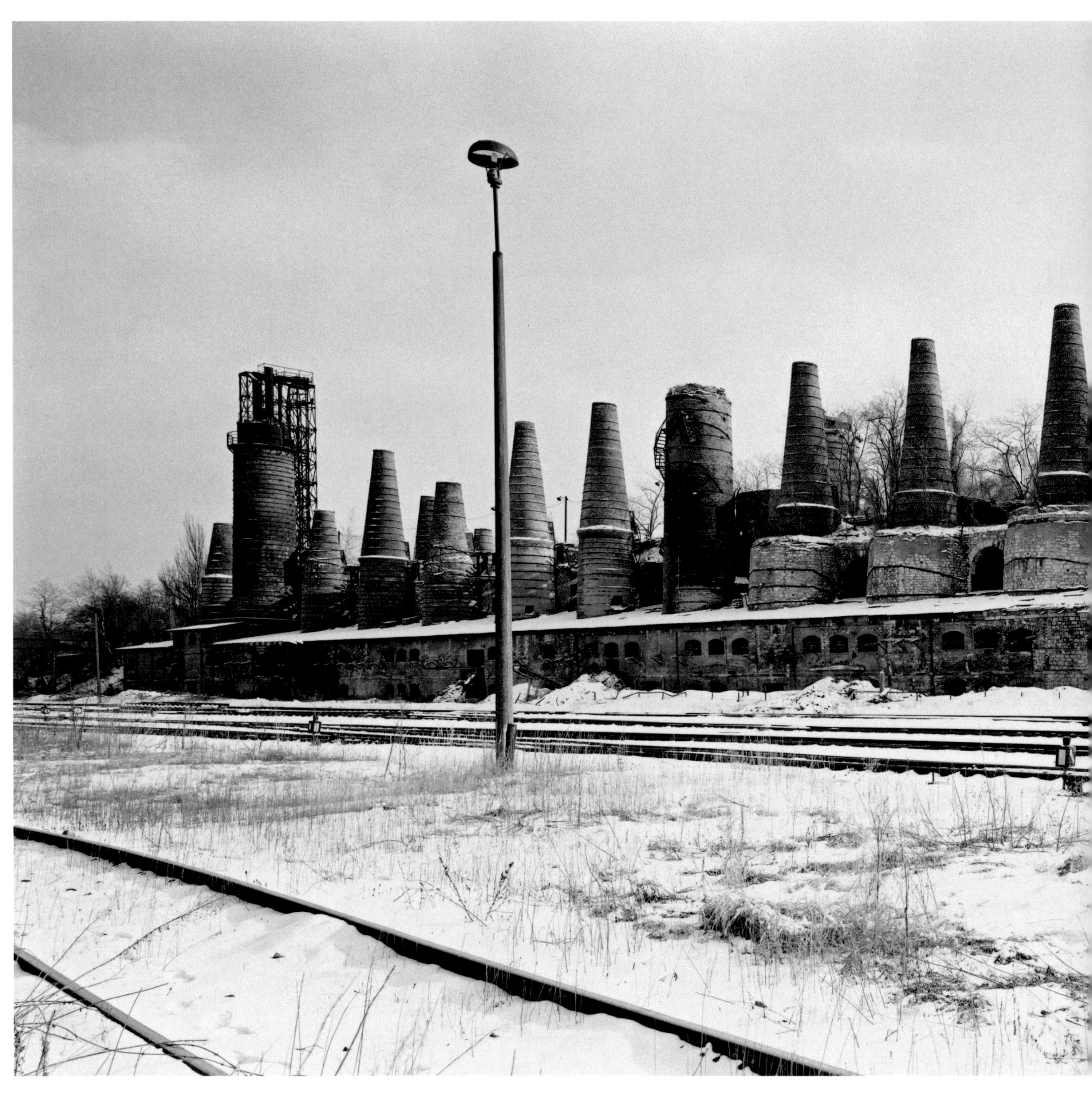

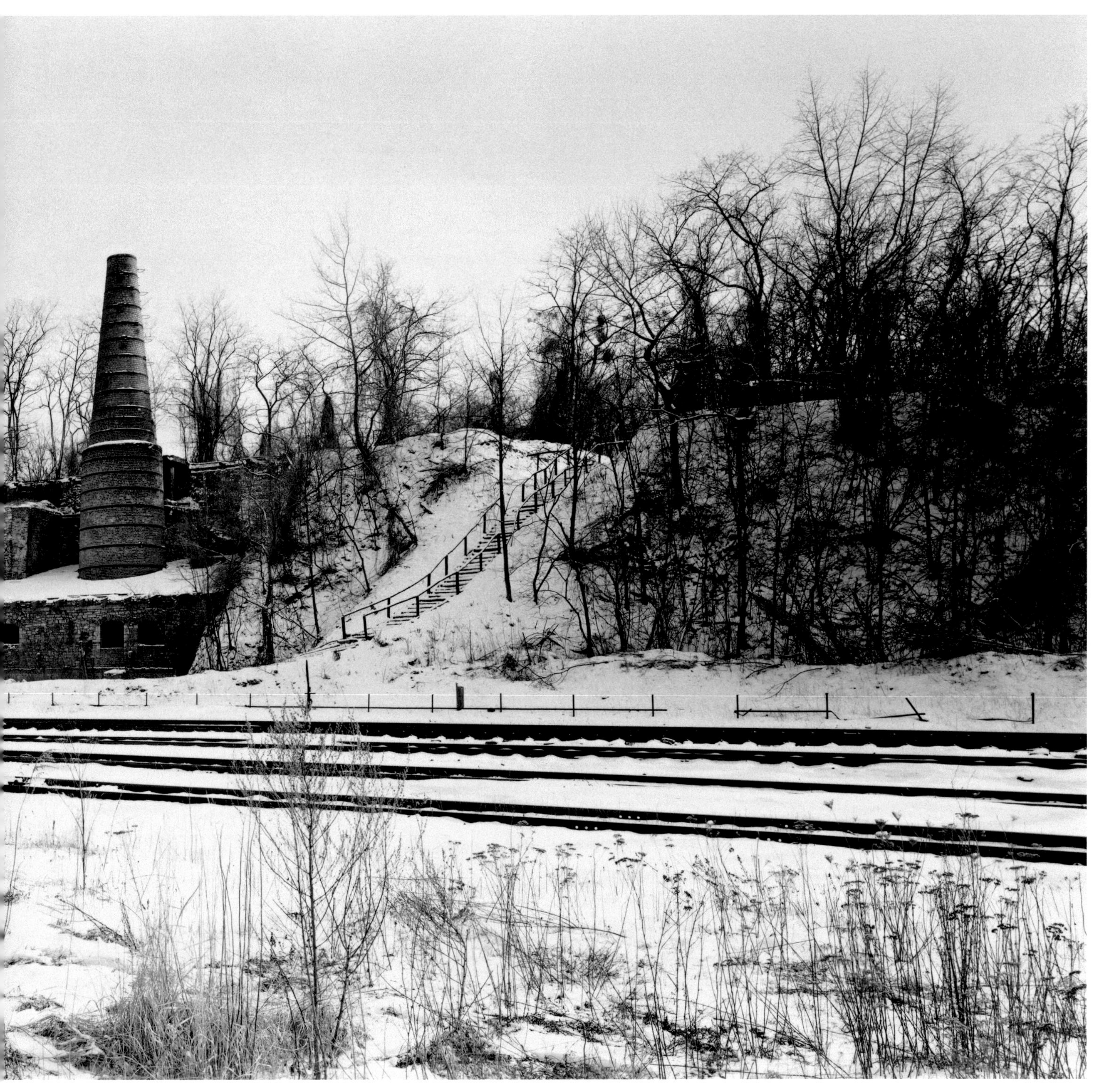

25

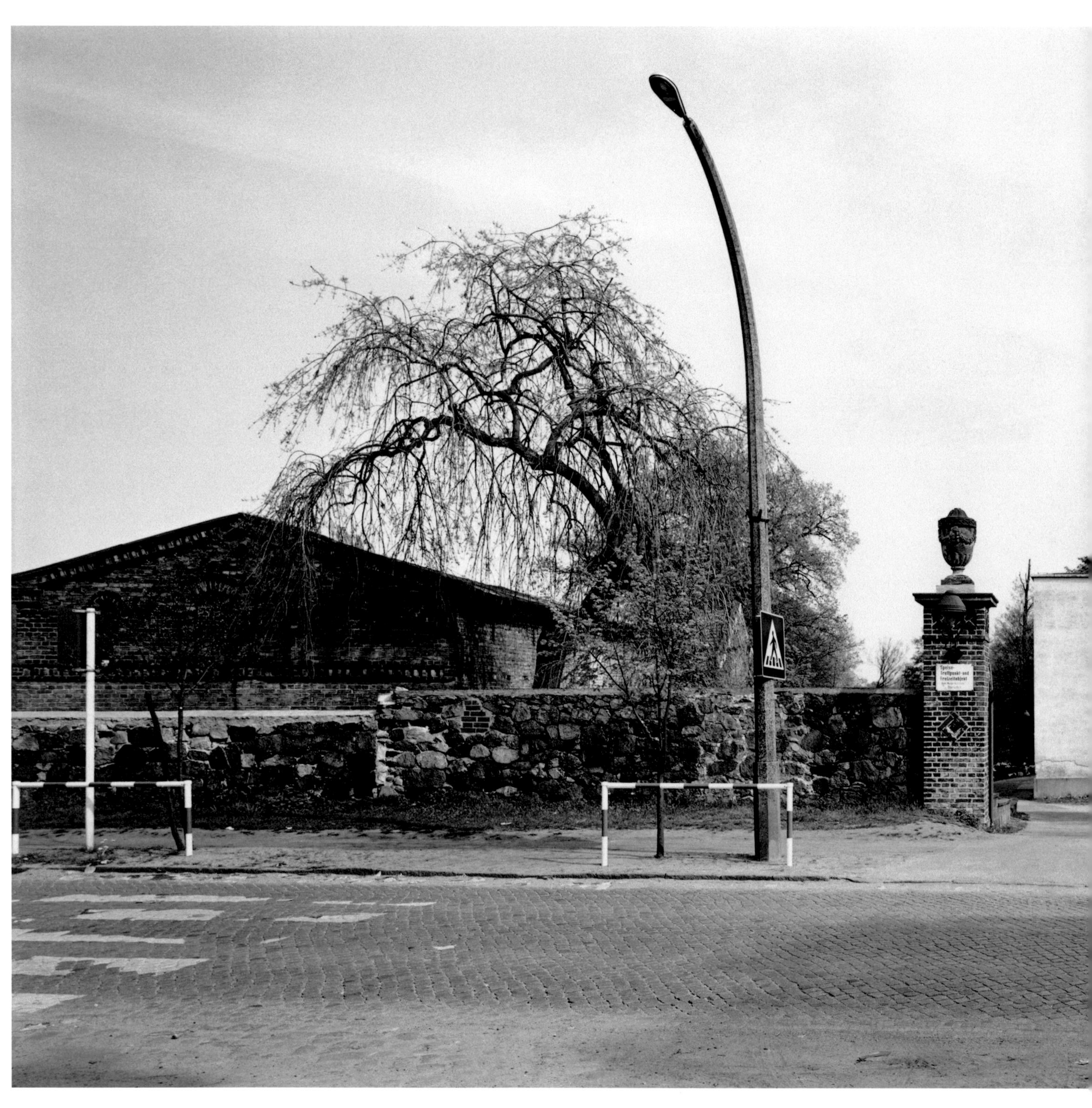

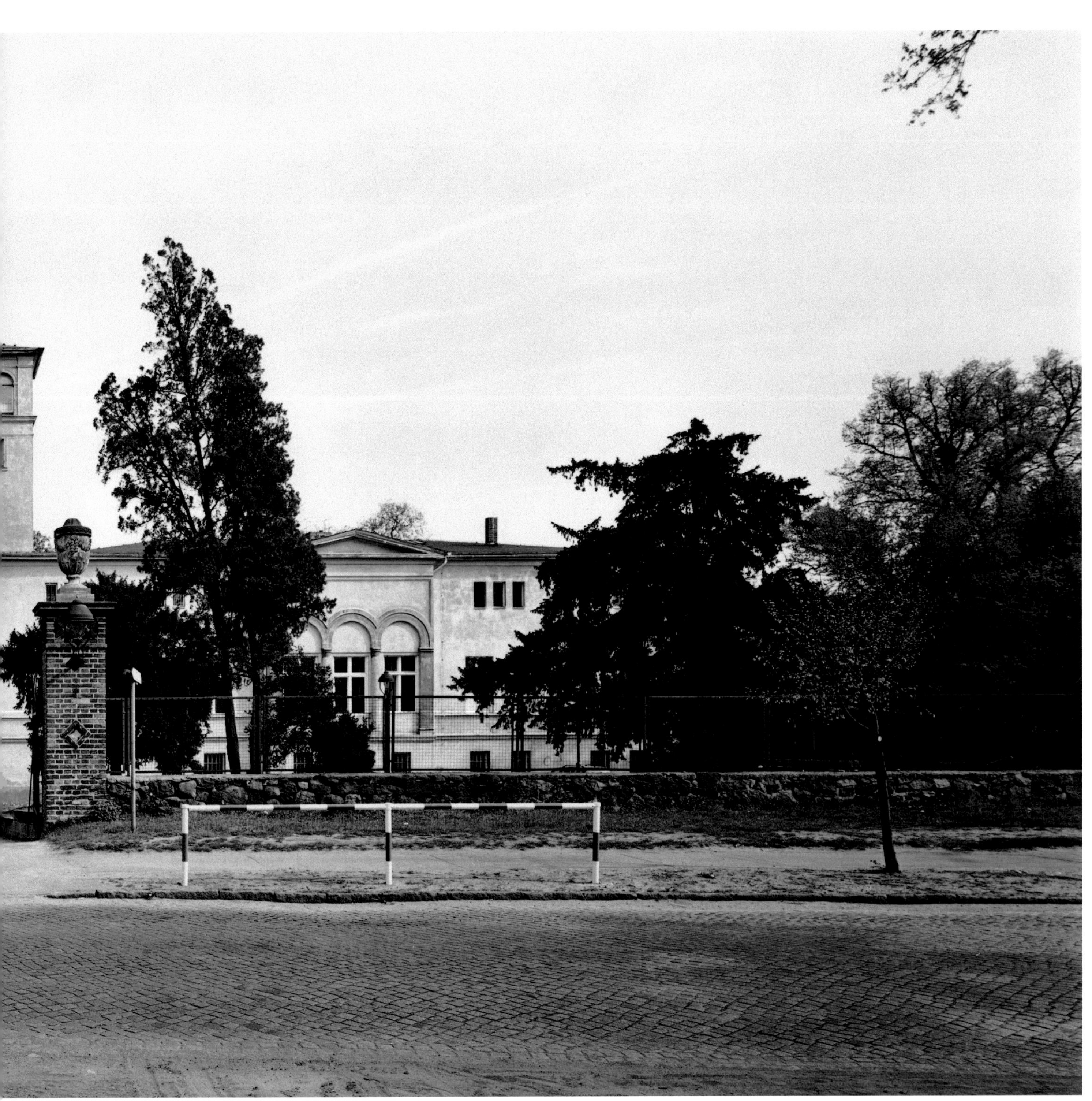

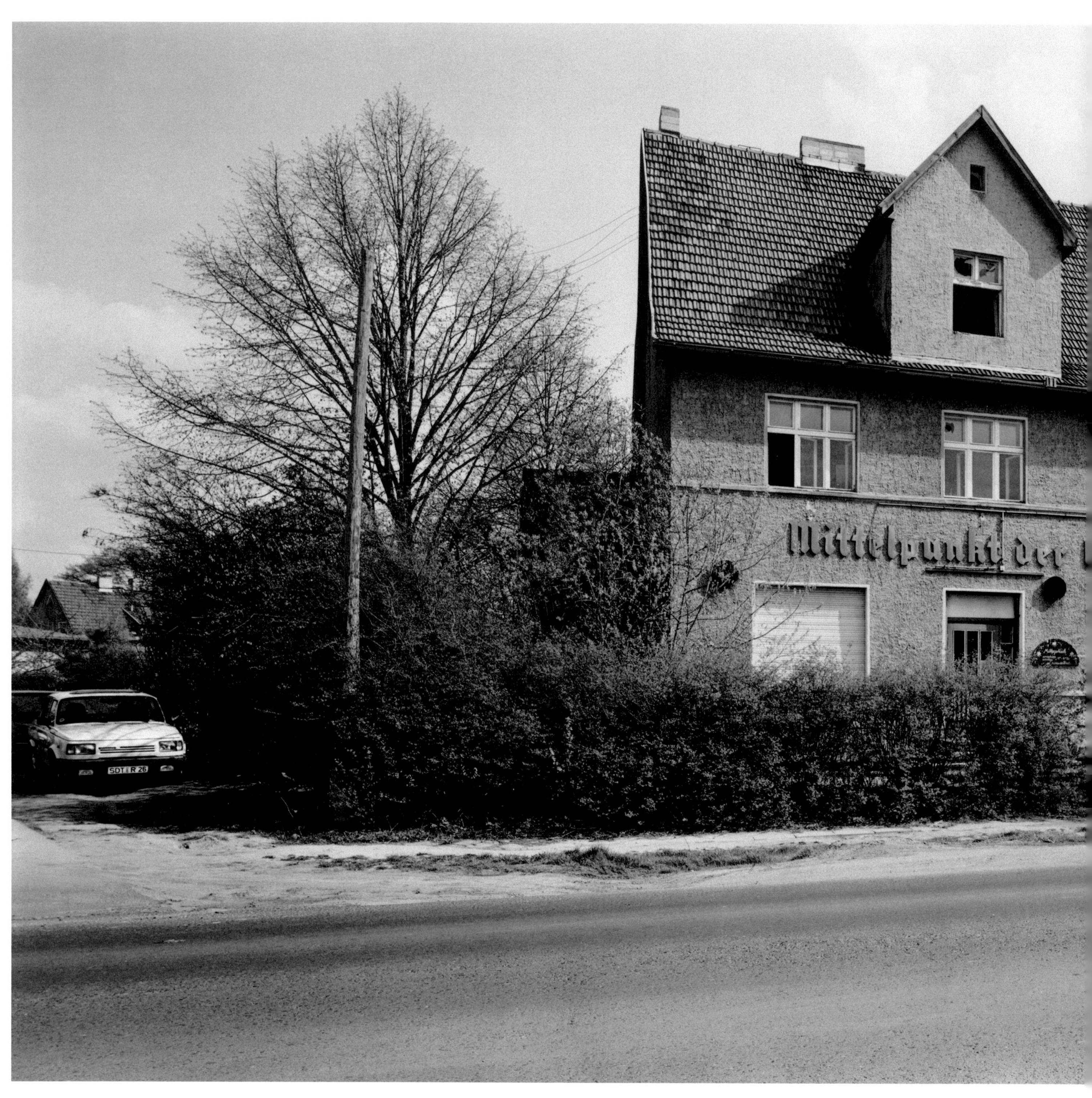
Mittelpunkt der

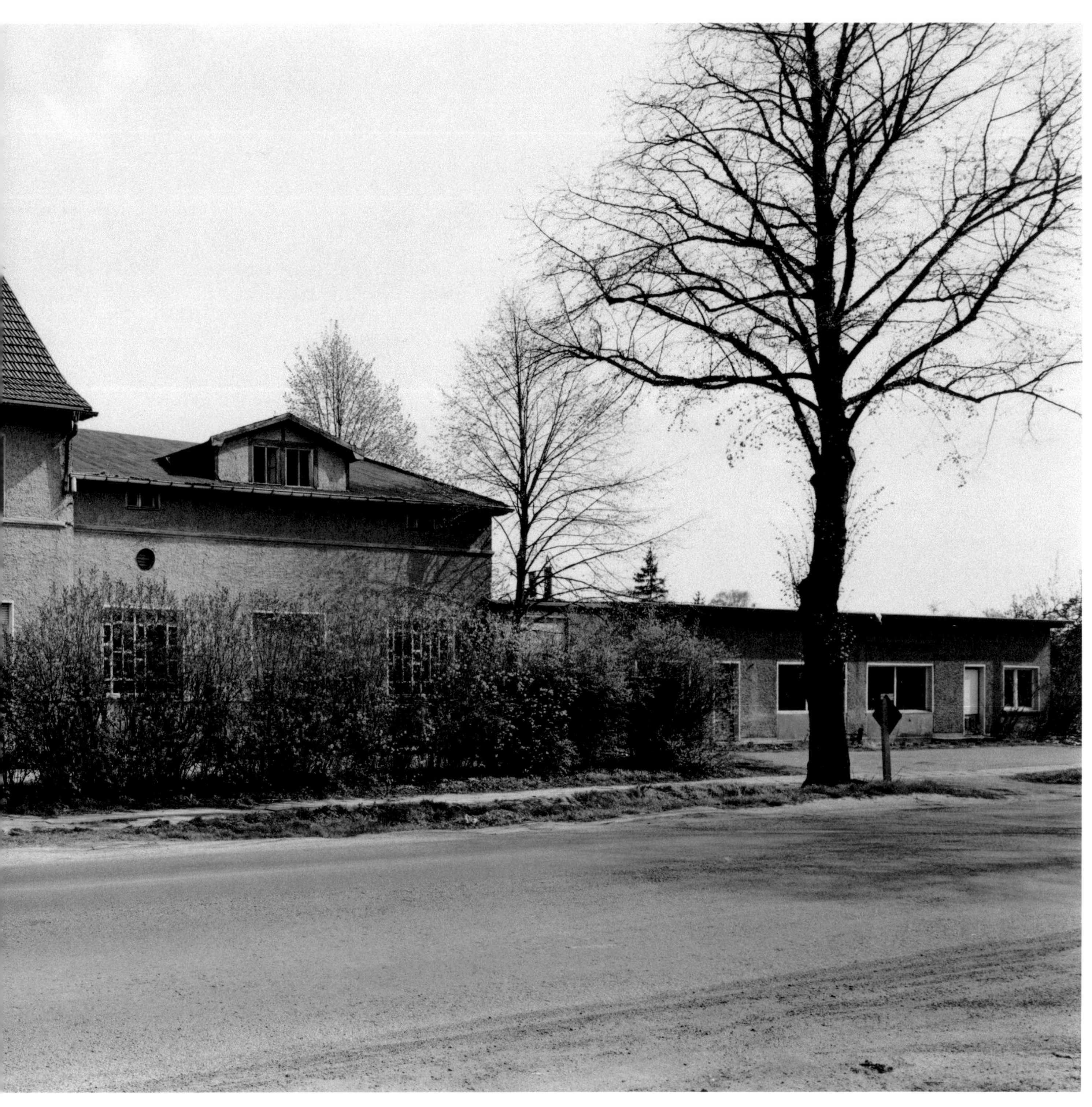

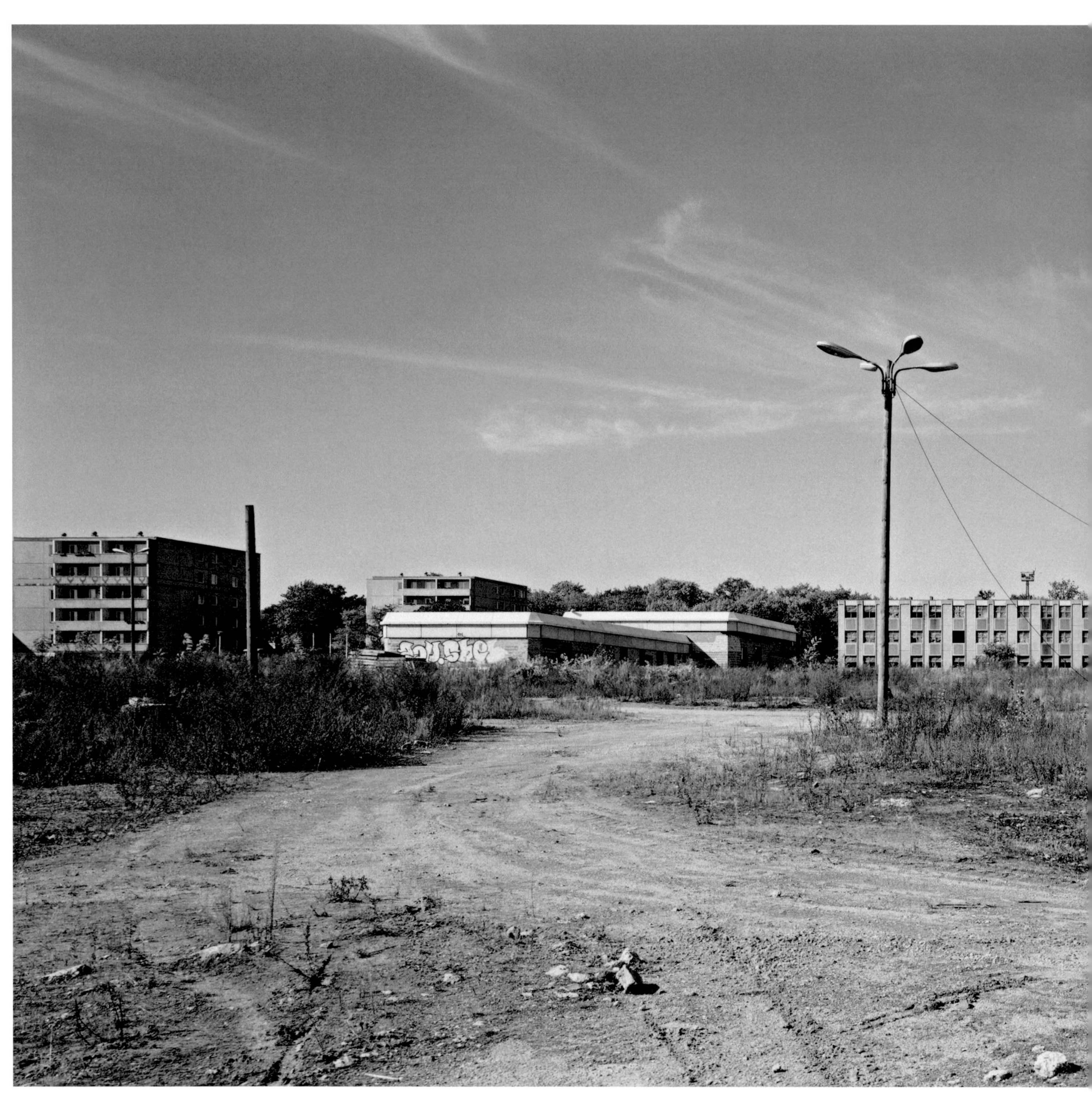

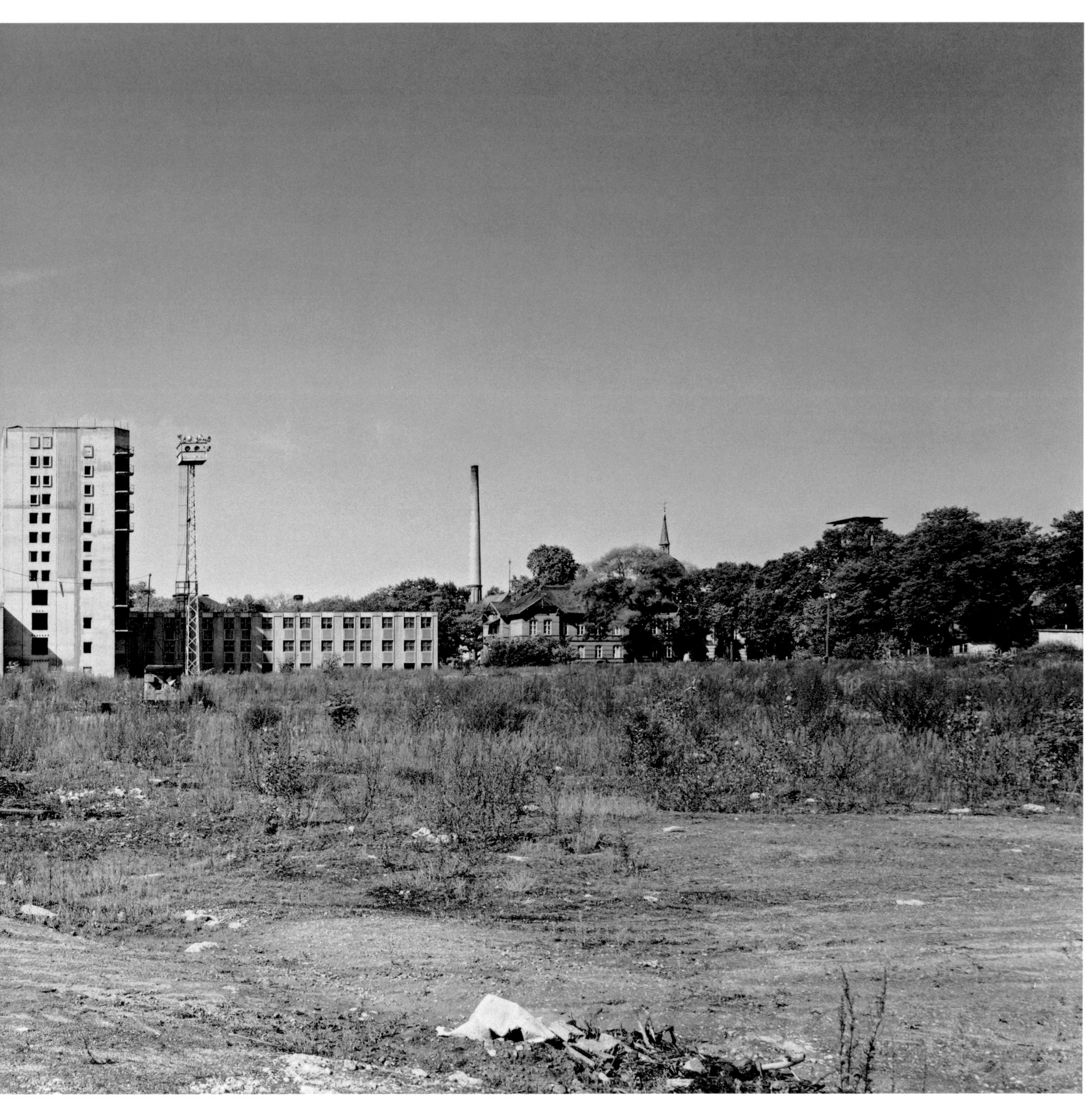

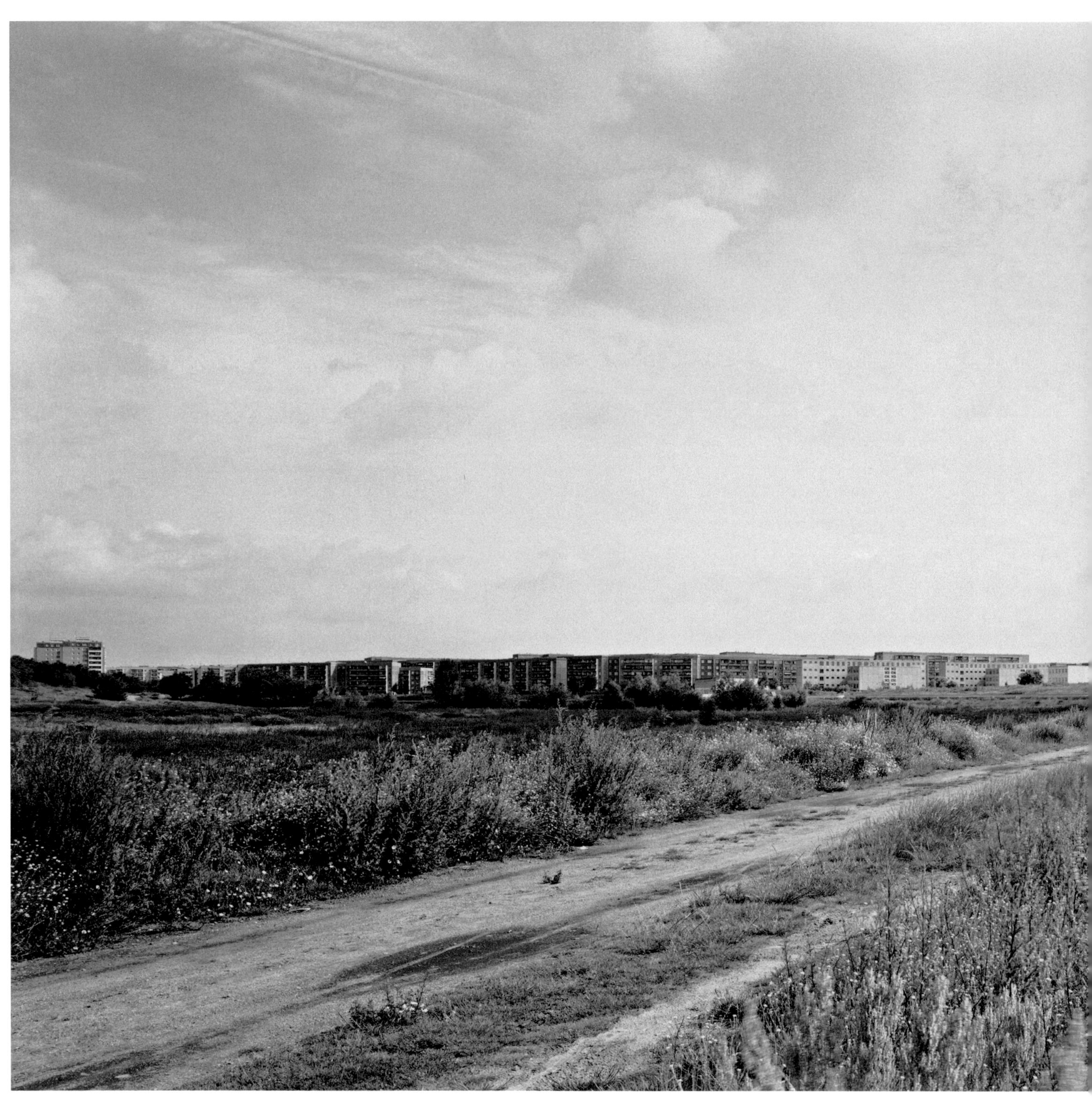

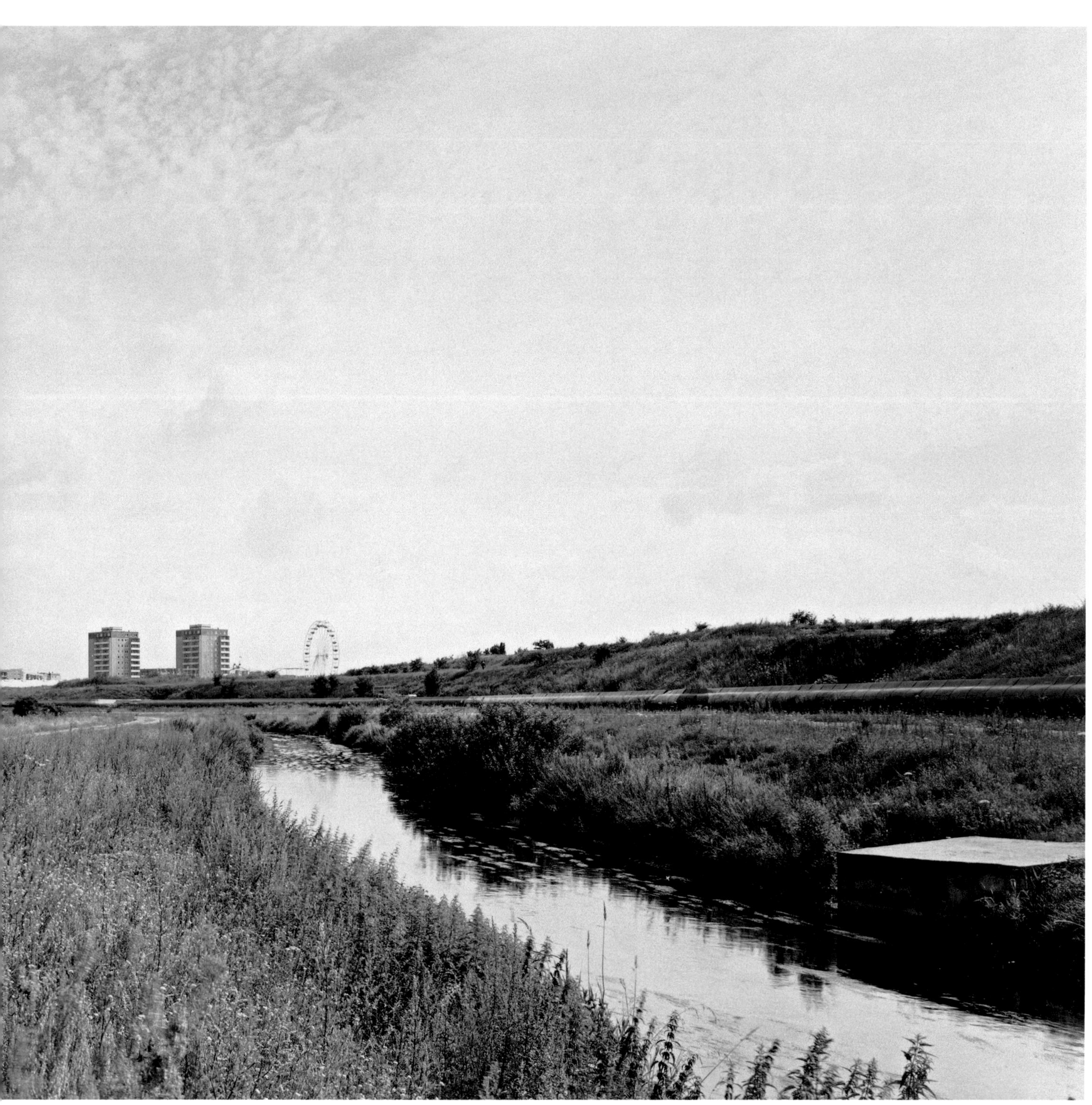

29

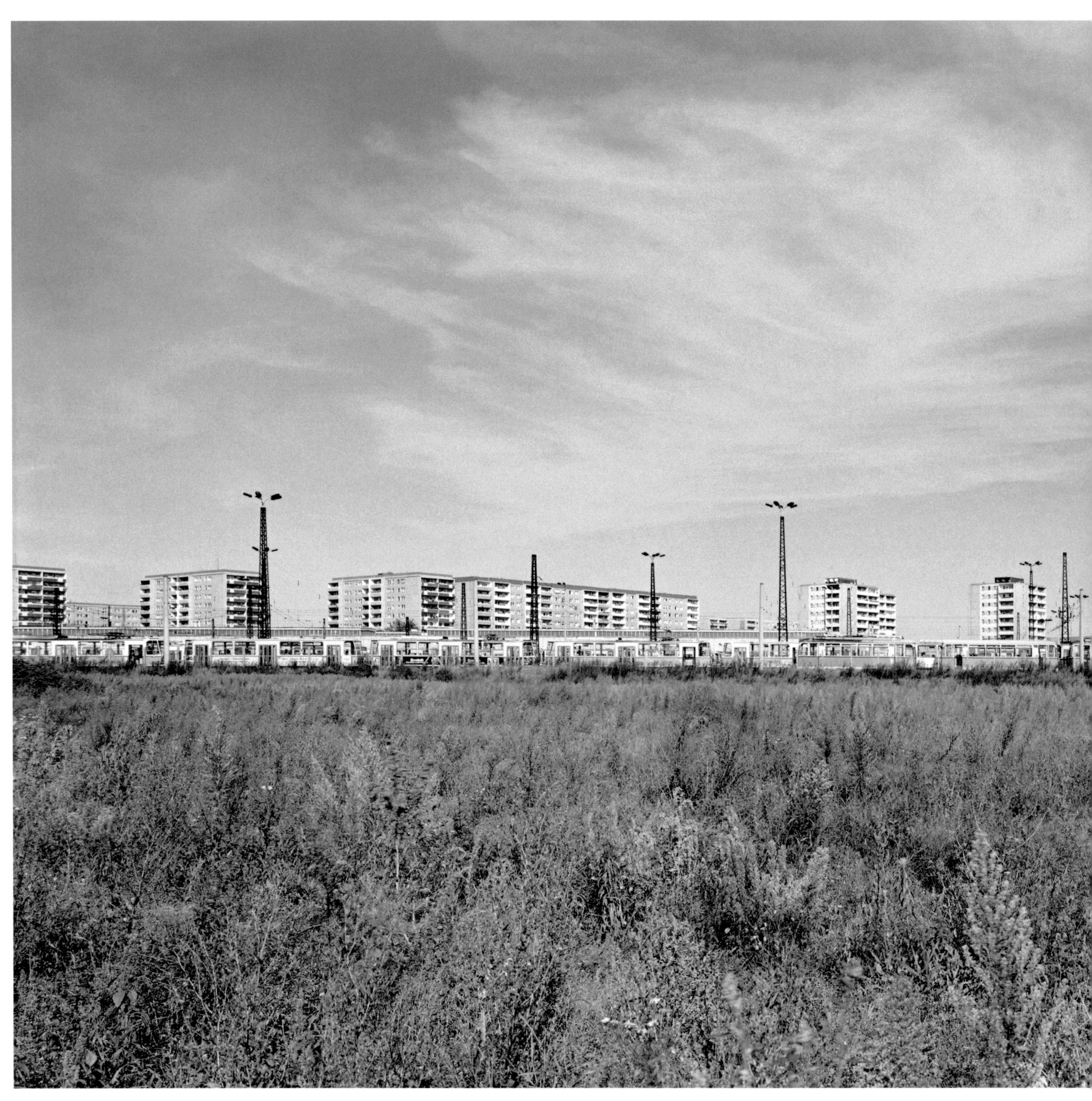

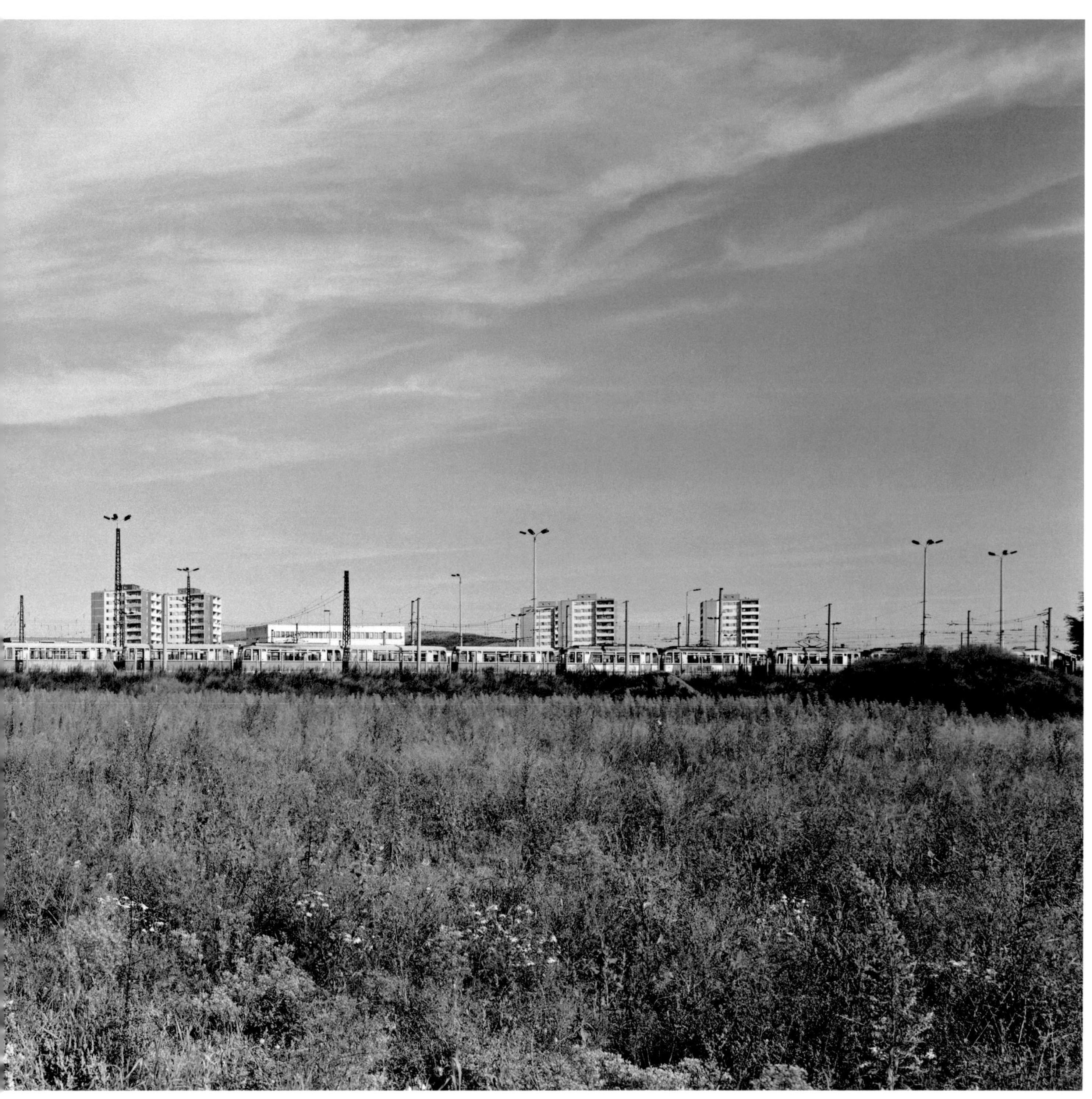

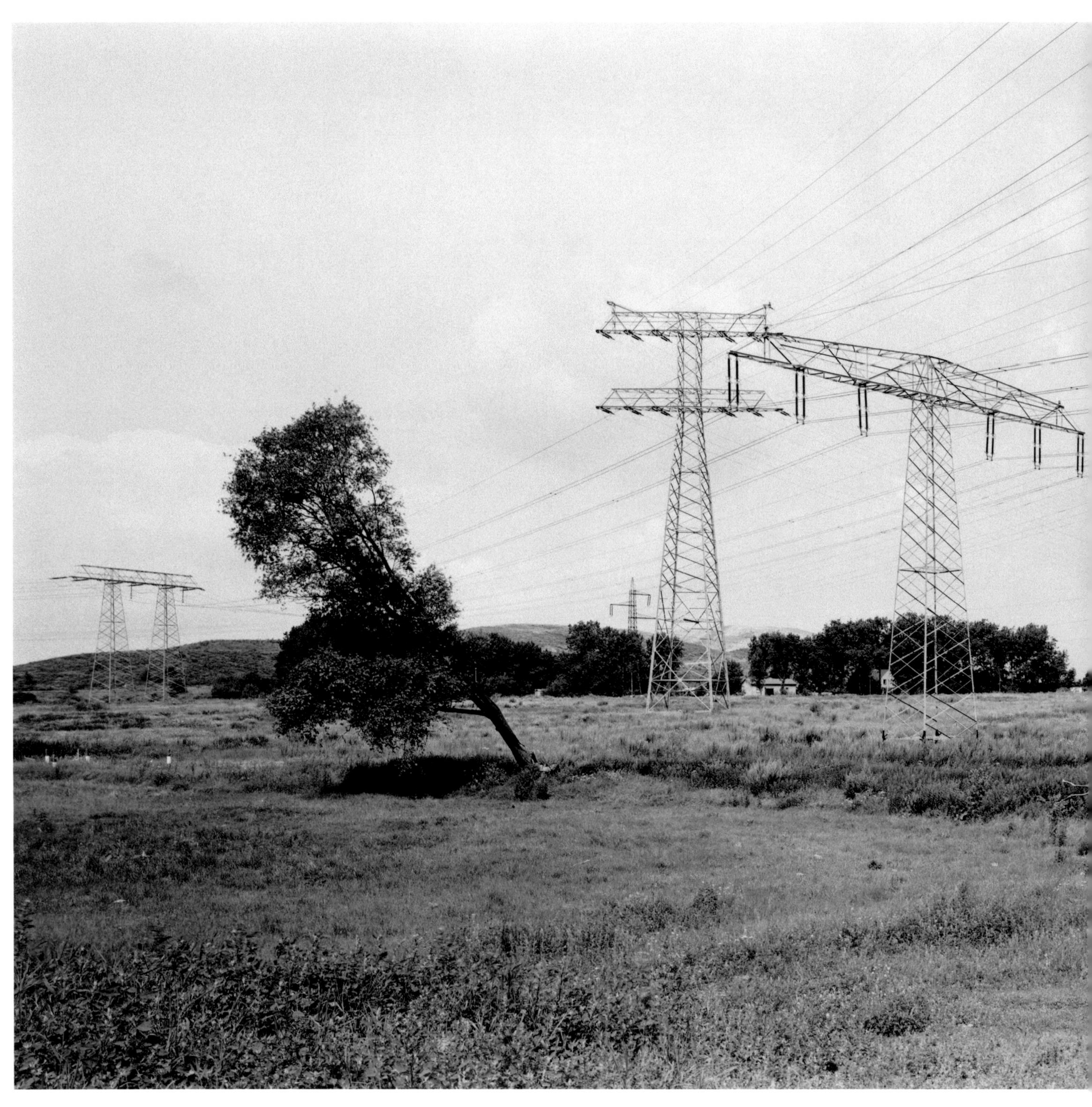

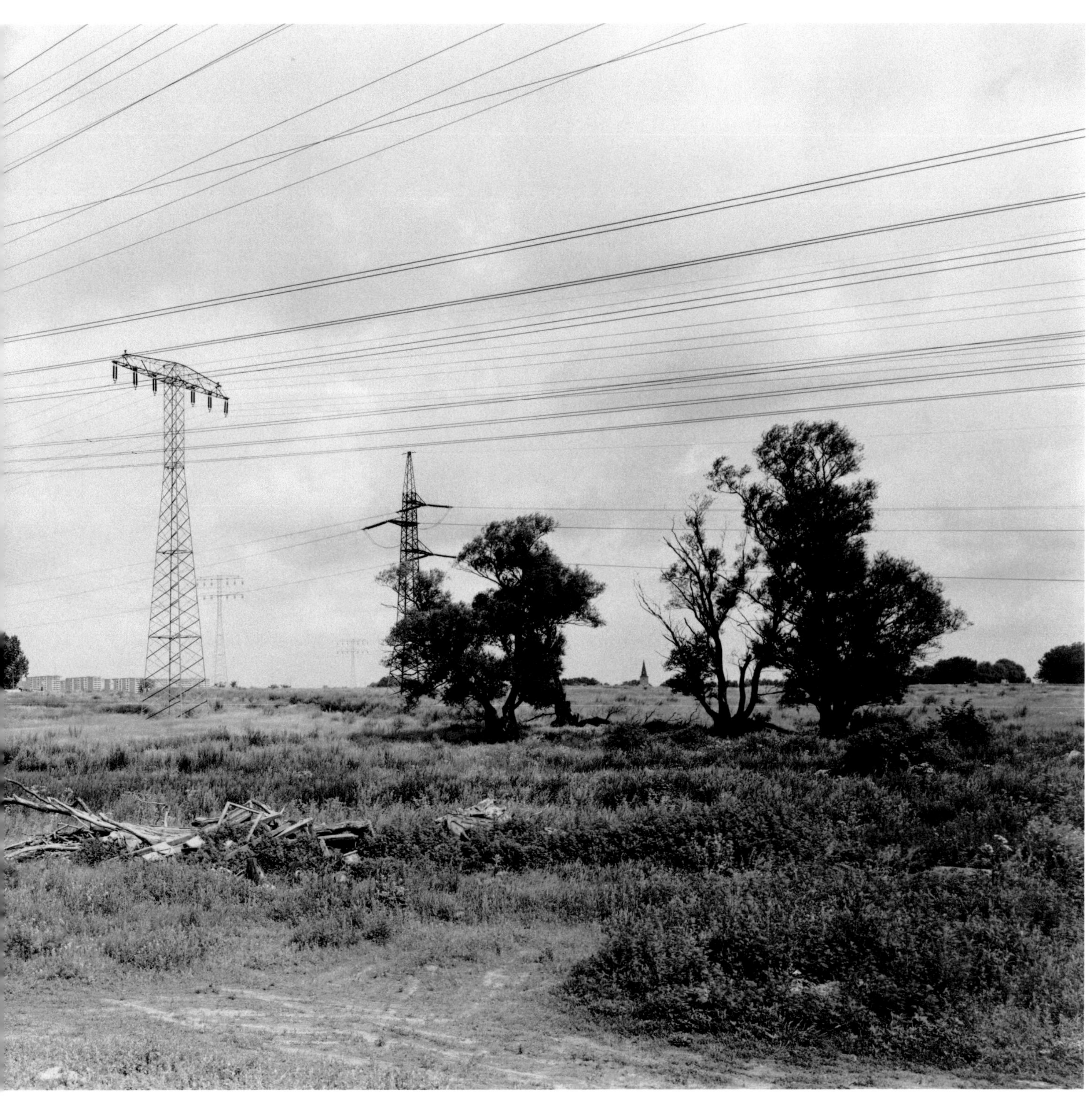

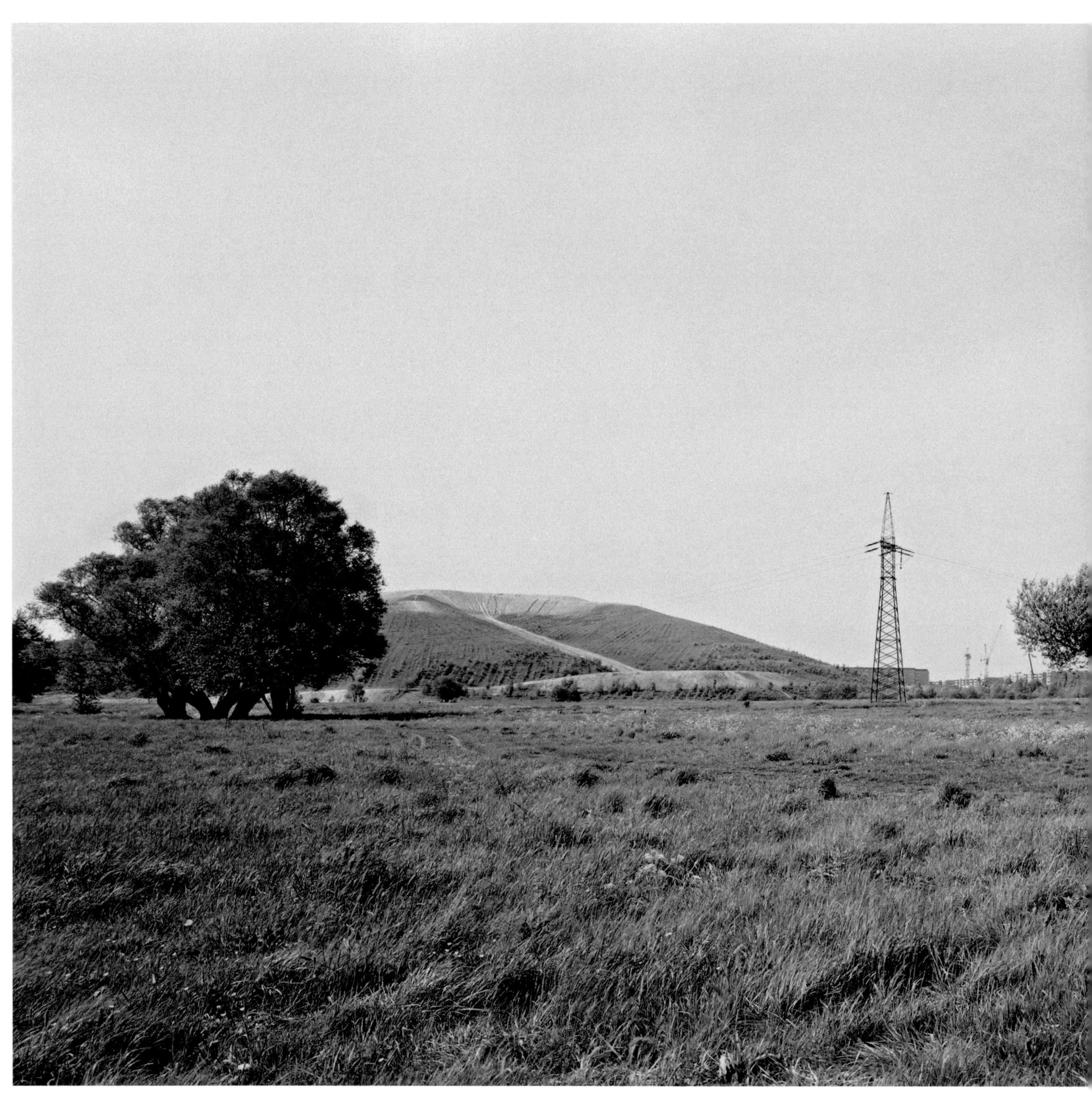

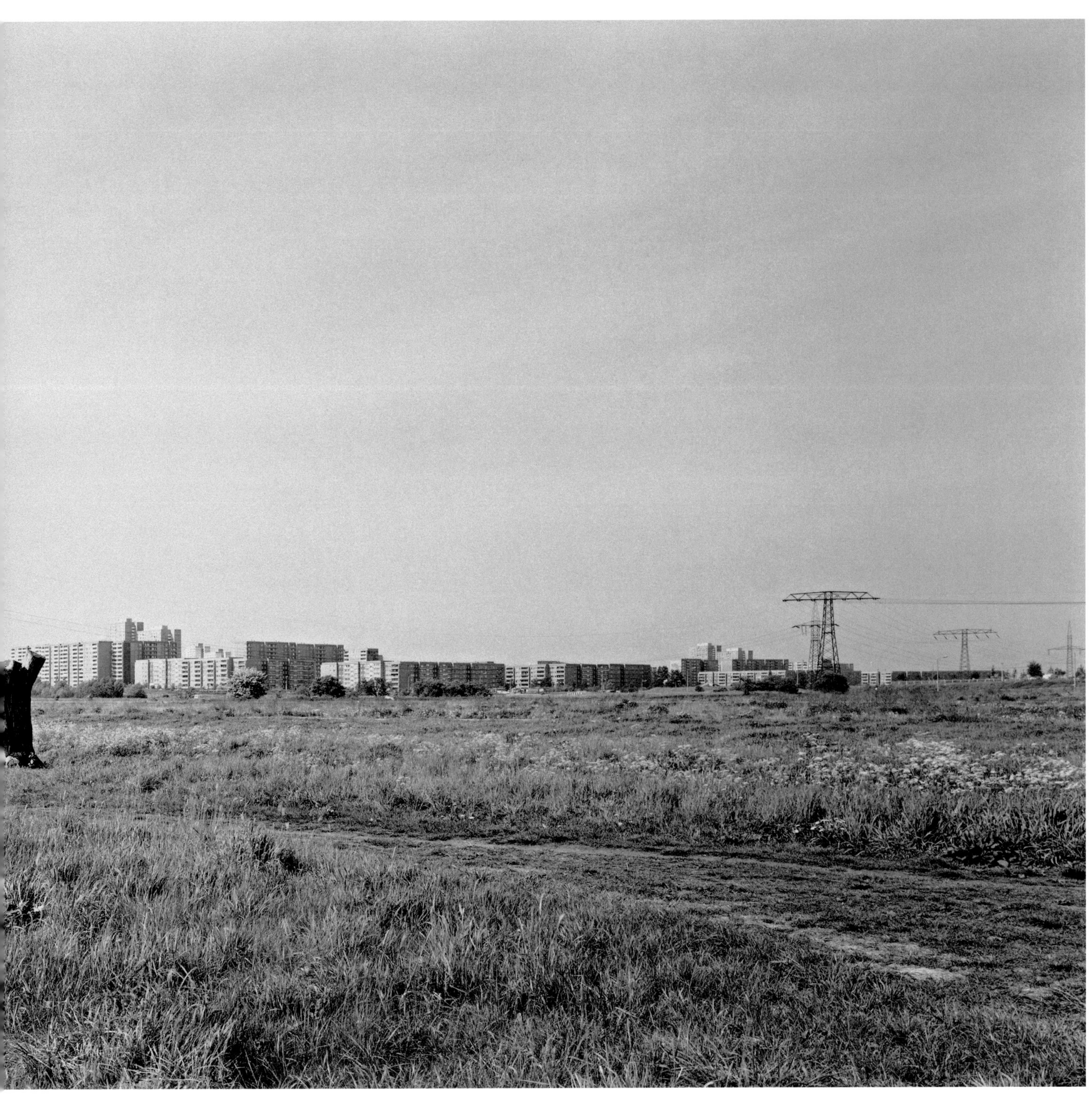

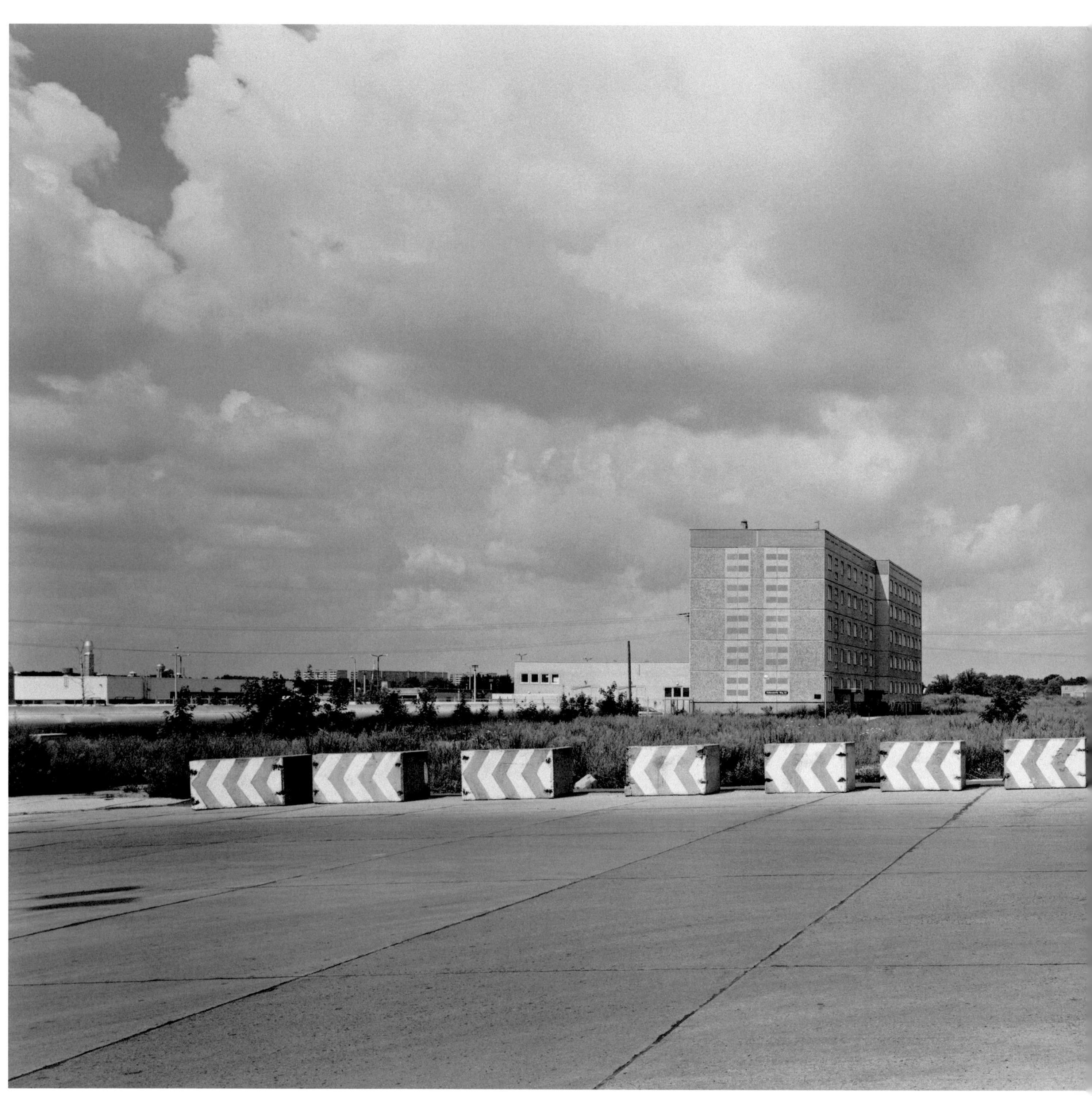

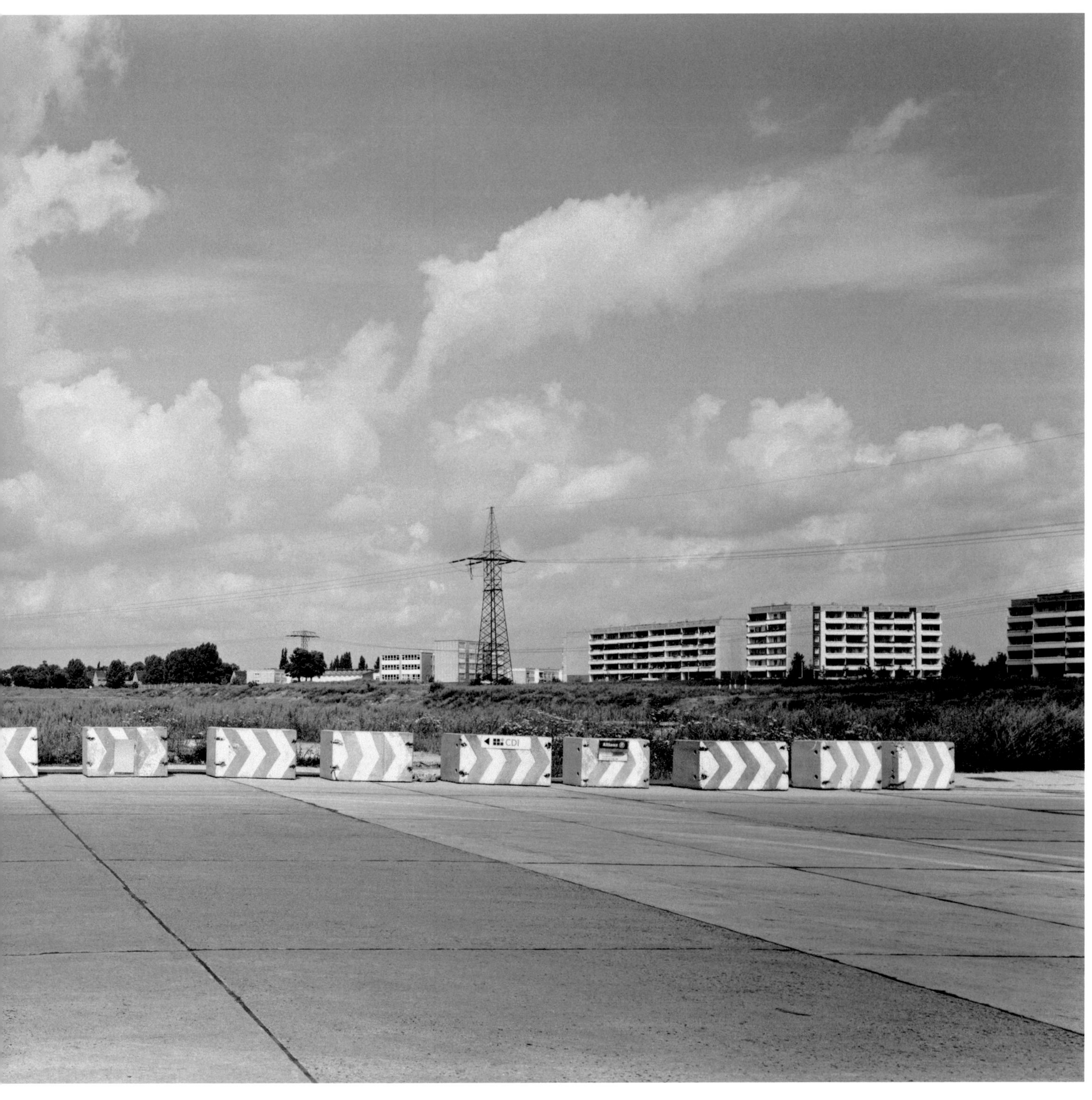
CDI

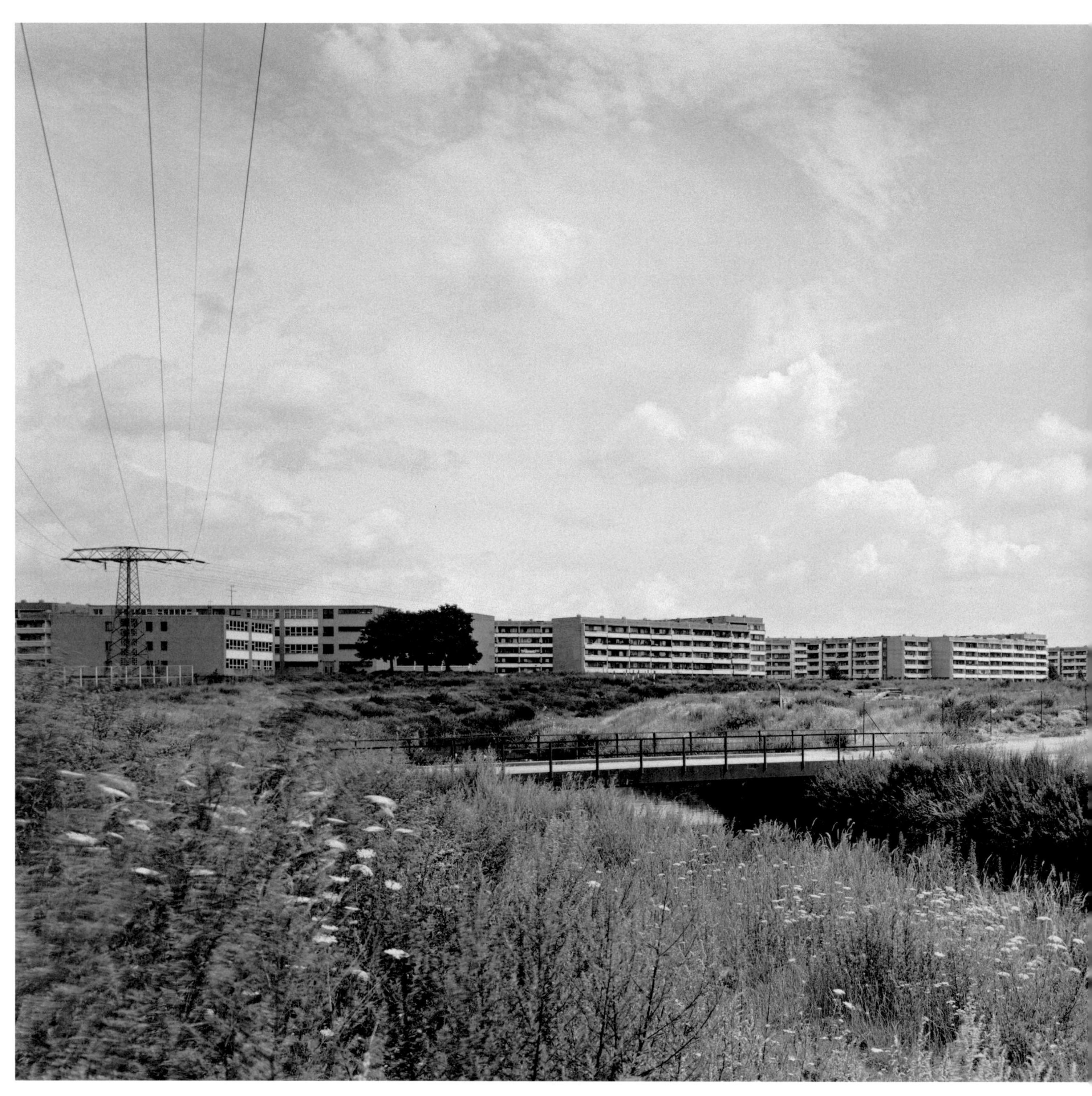

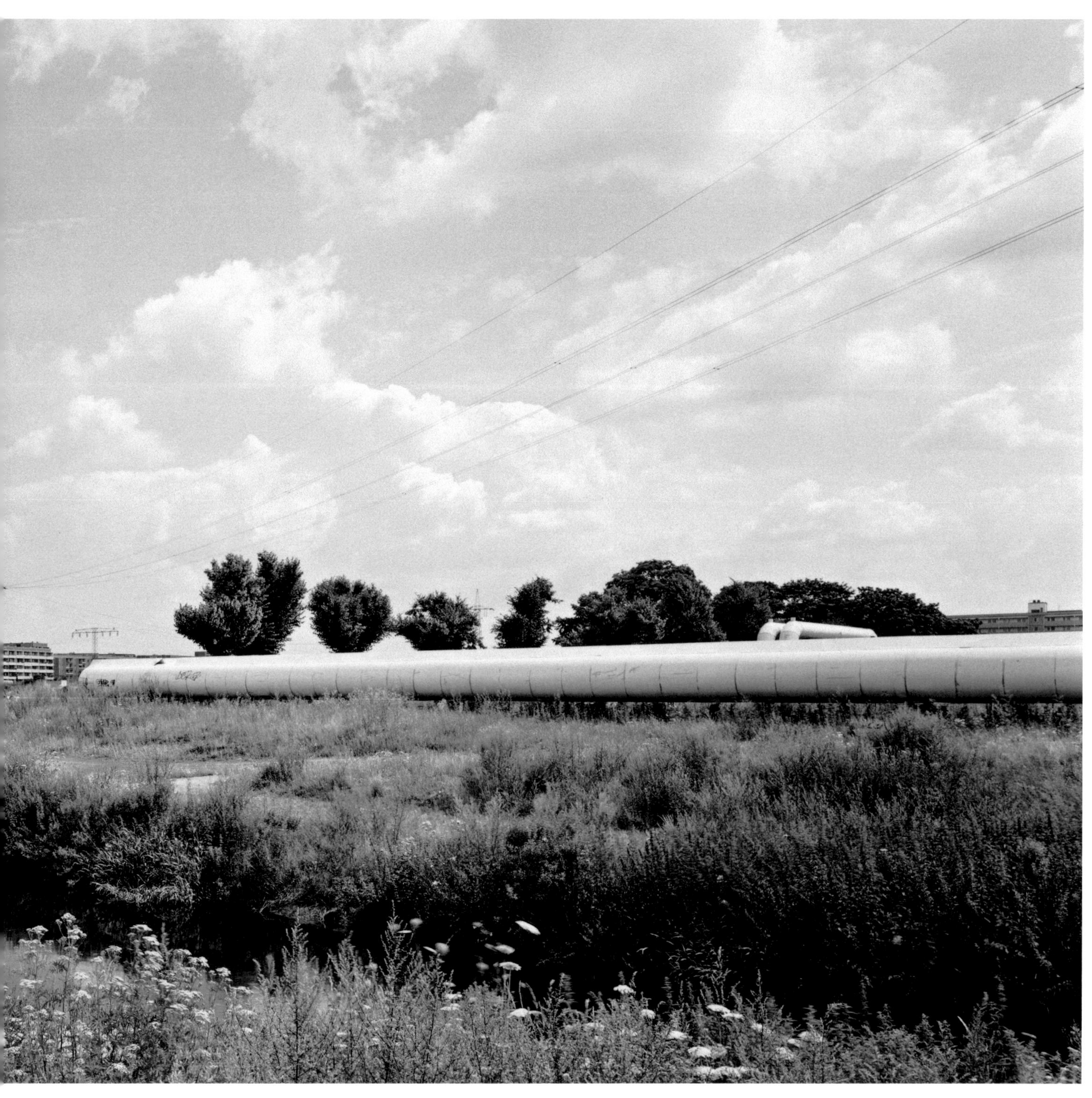

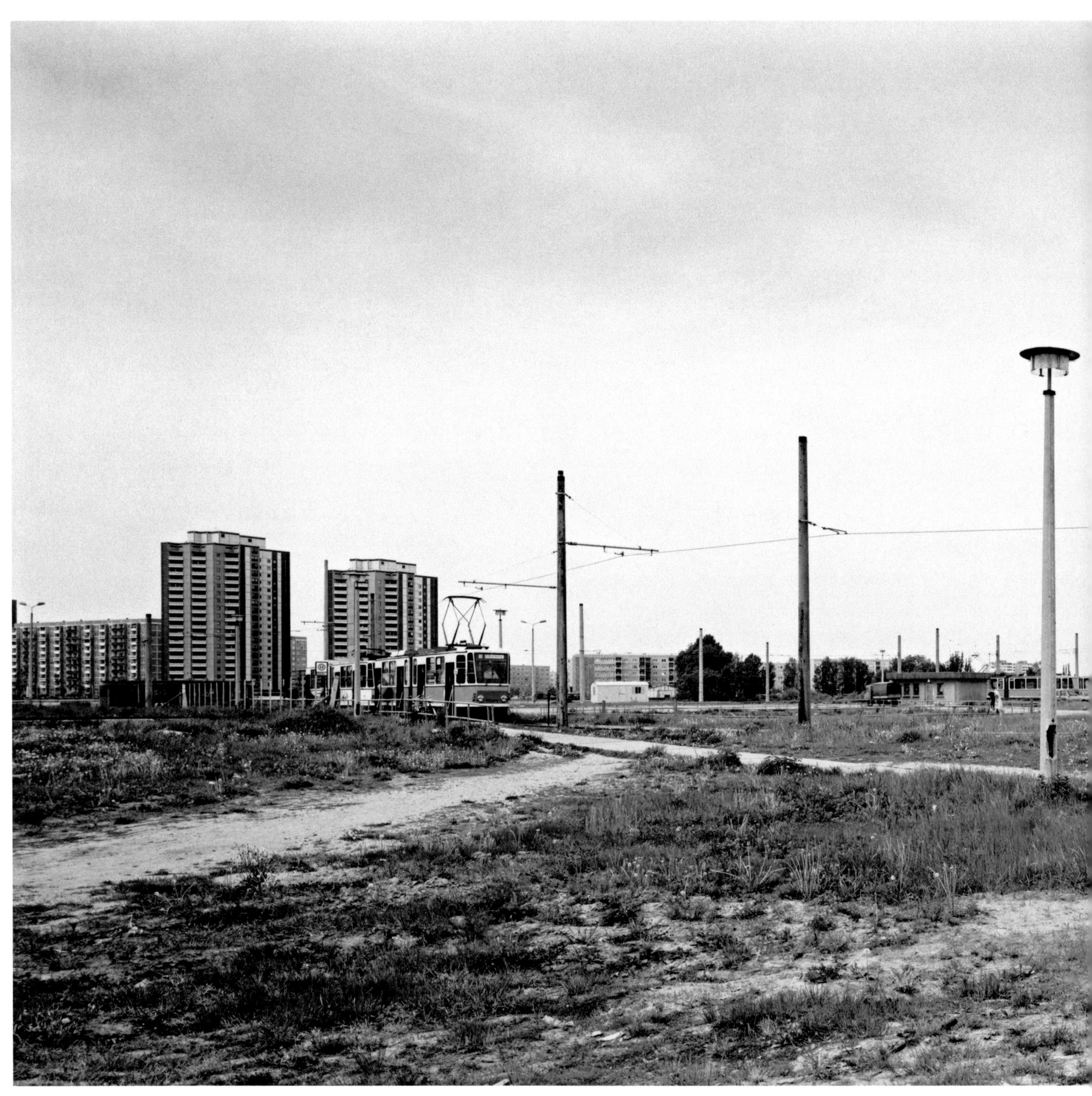

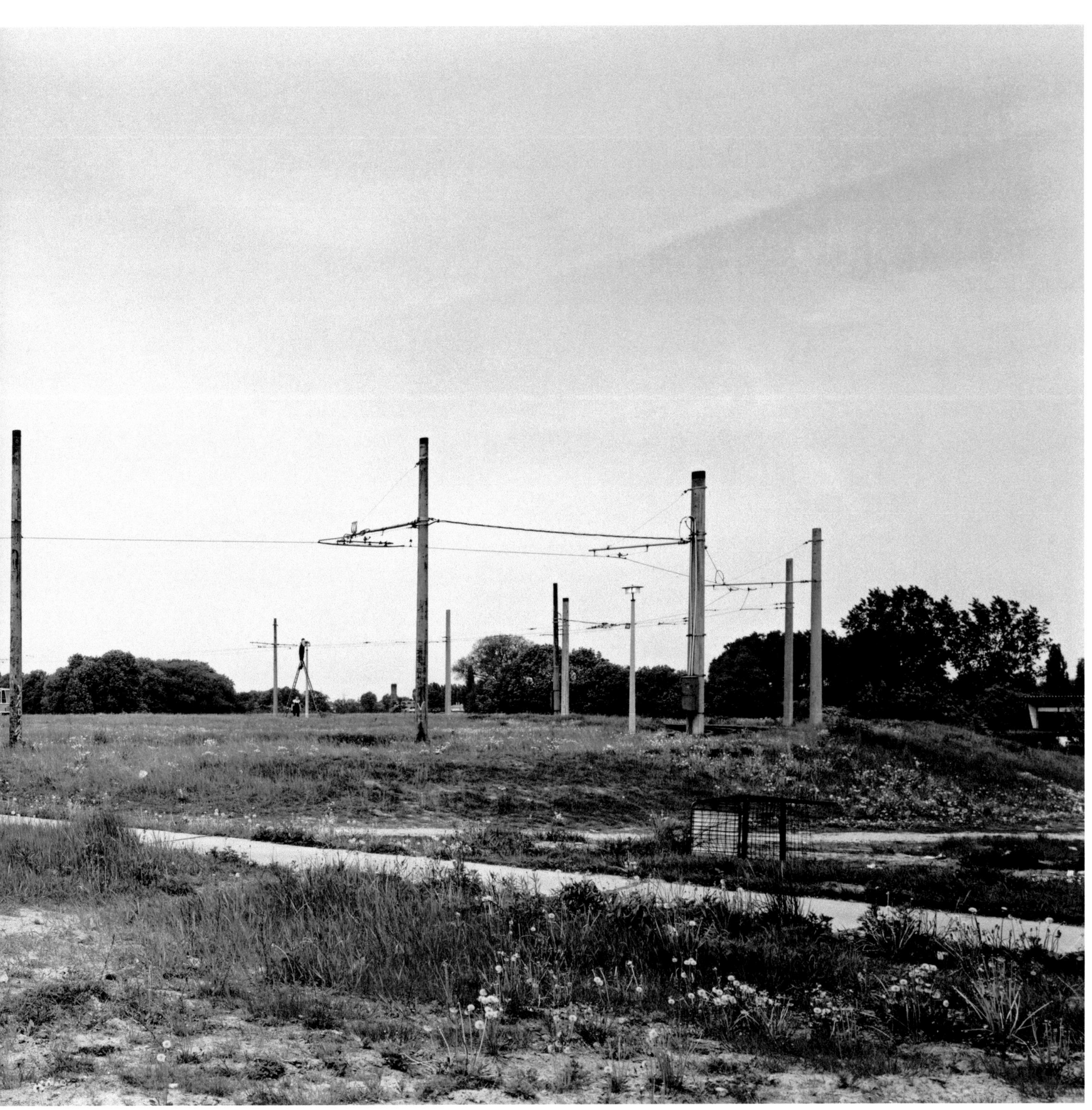

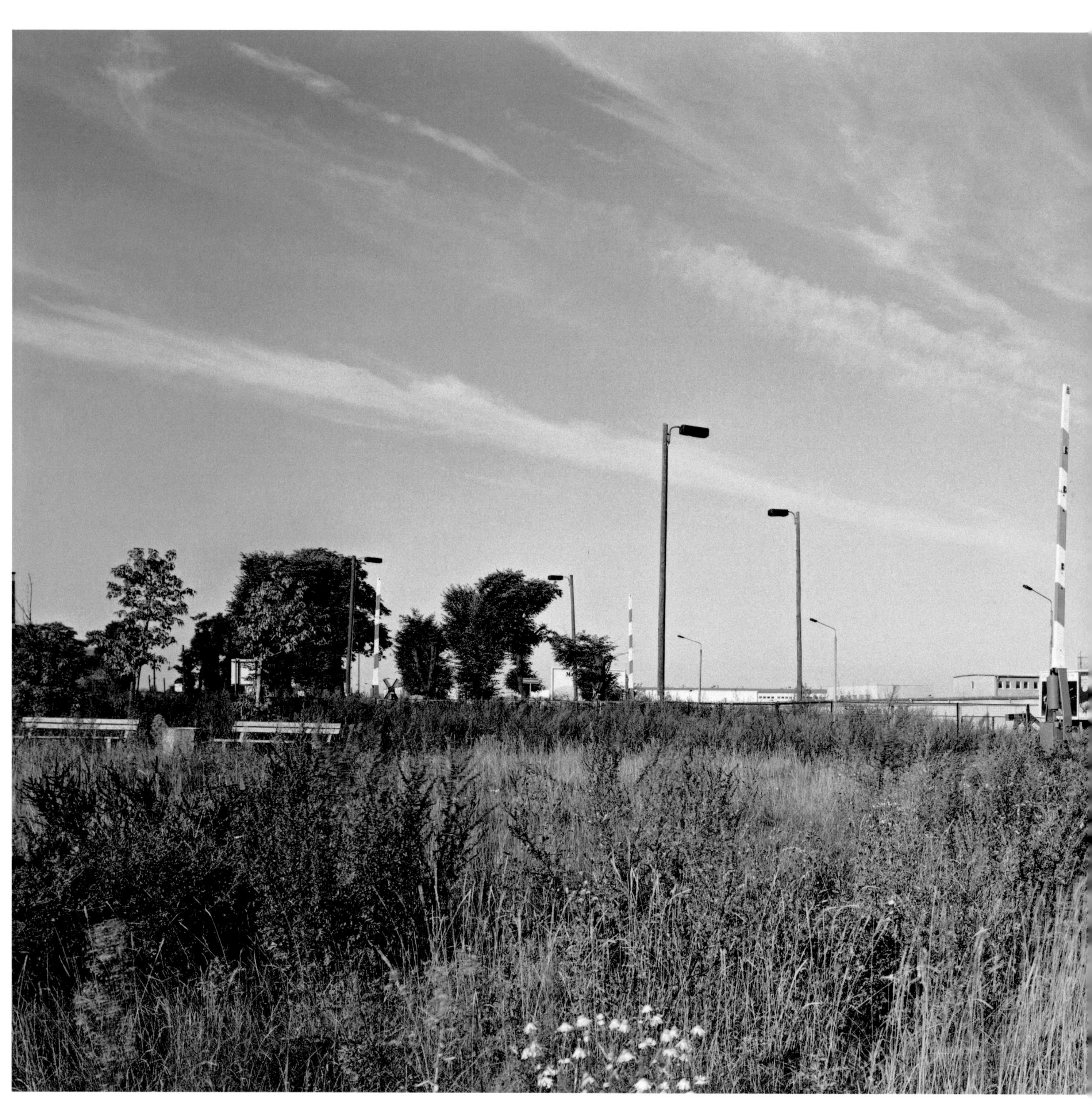

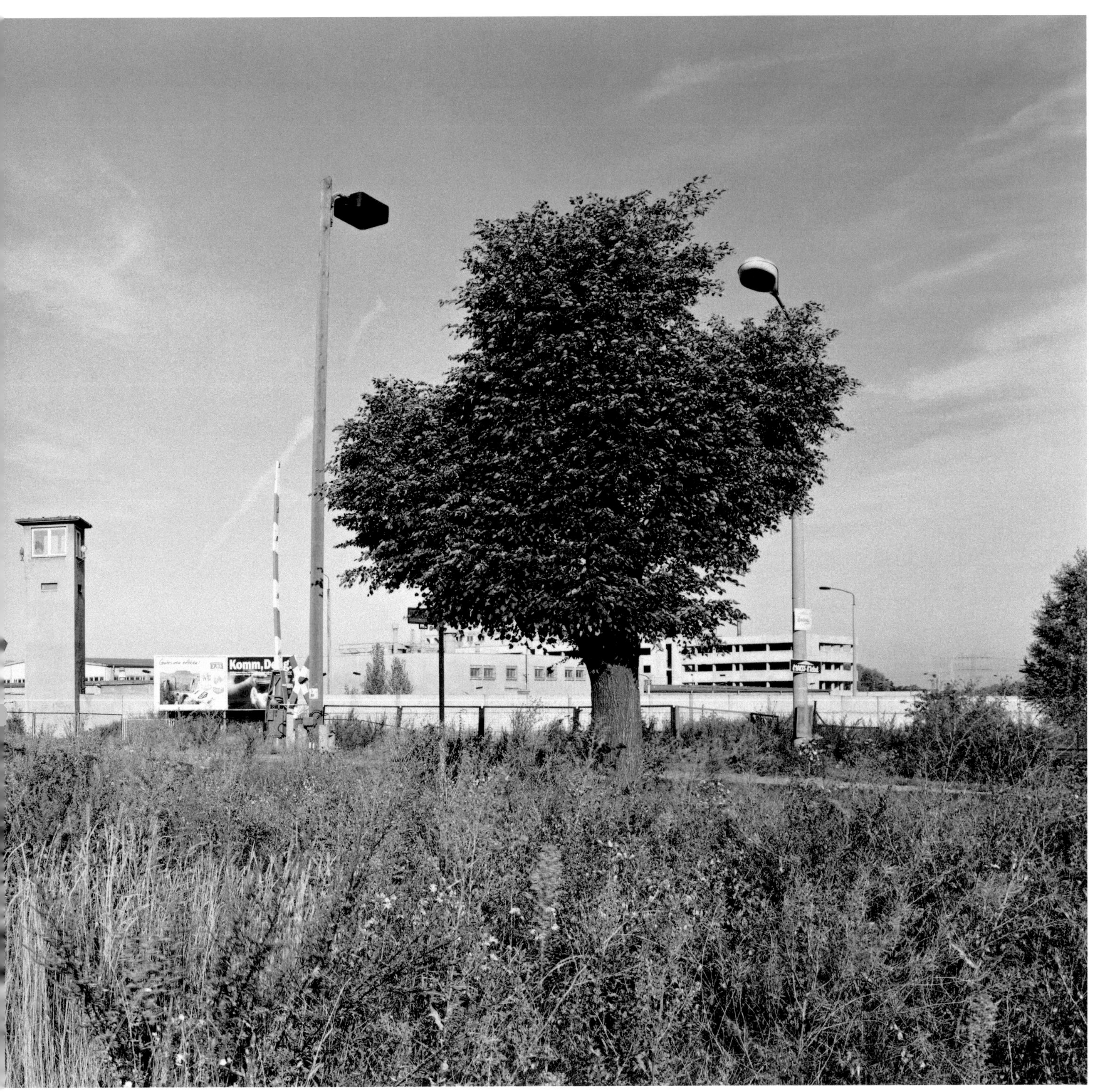
Komm,

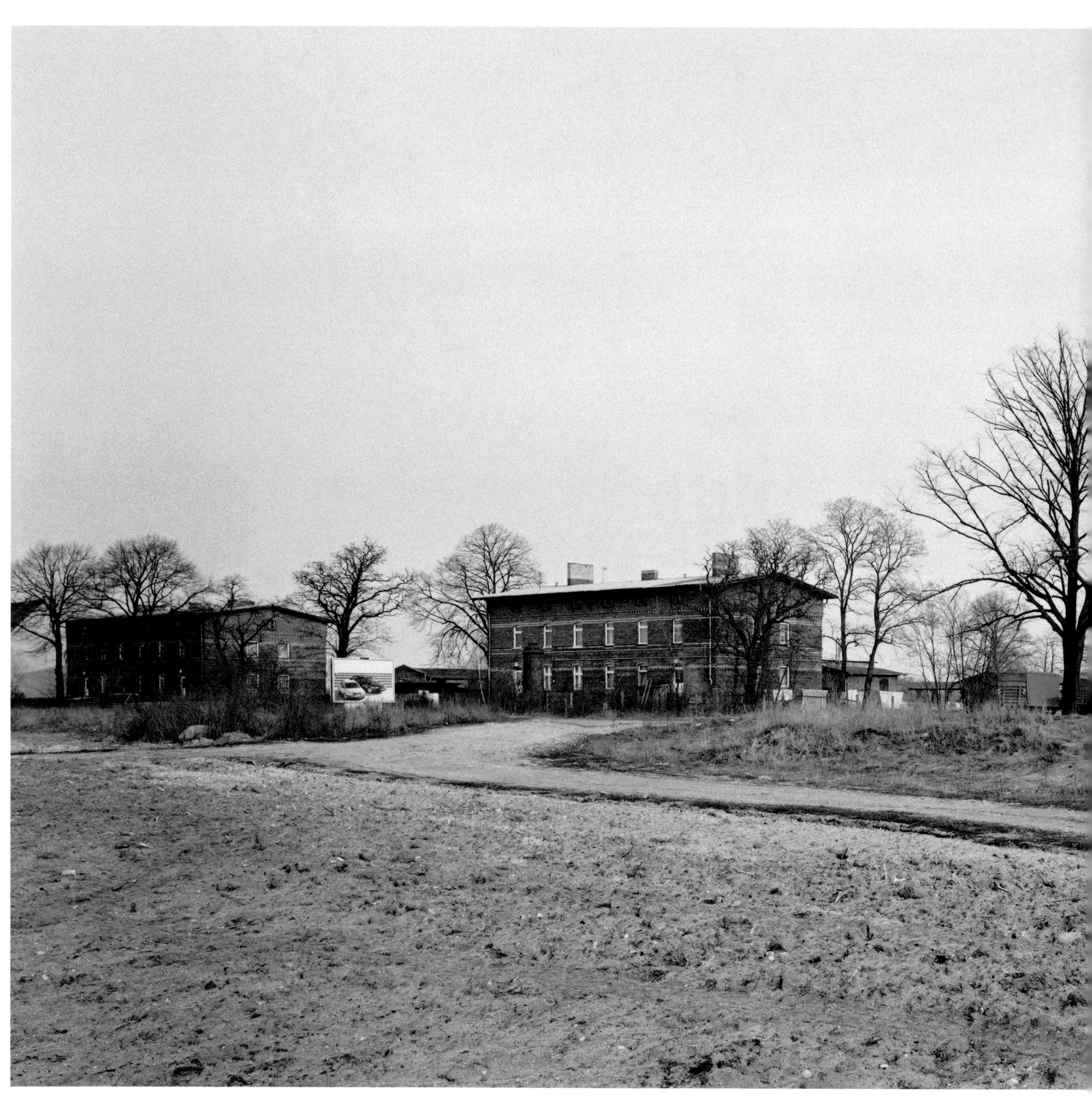

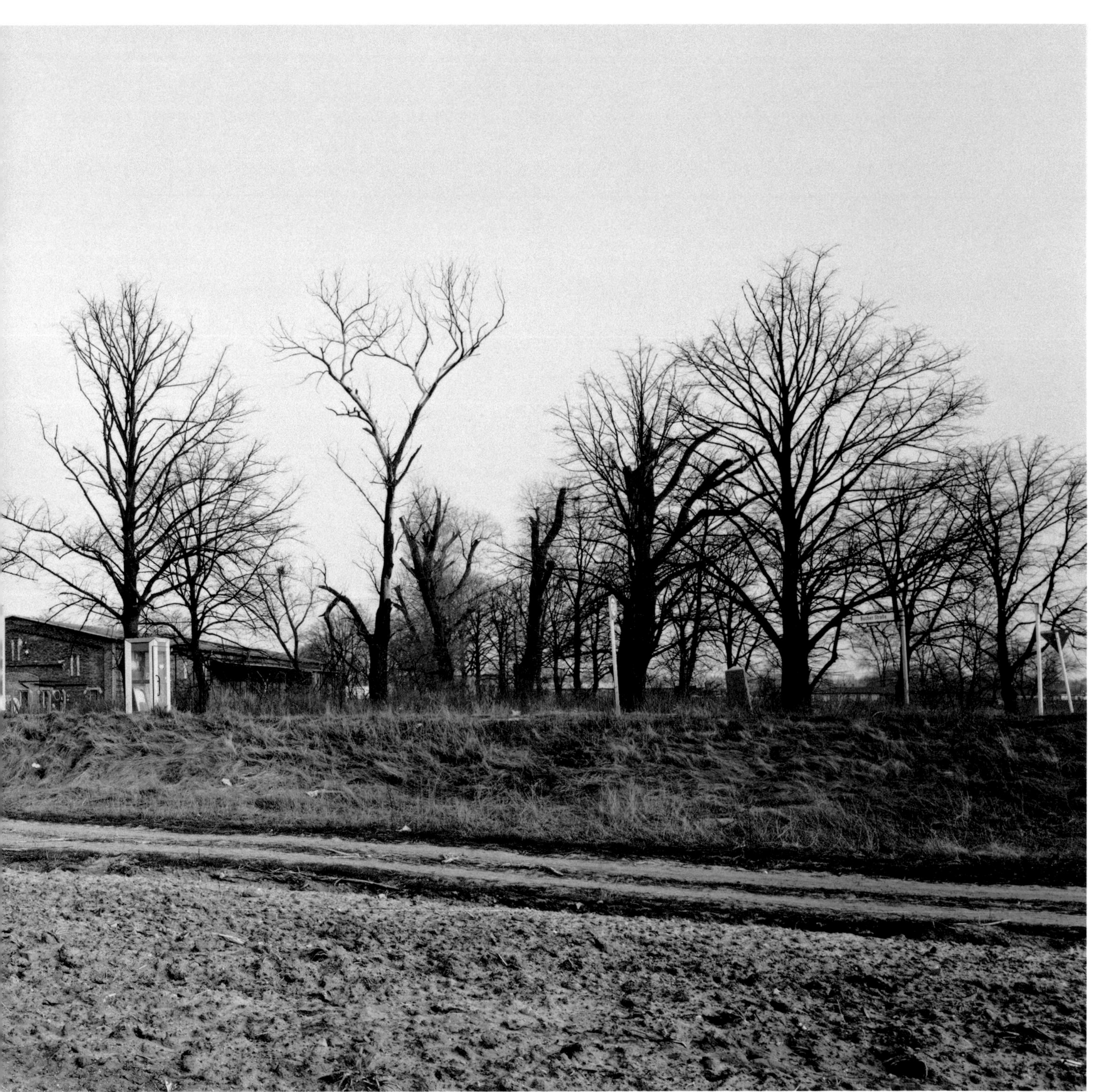
Bucher Straße

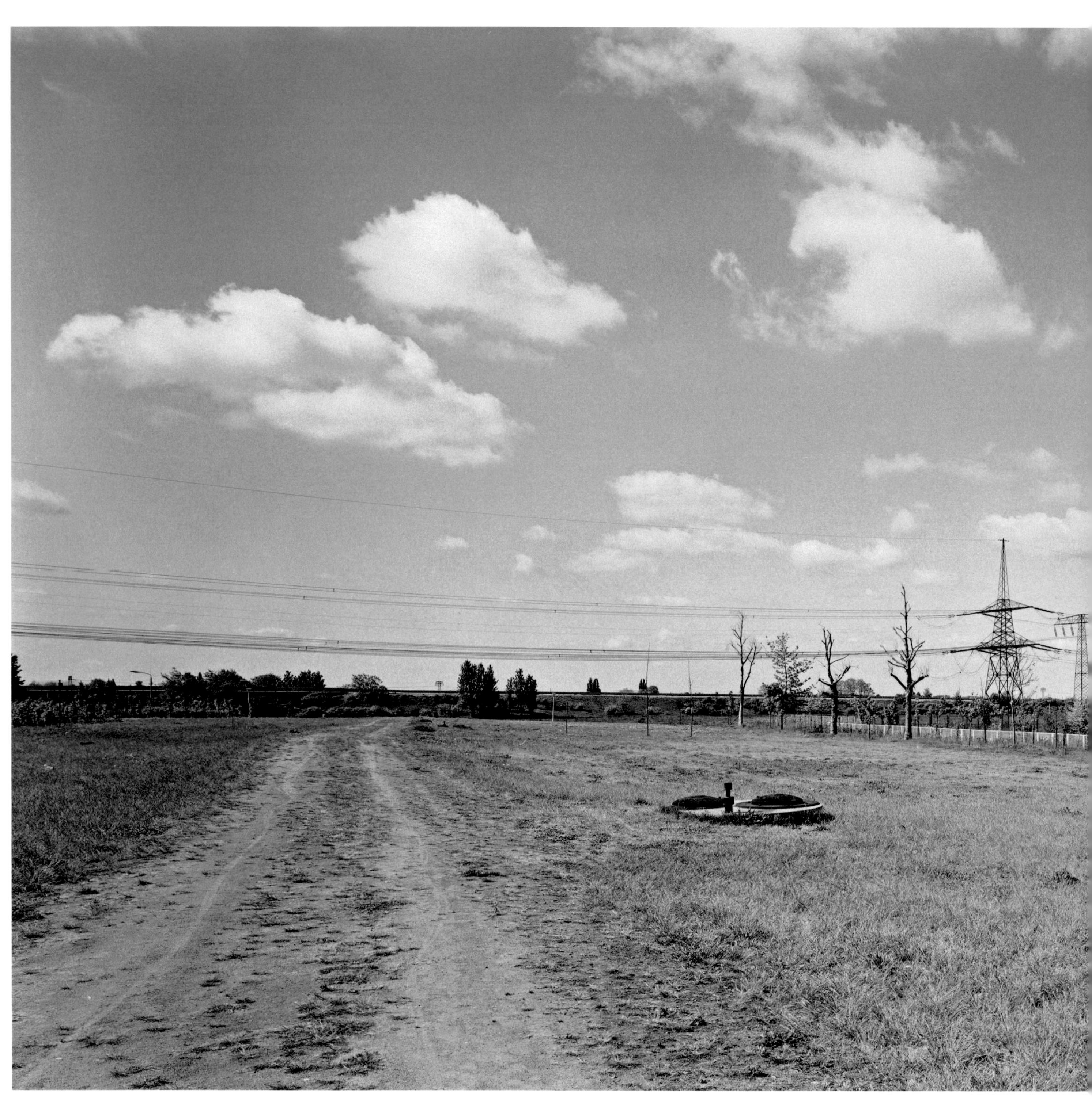

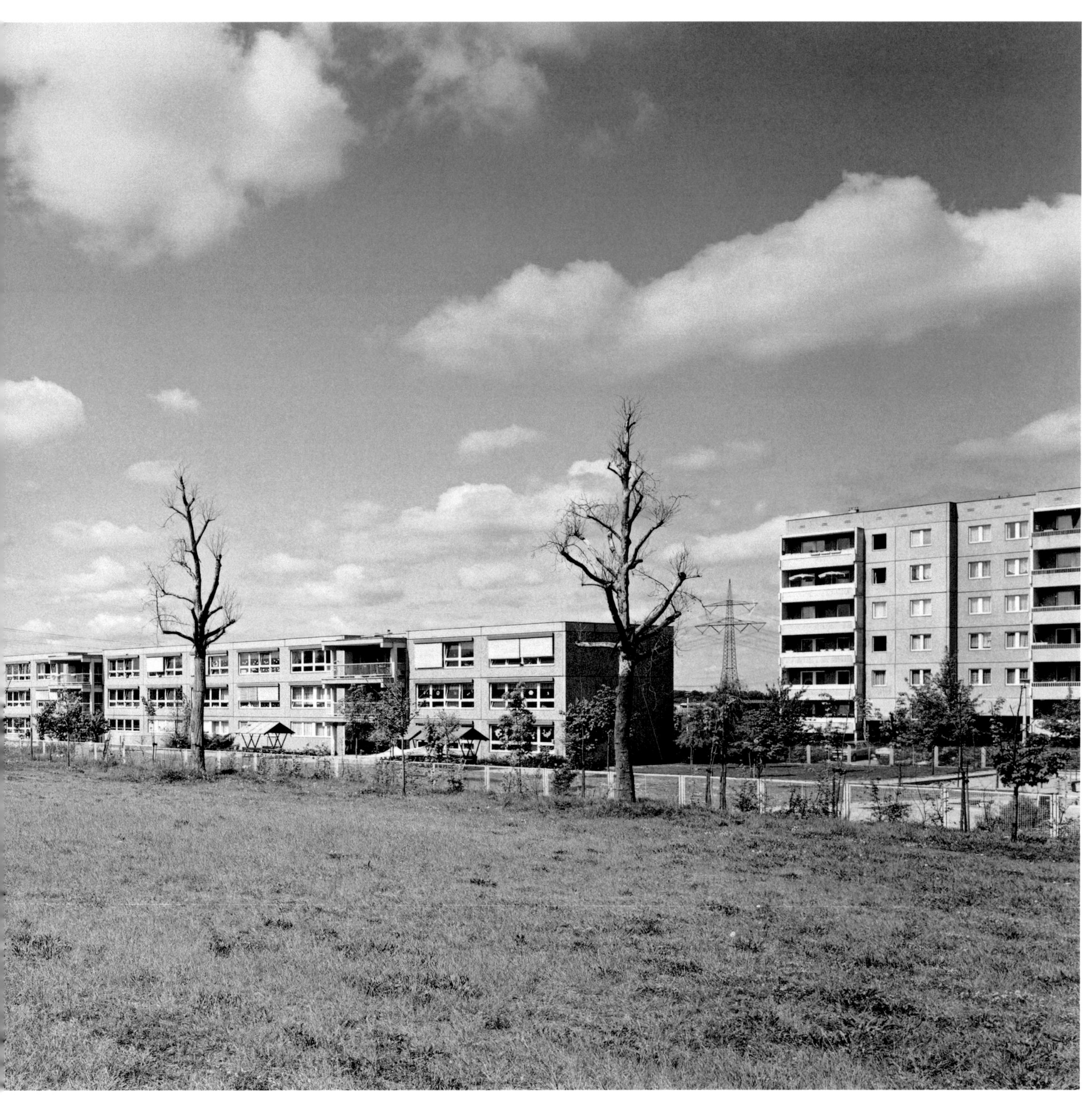

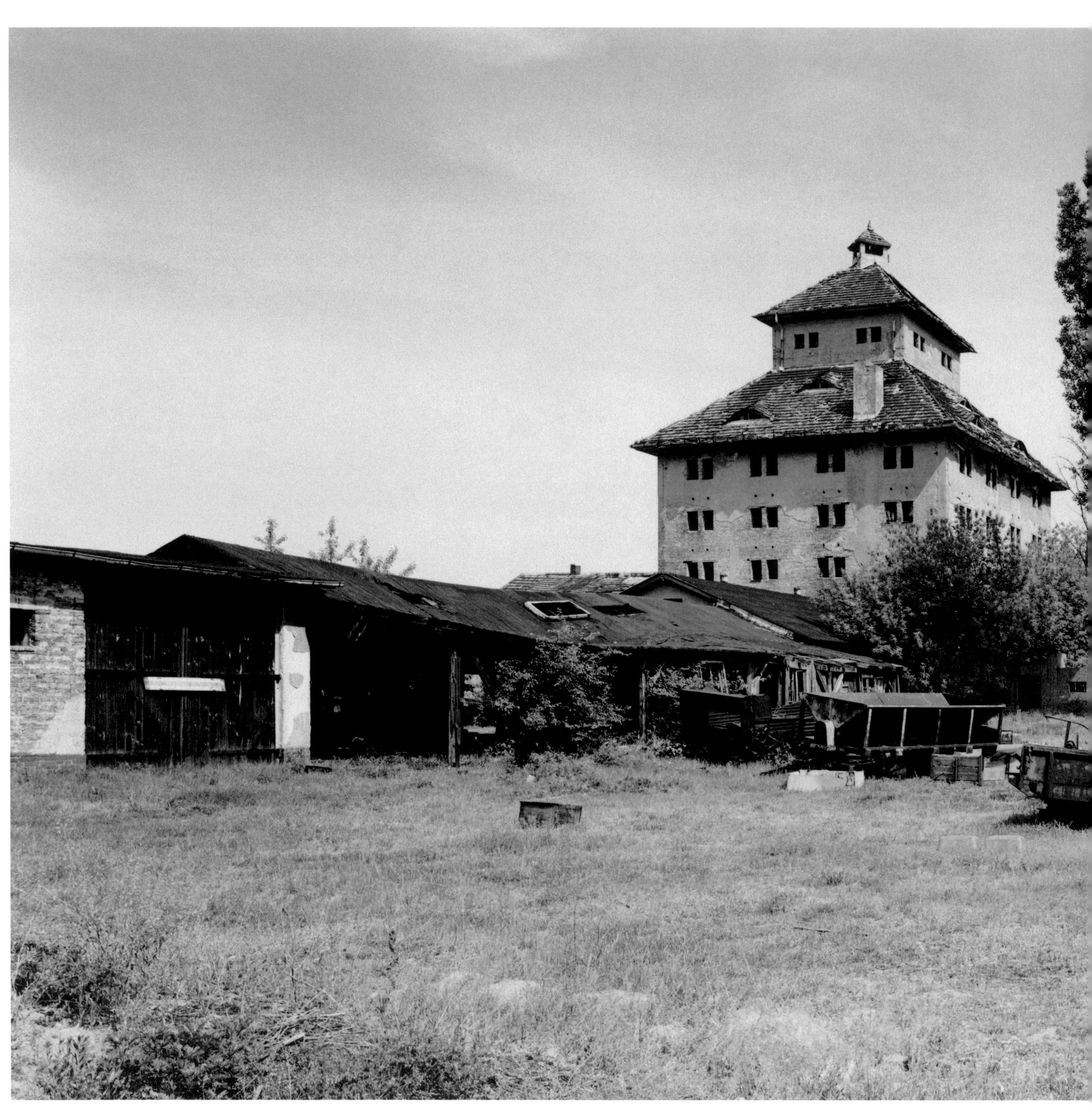

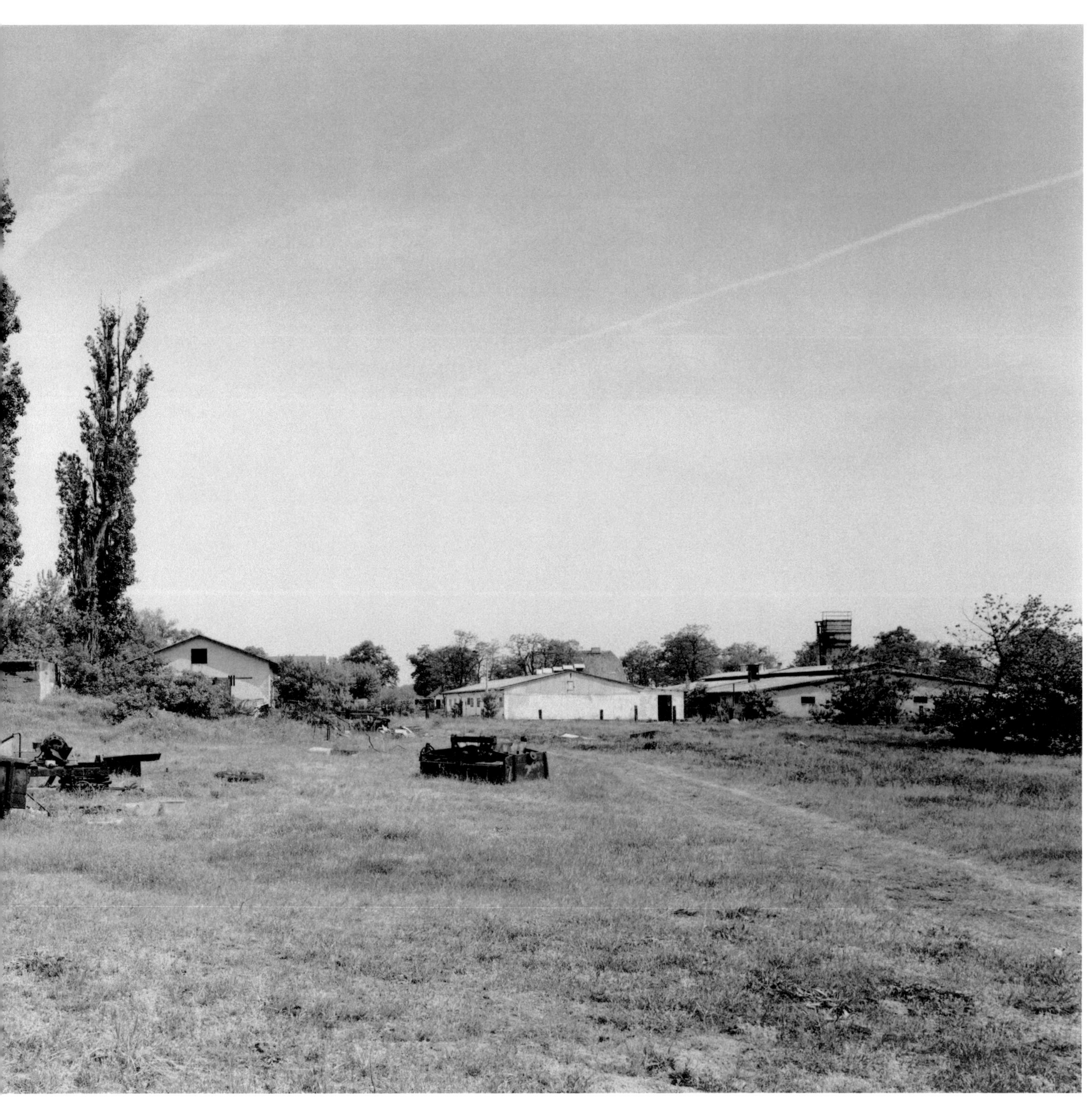

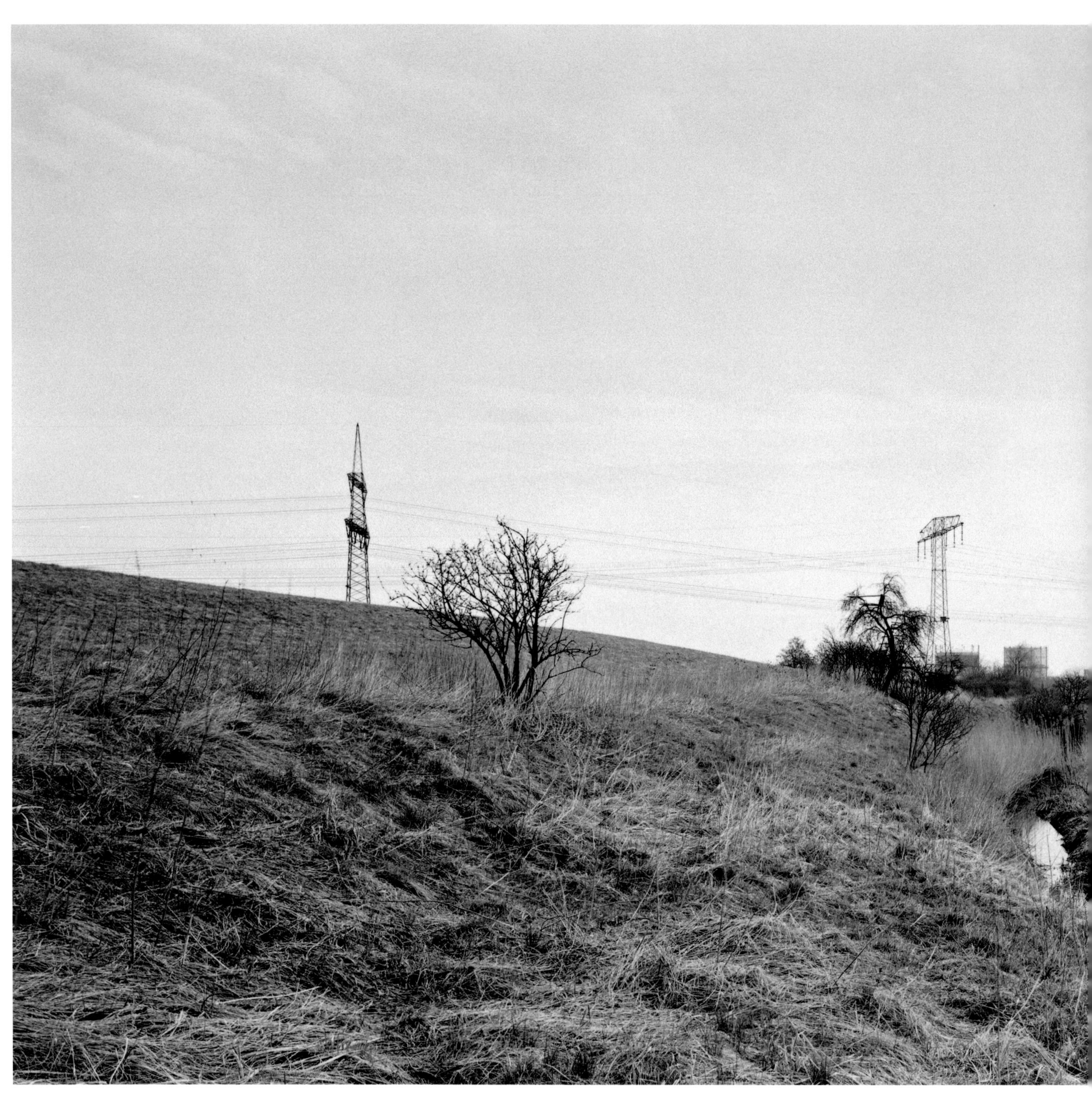

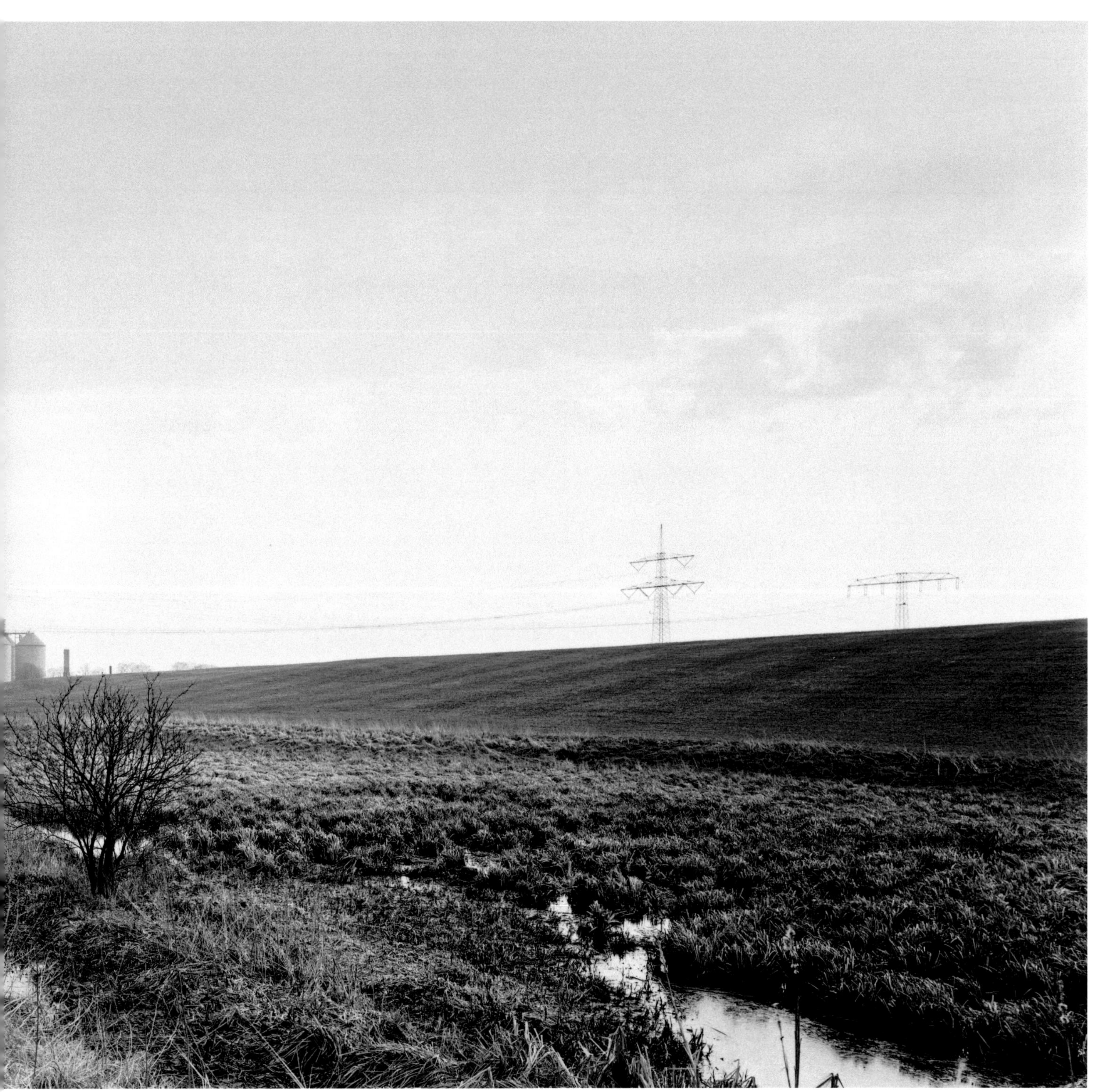

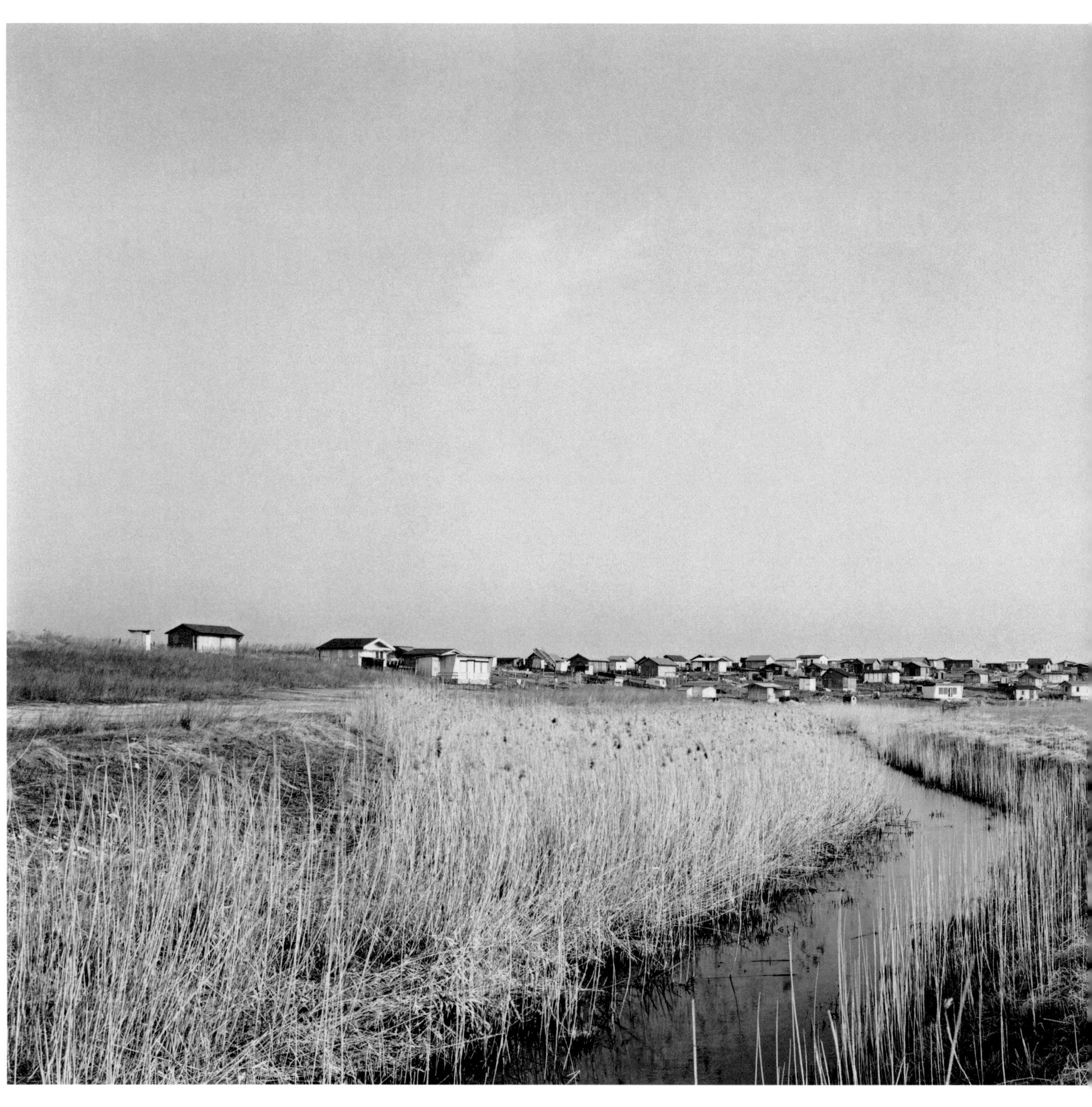

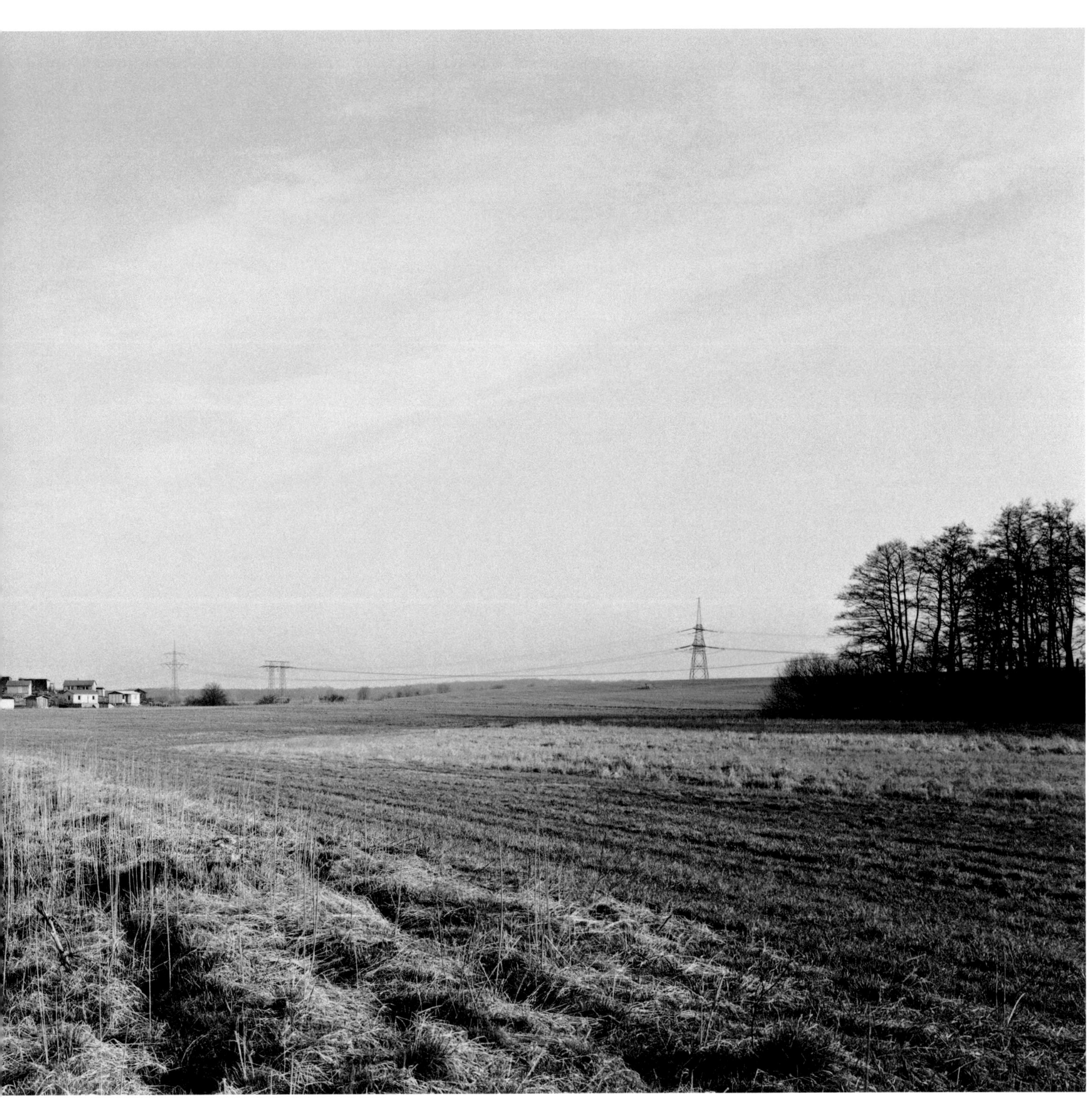

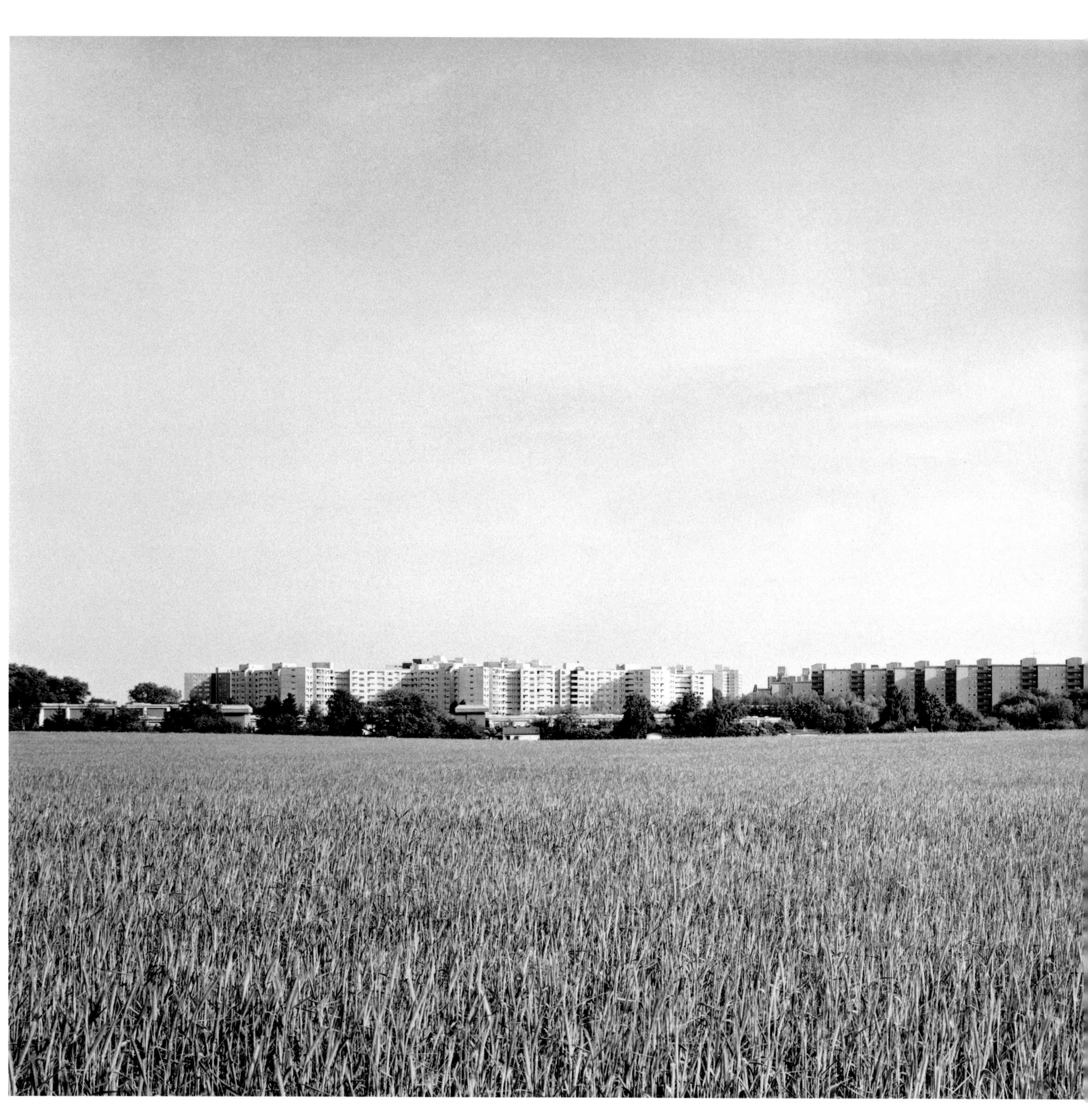

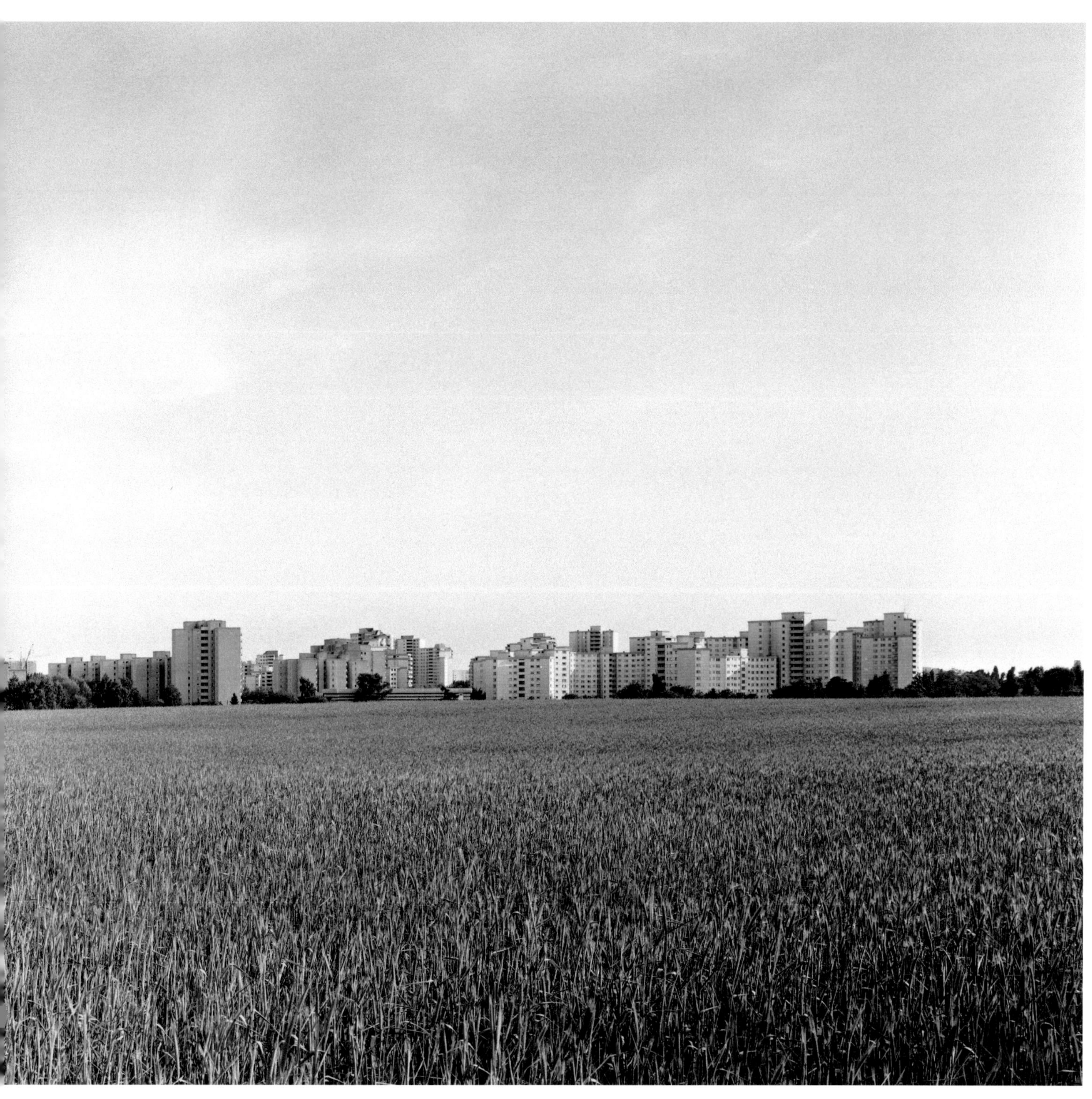

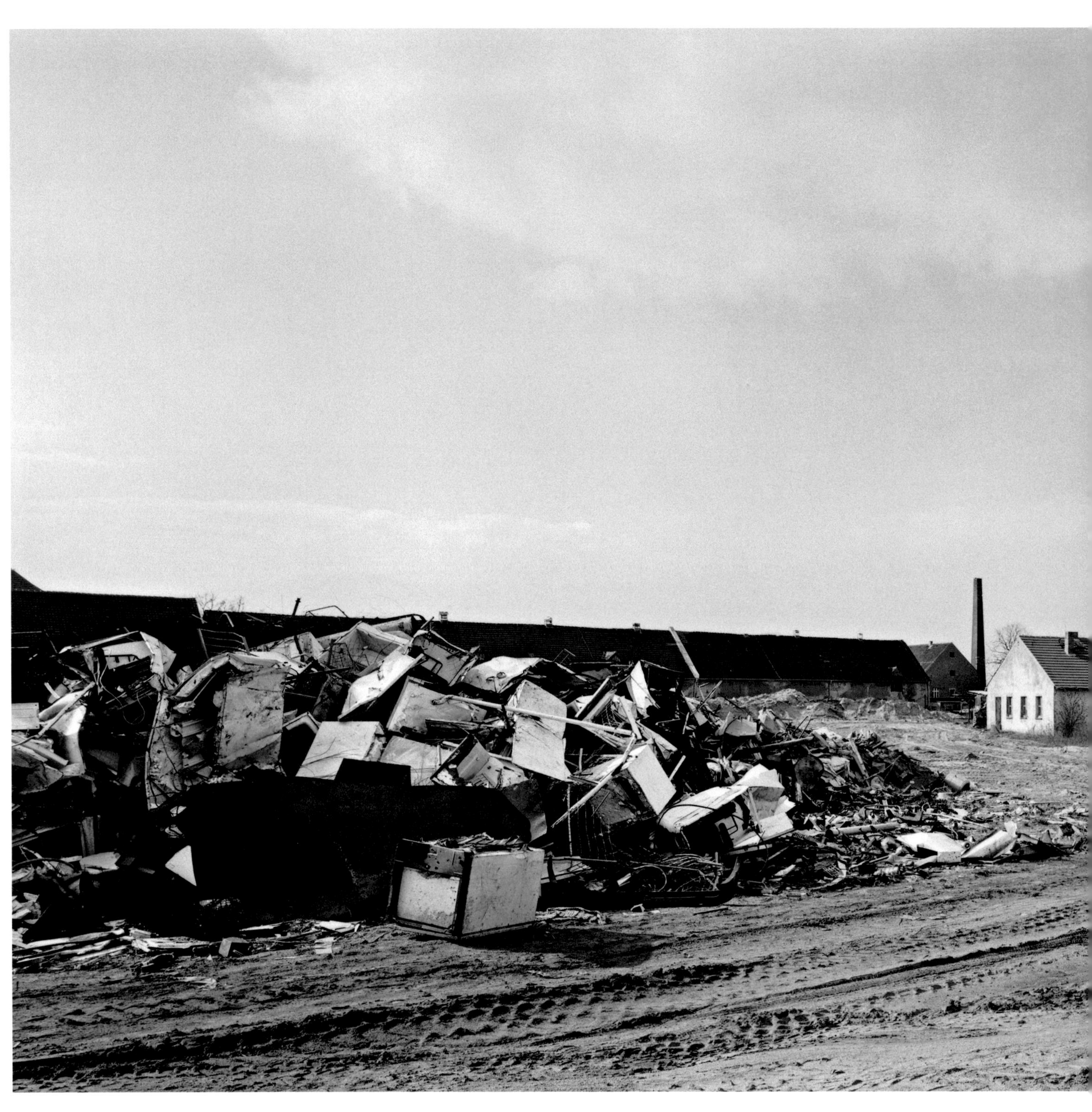

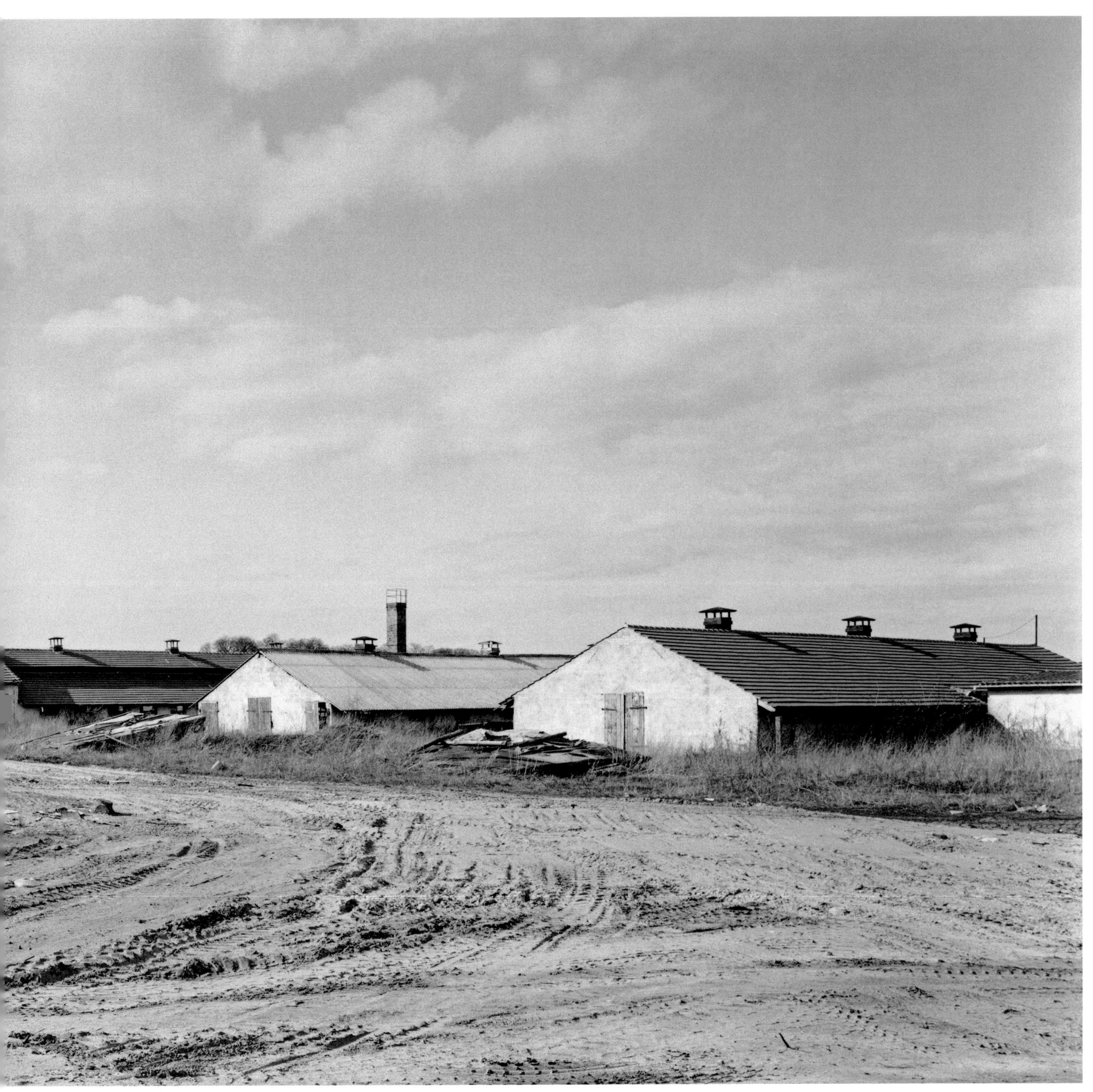

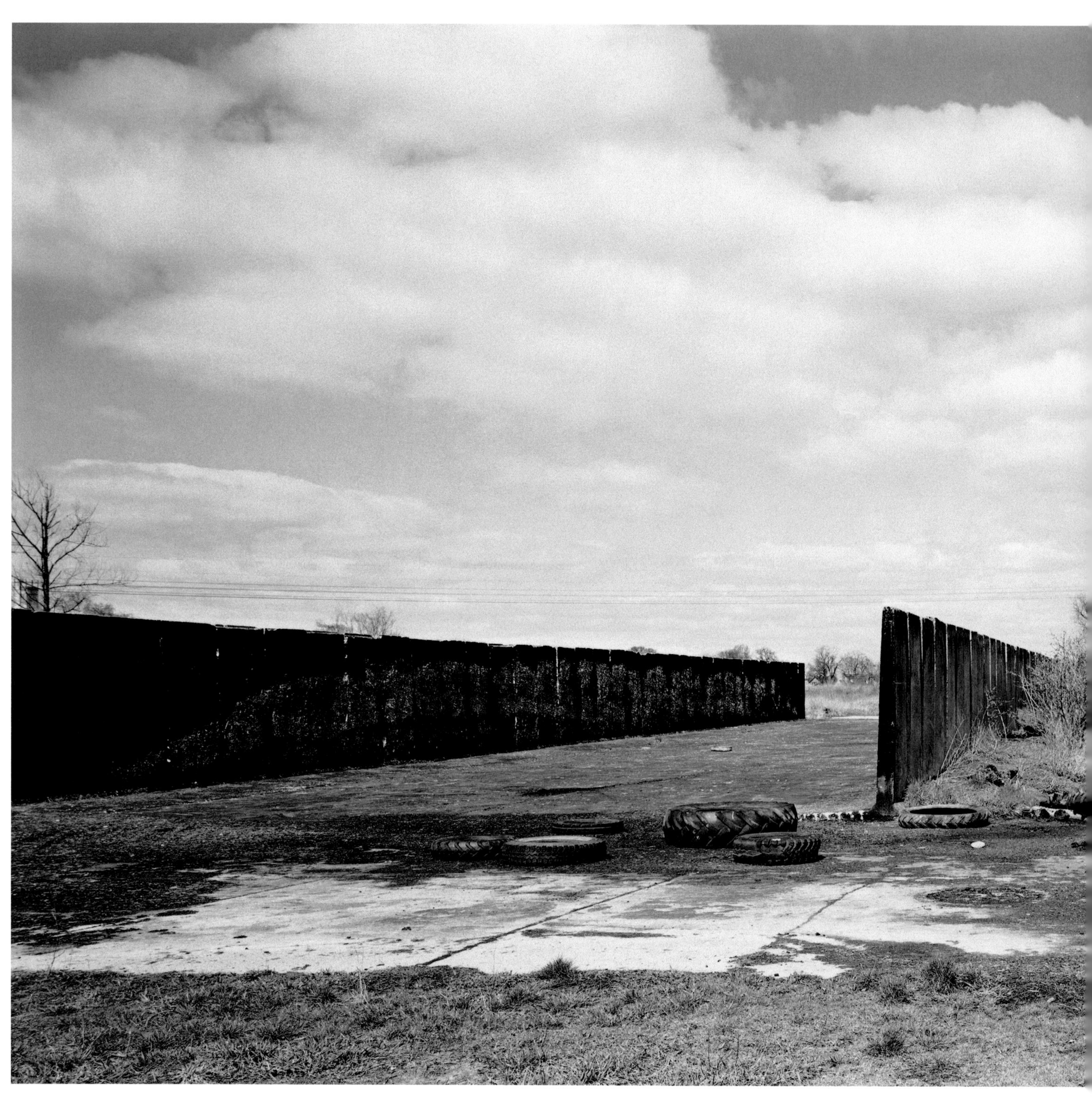

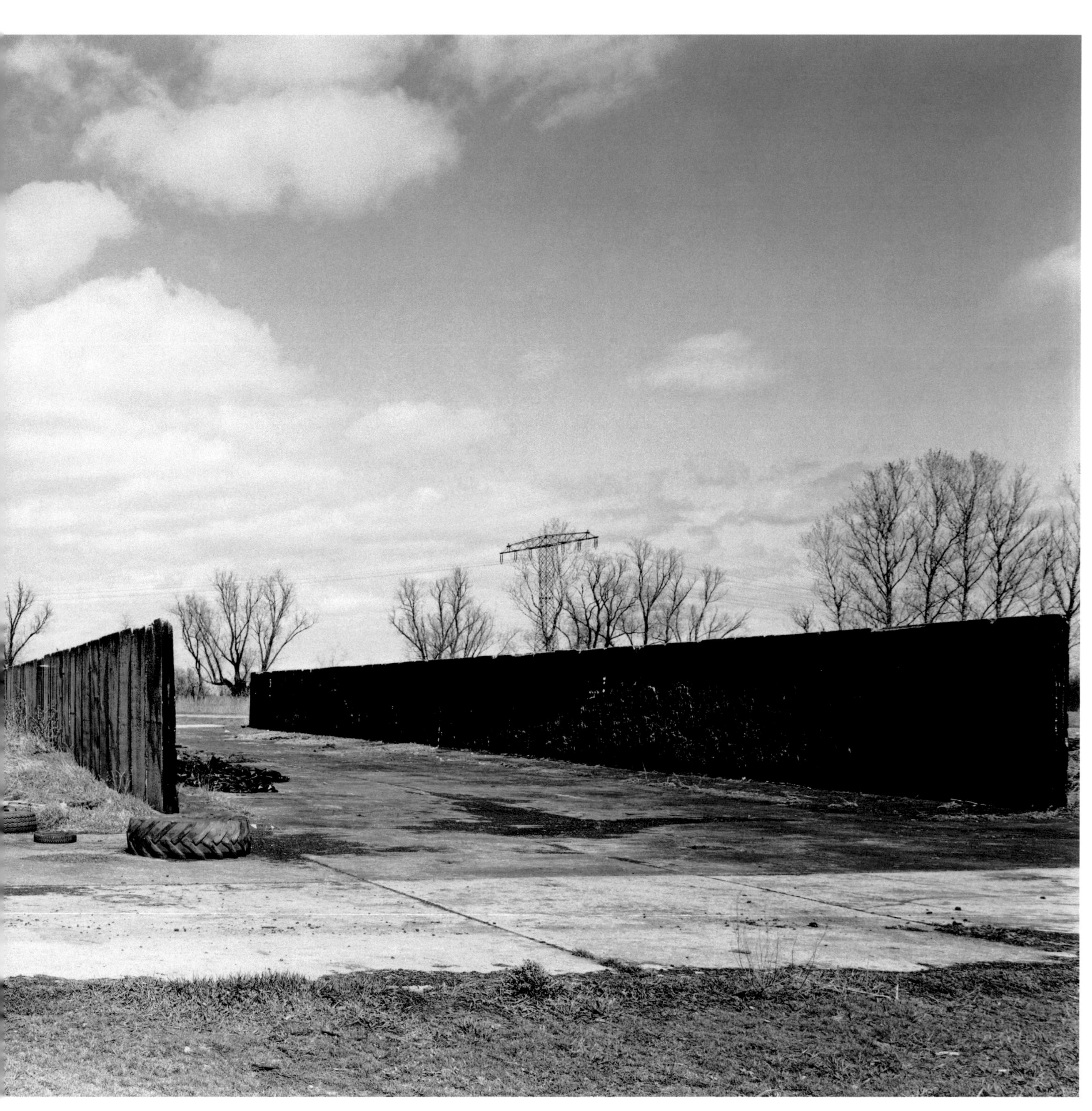

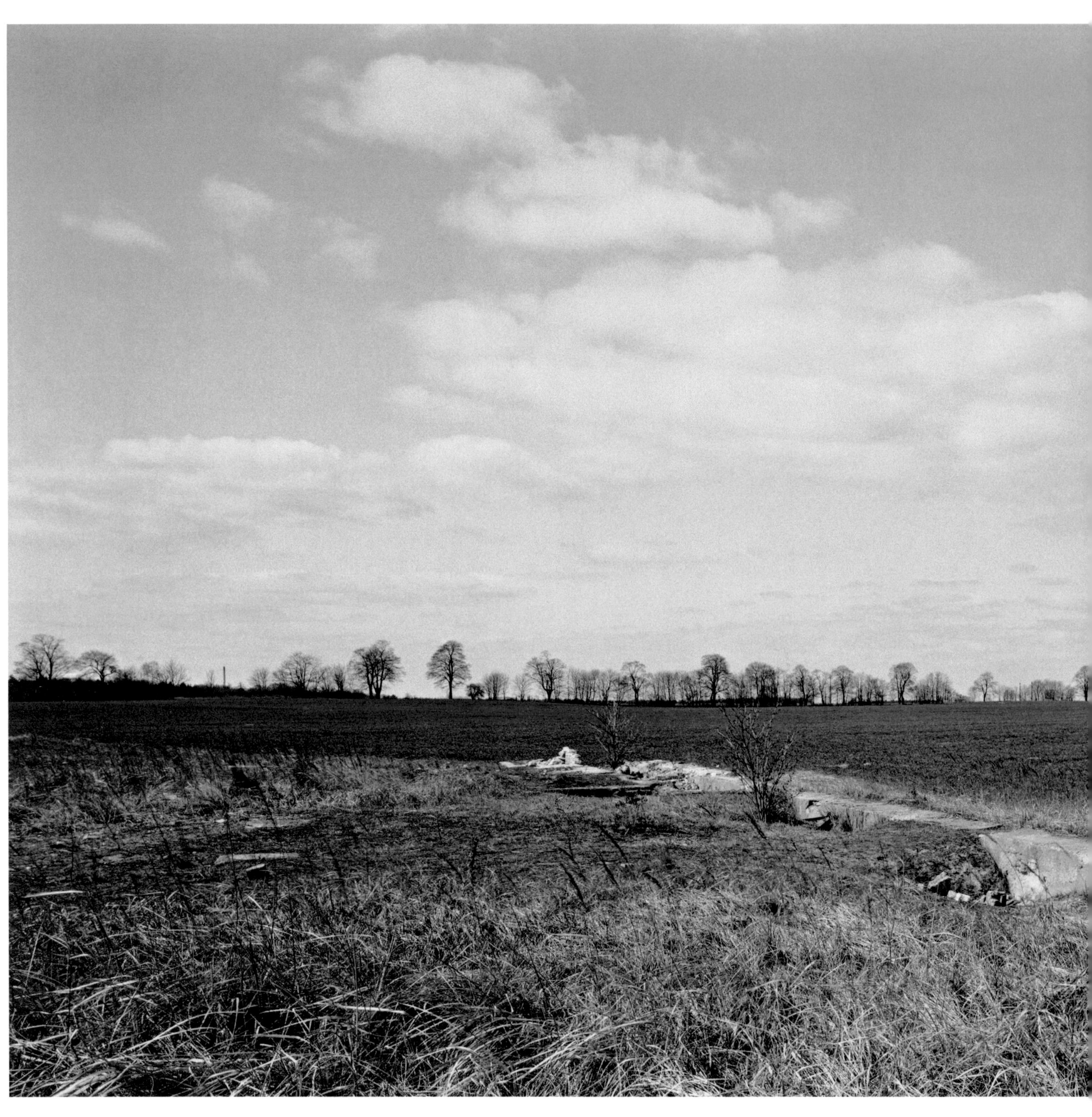

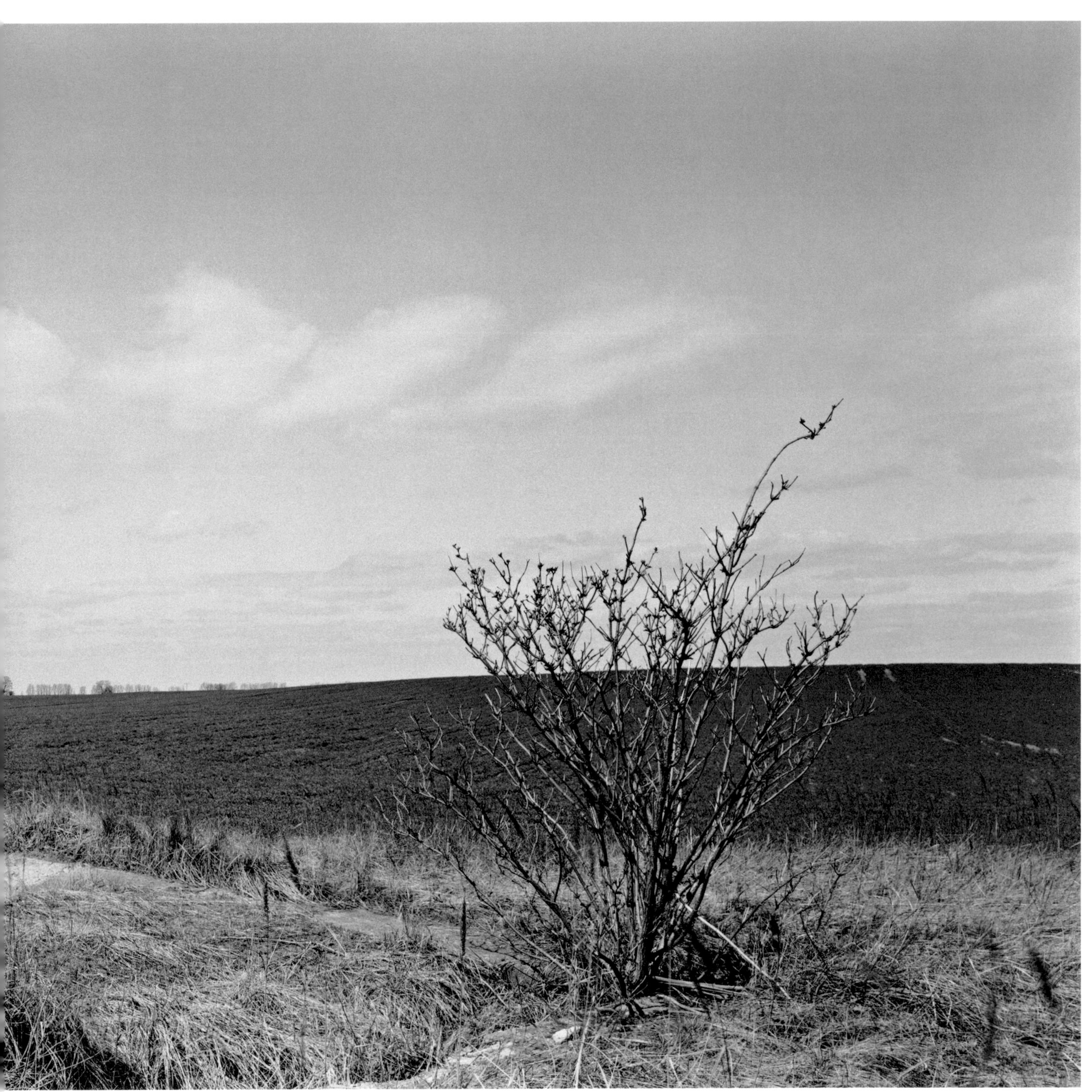

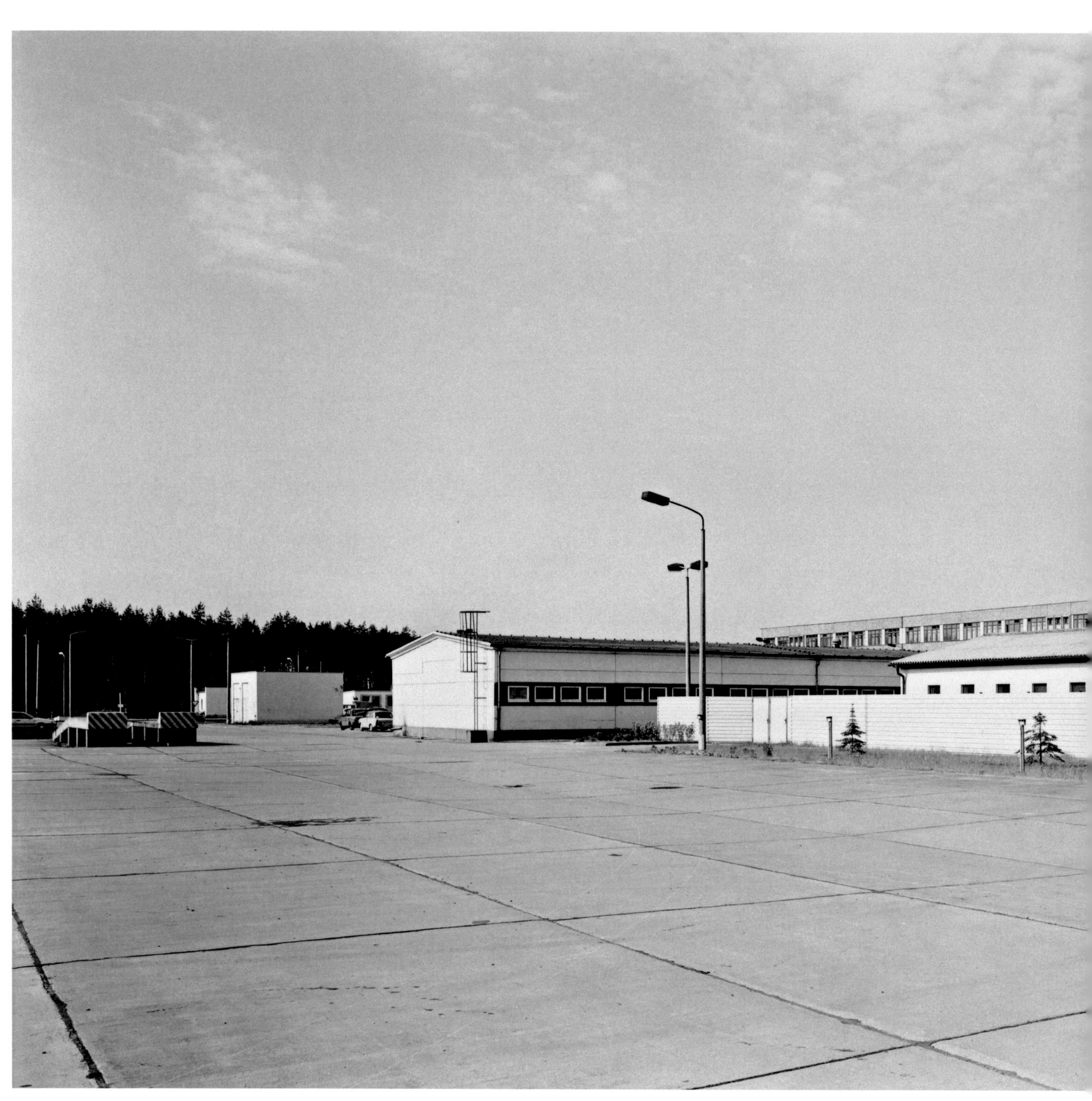

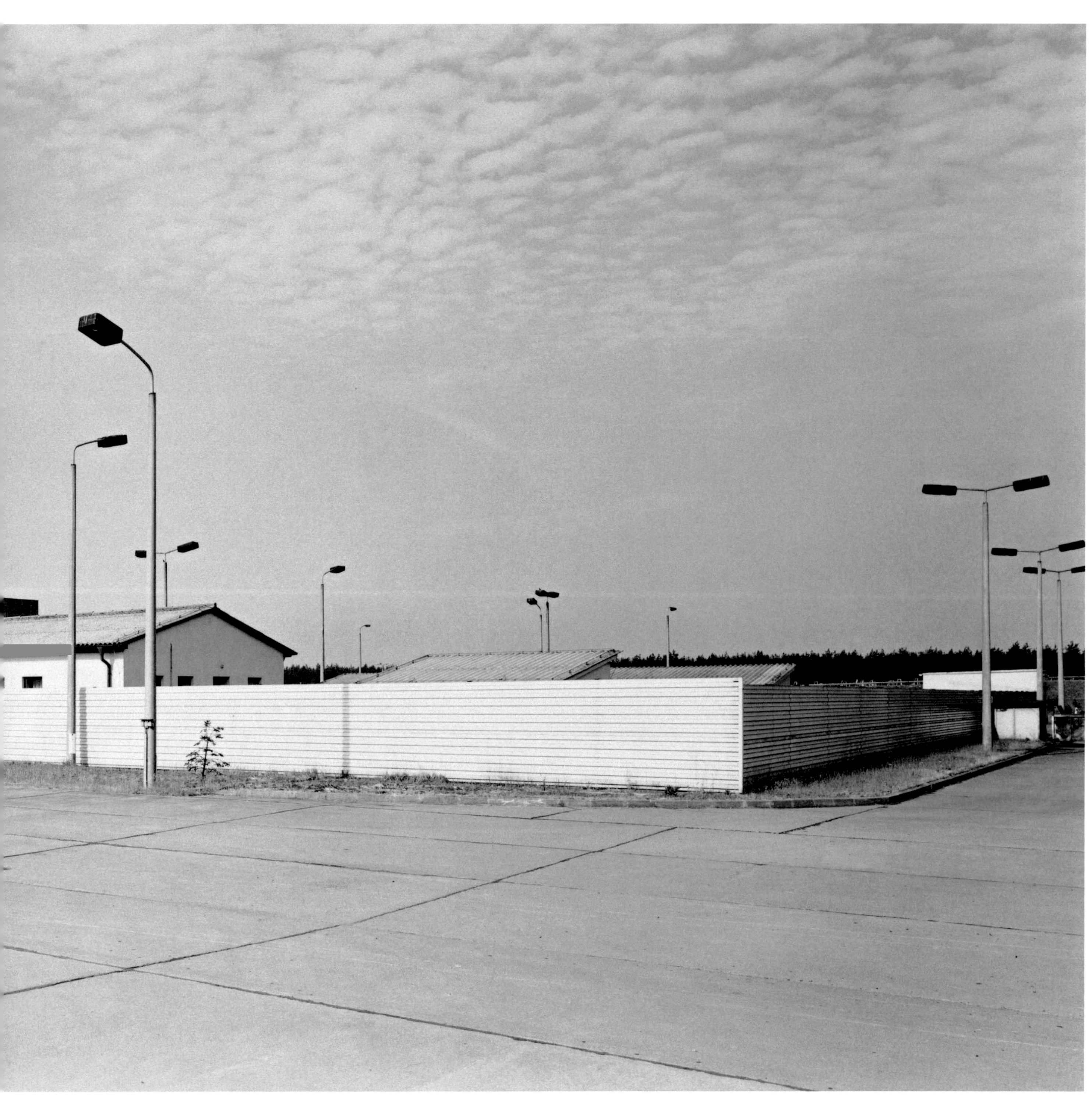

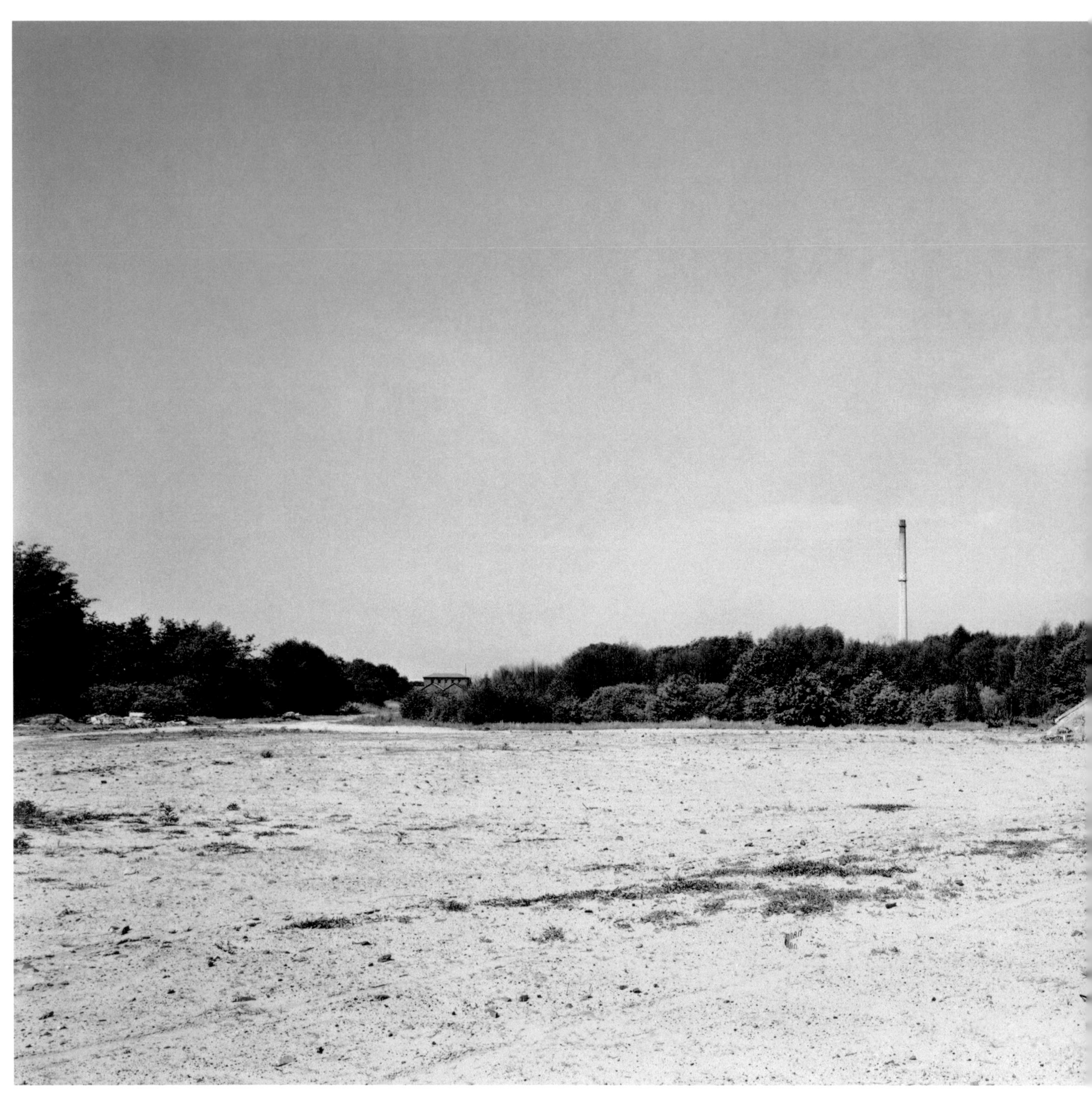

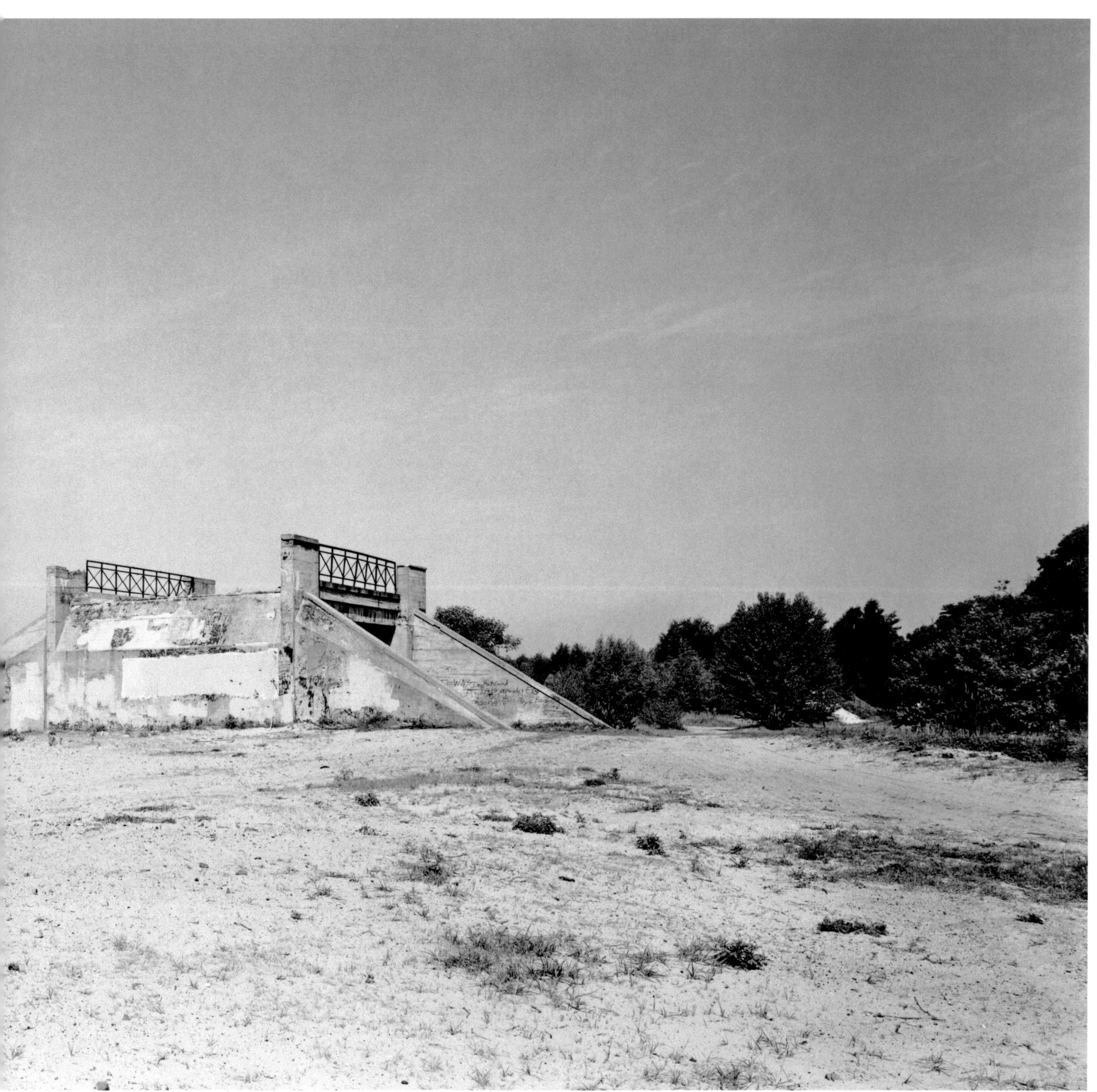

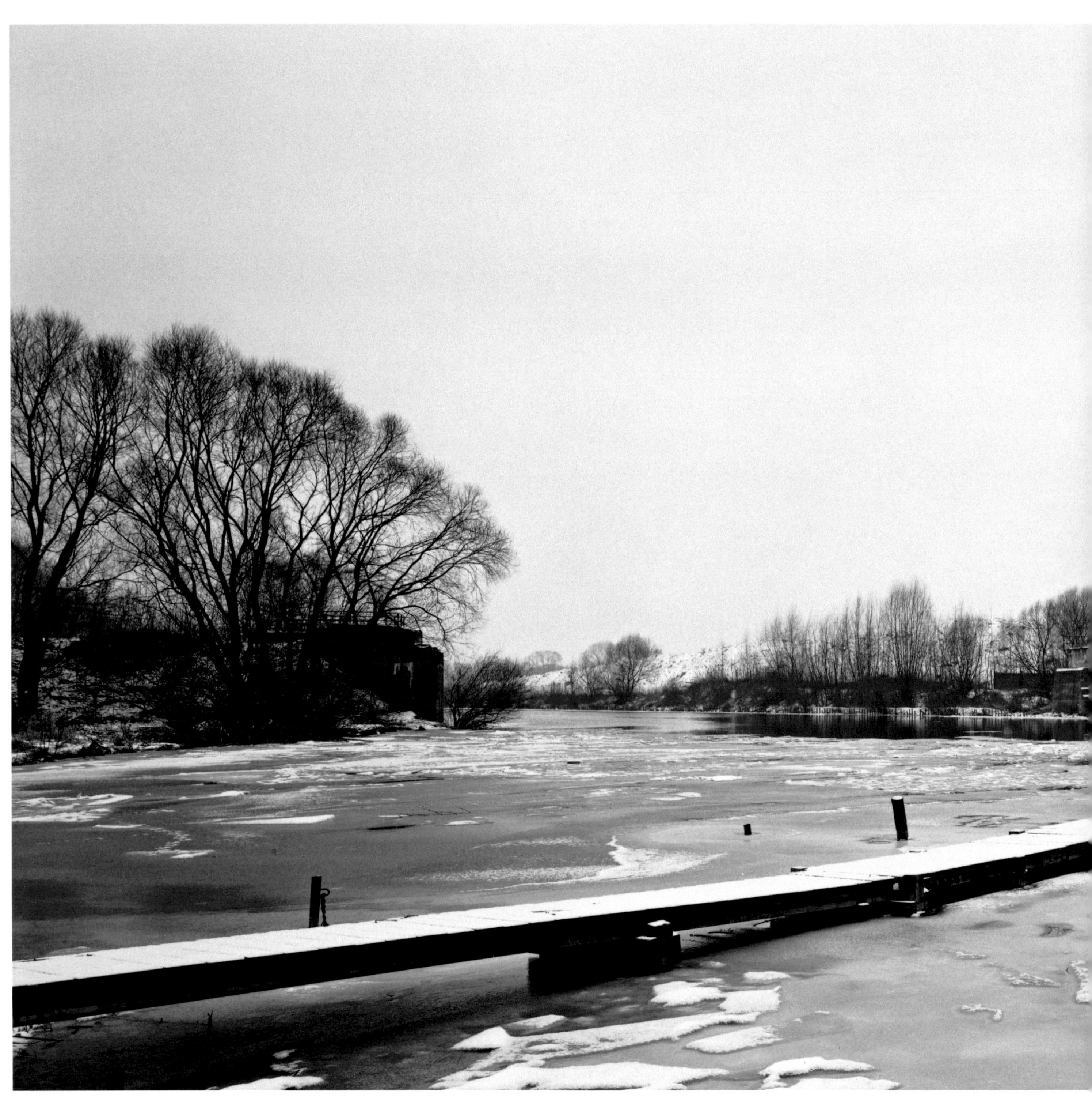

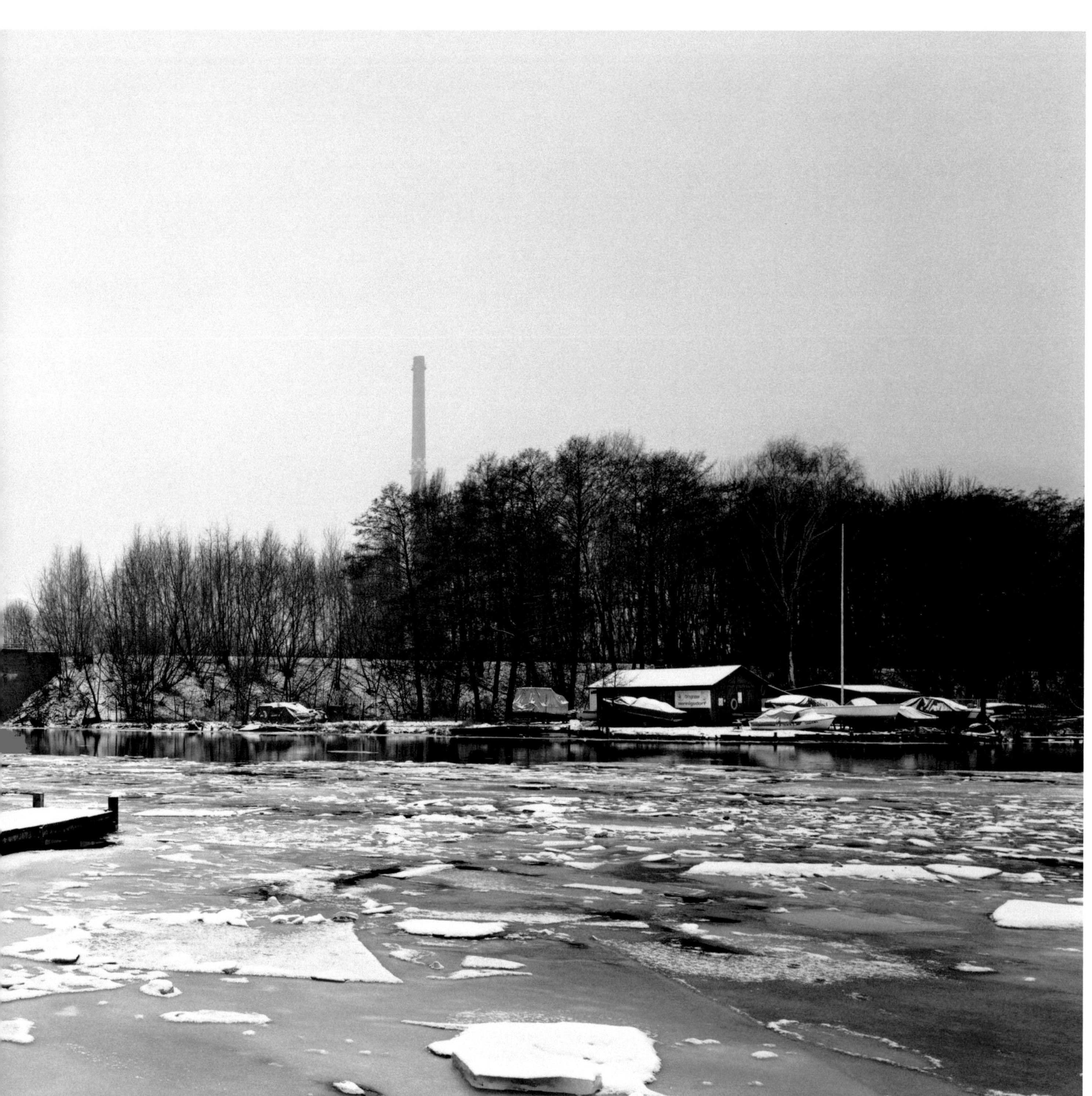
Hennigsdorf

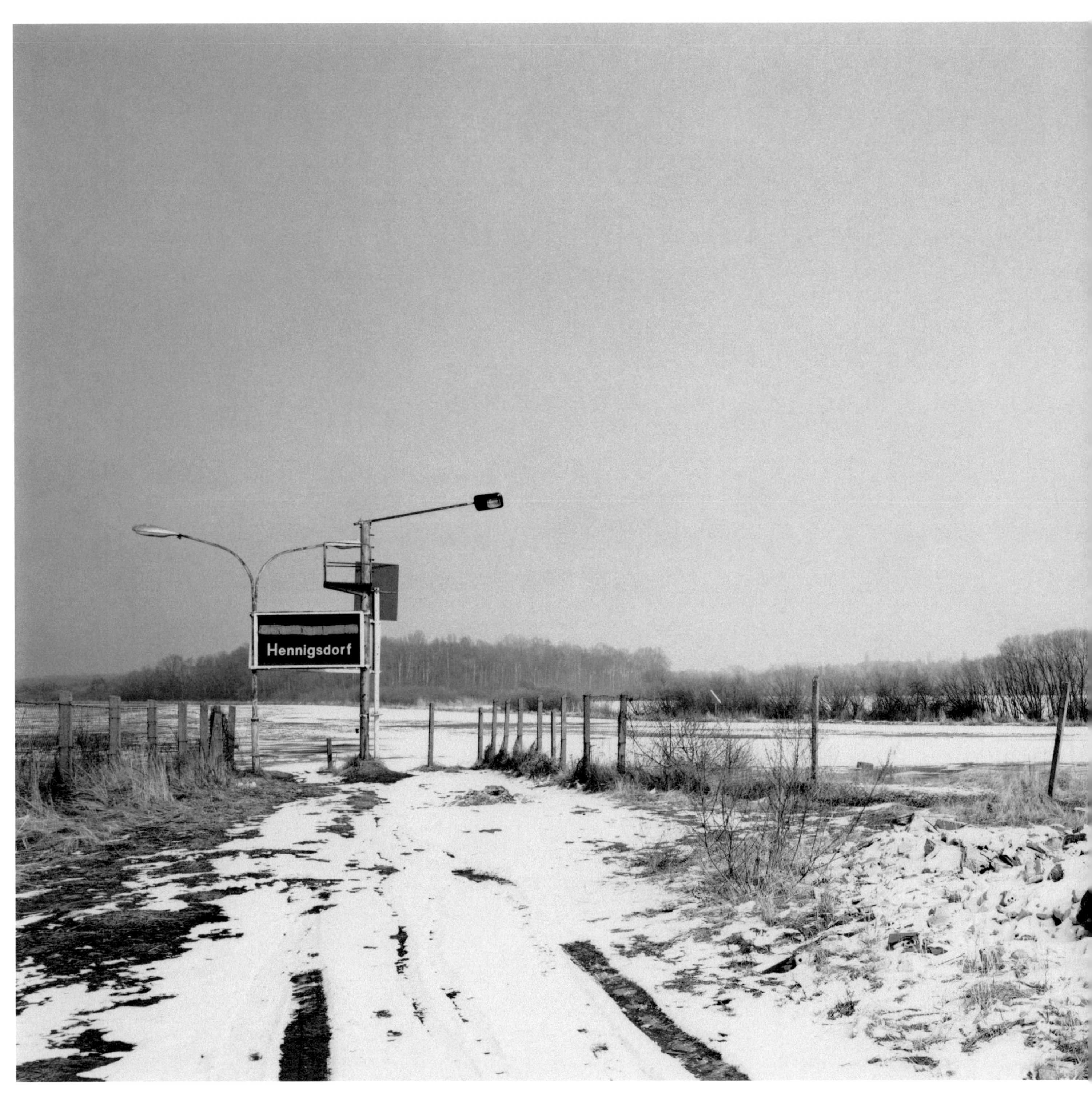
Hennigsdorf

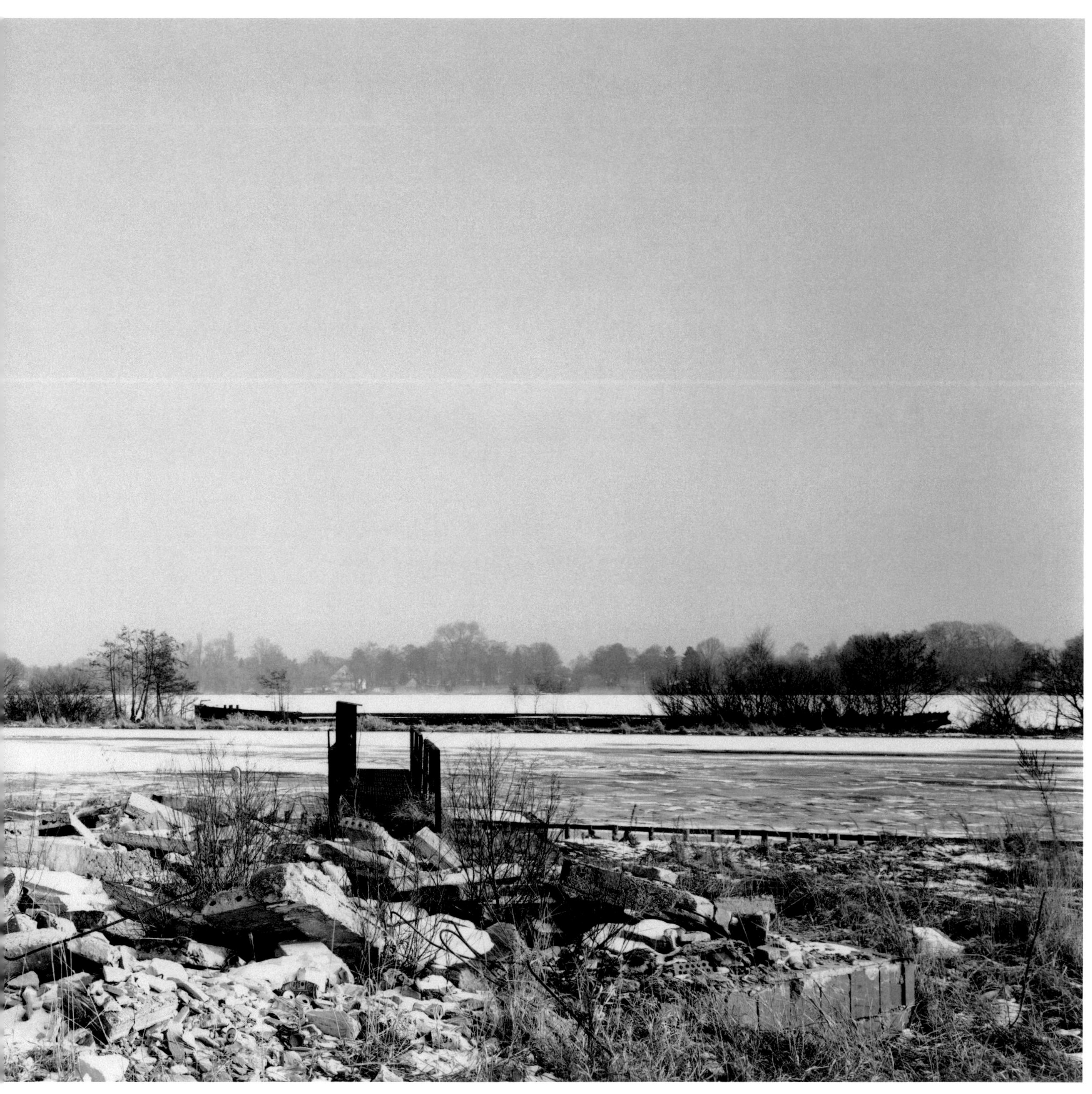

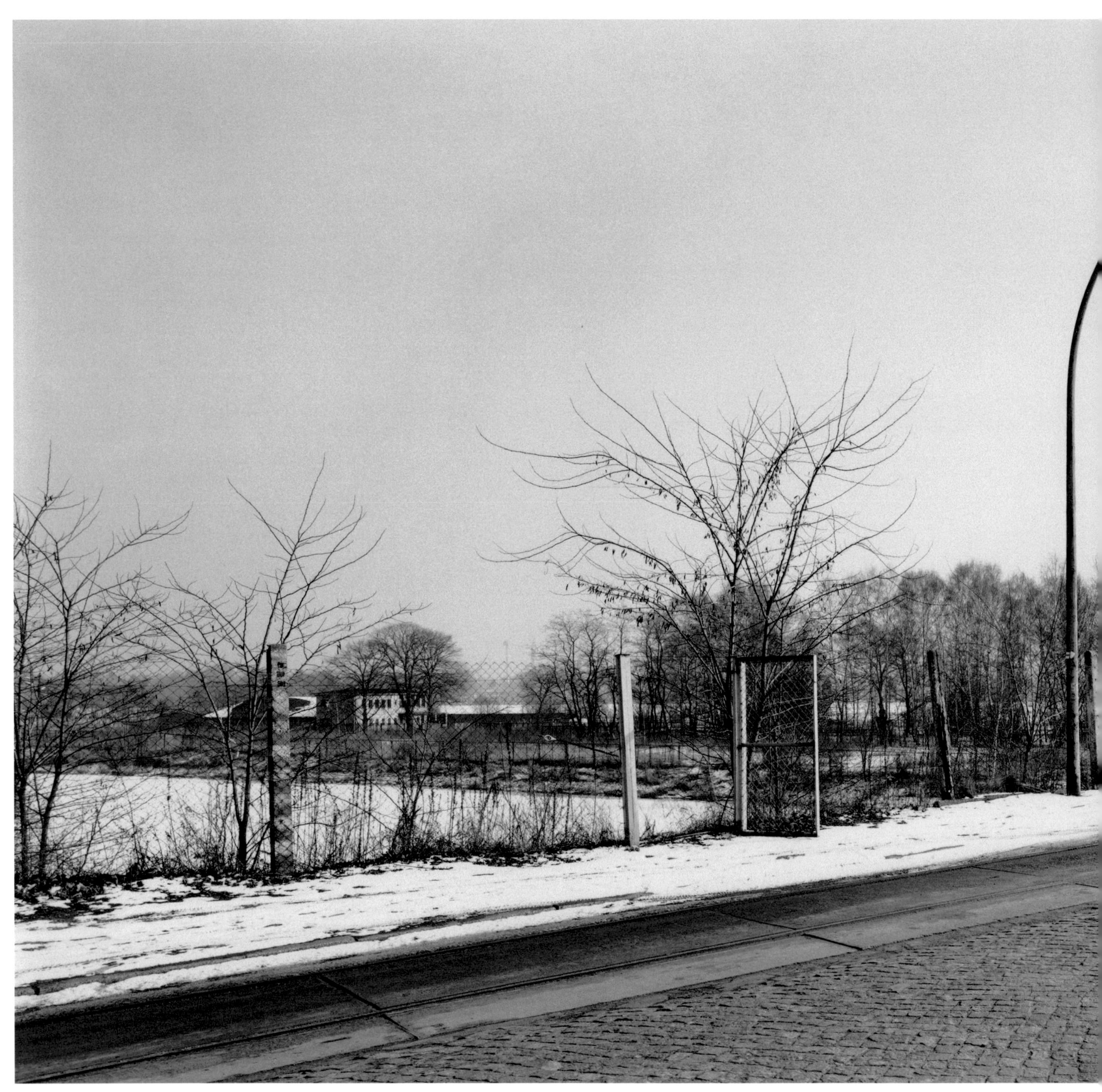

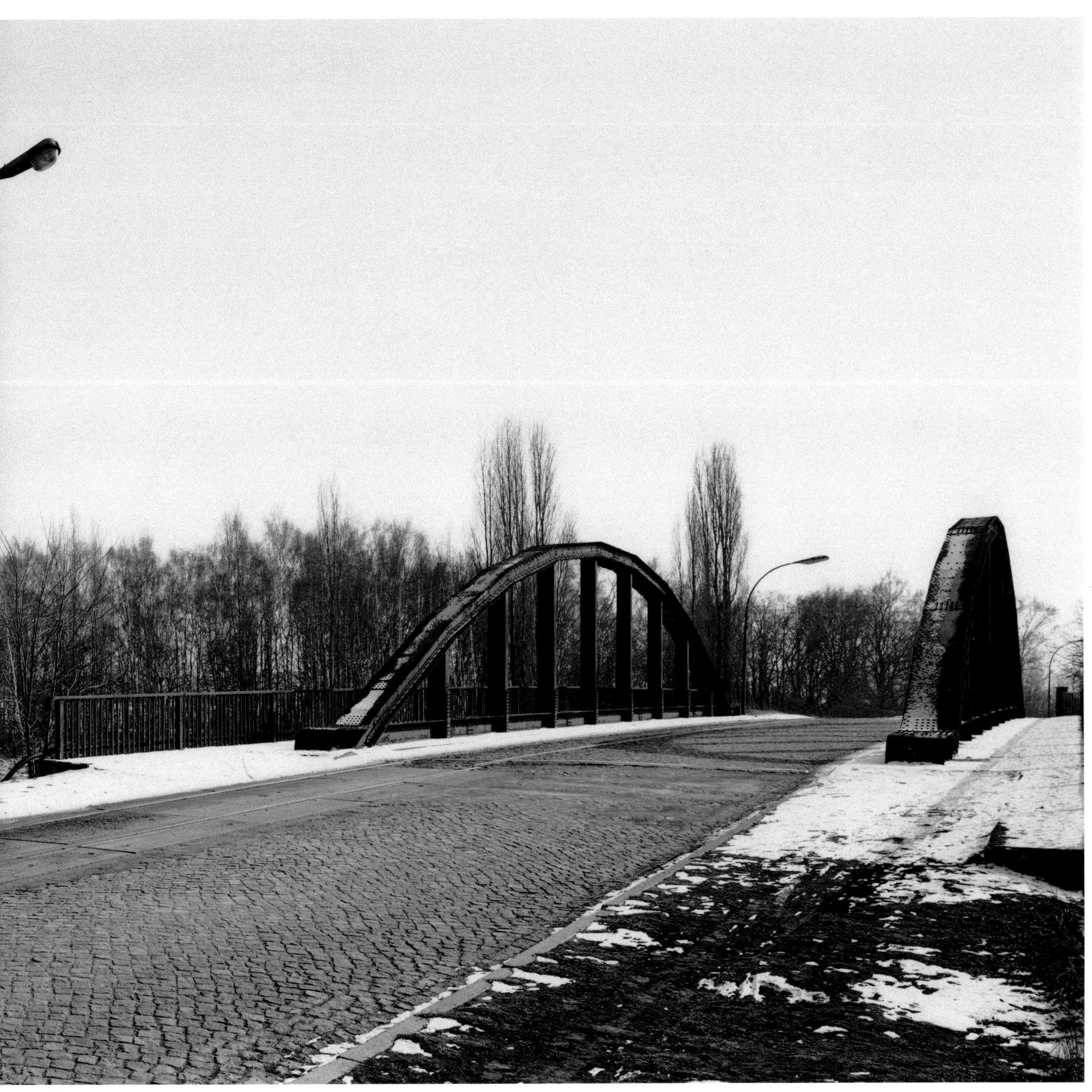

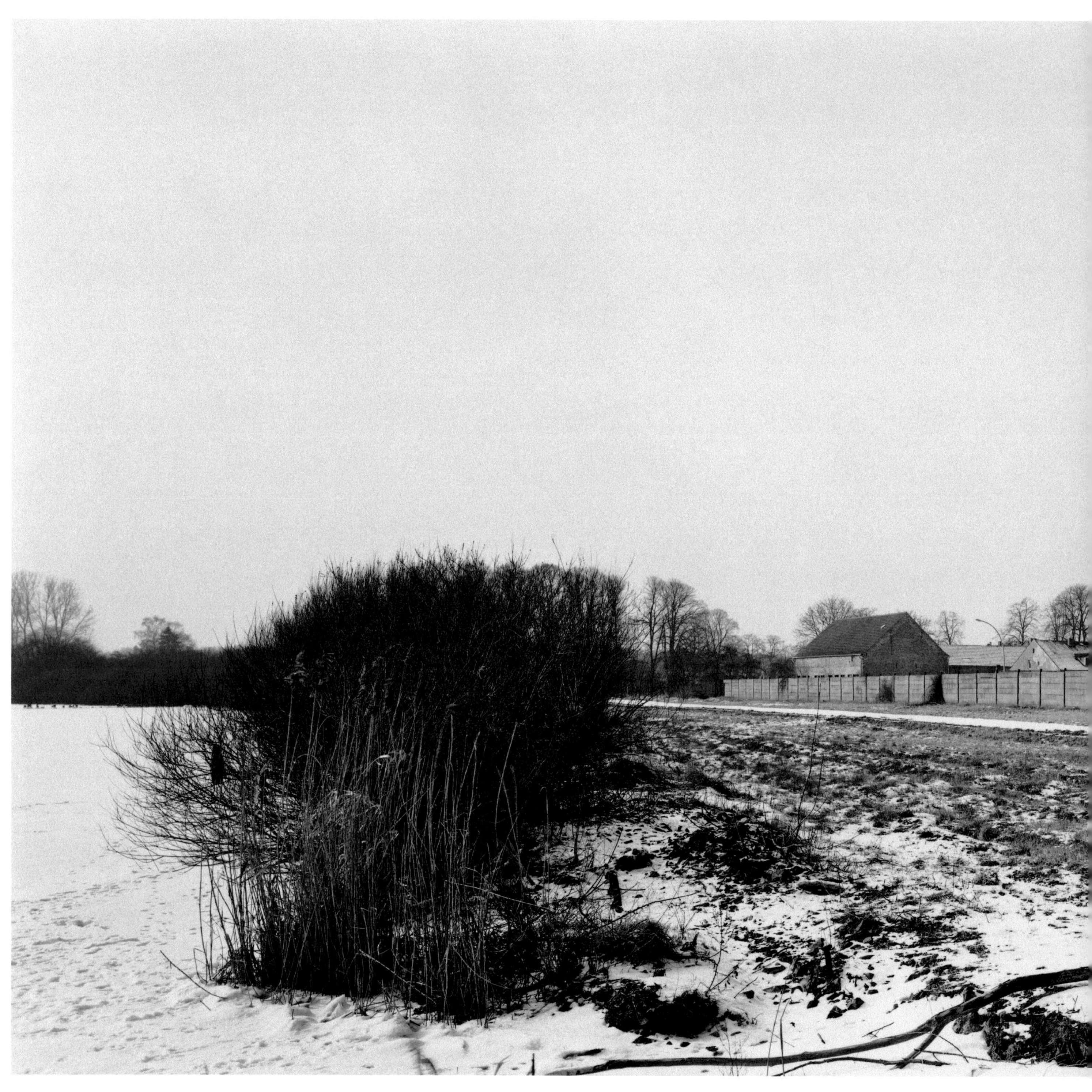

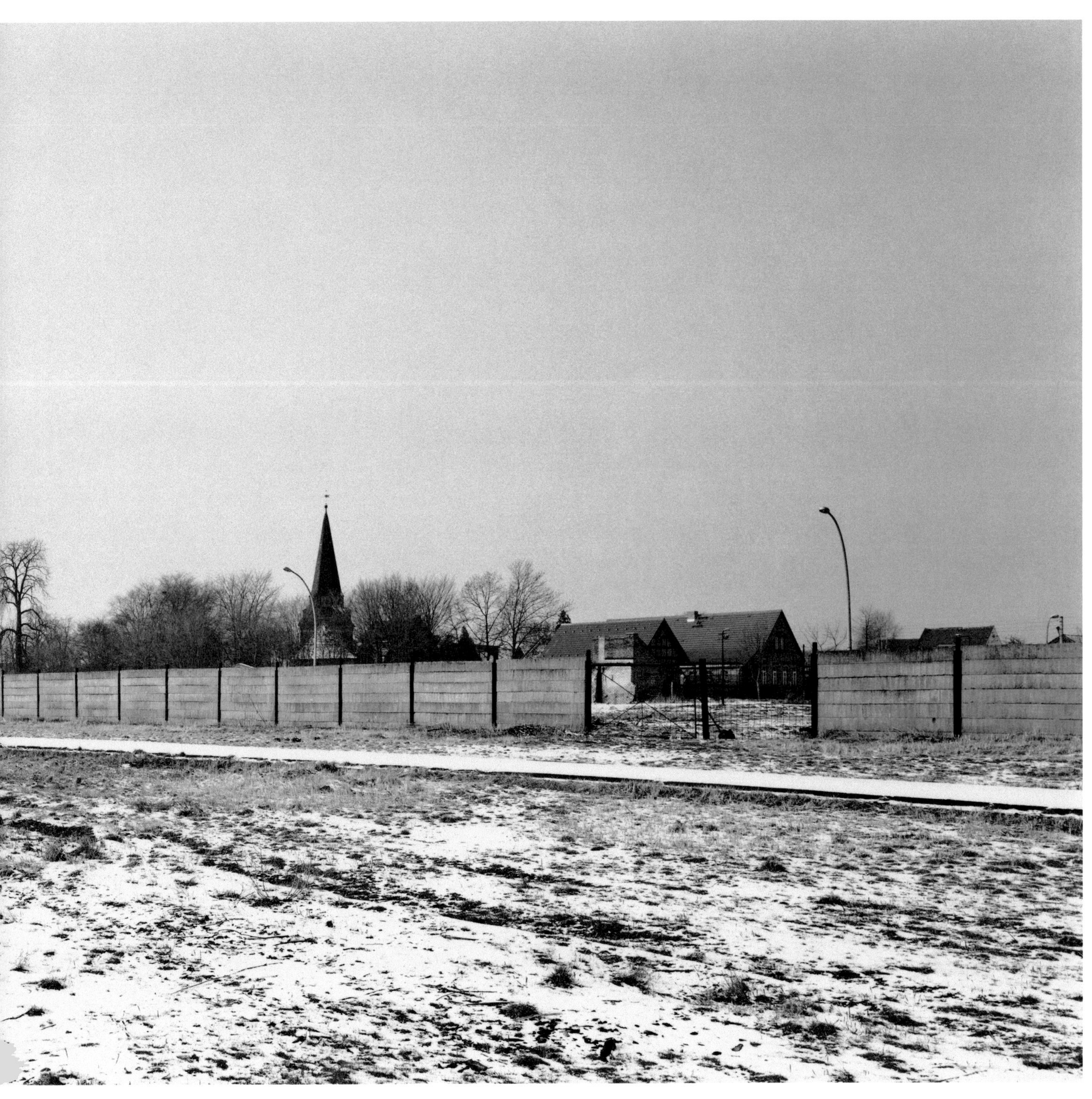

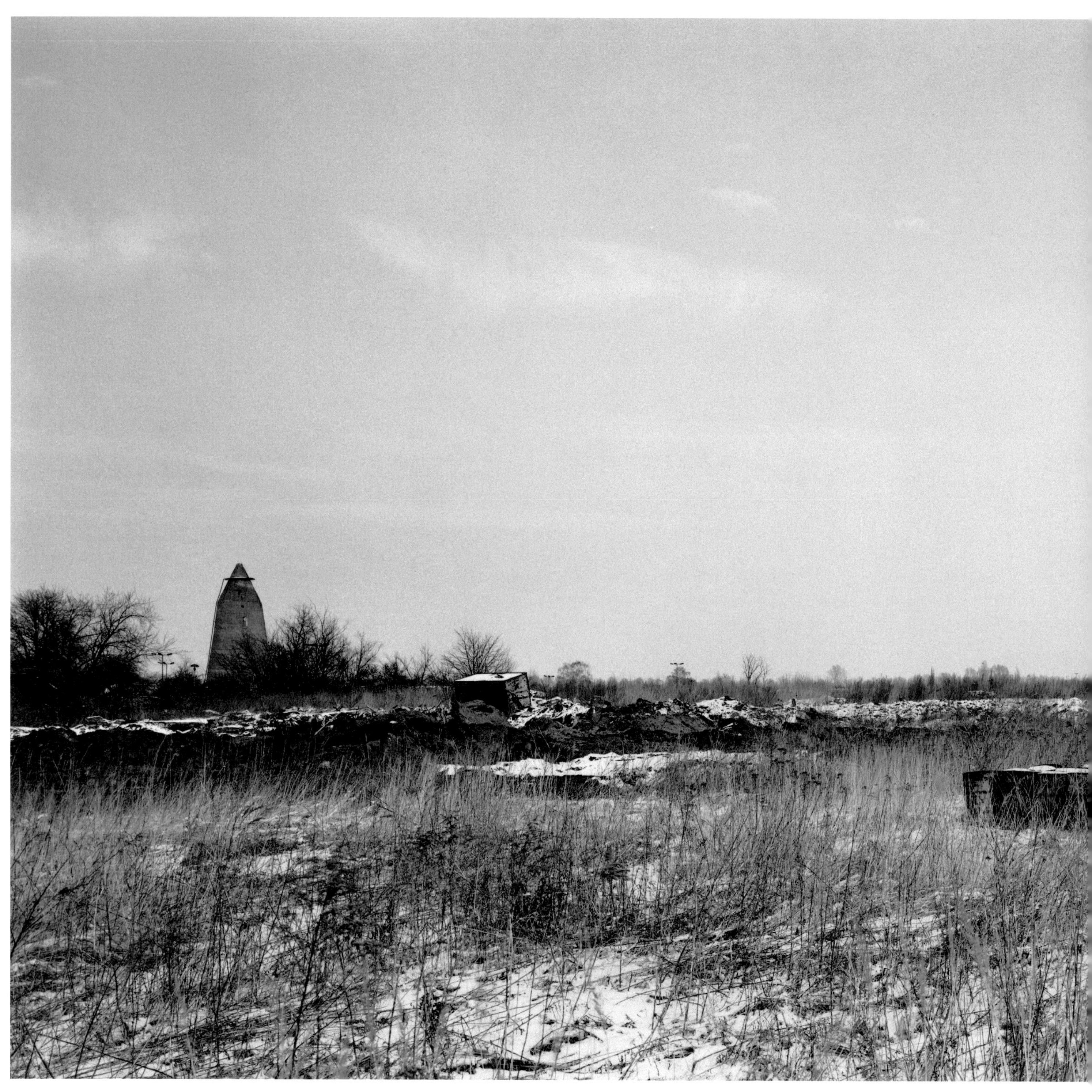

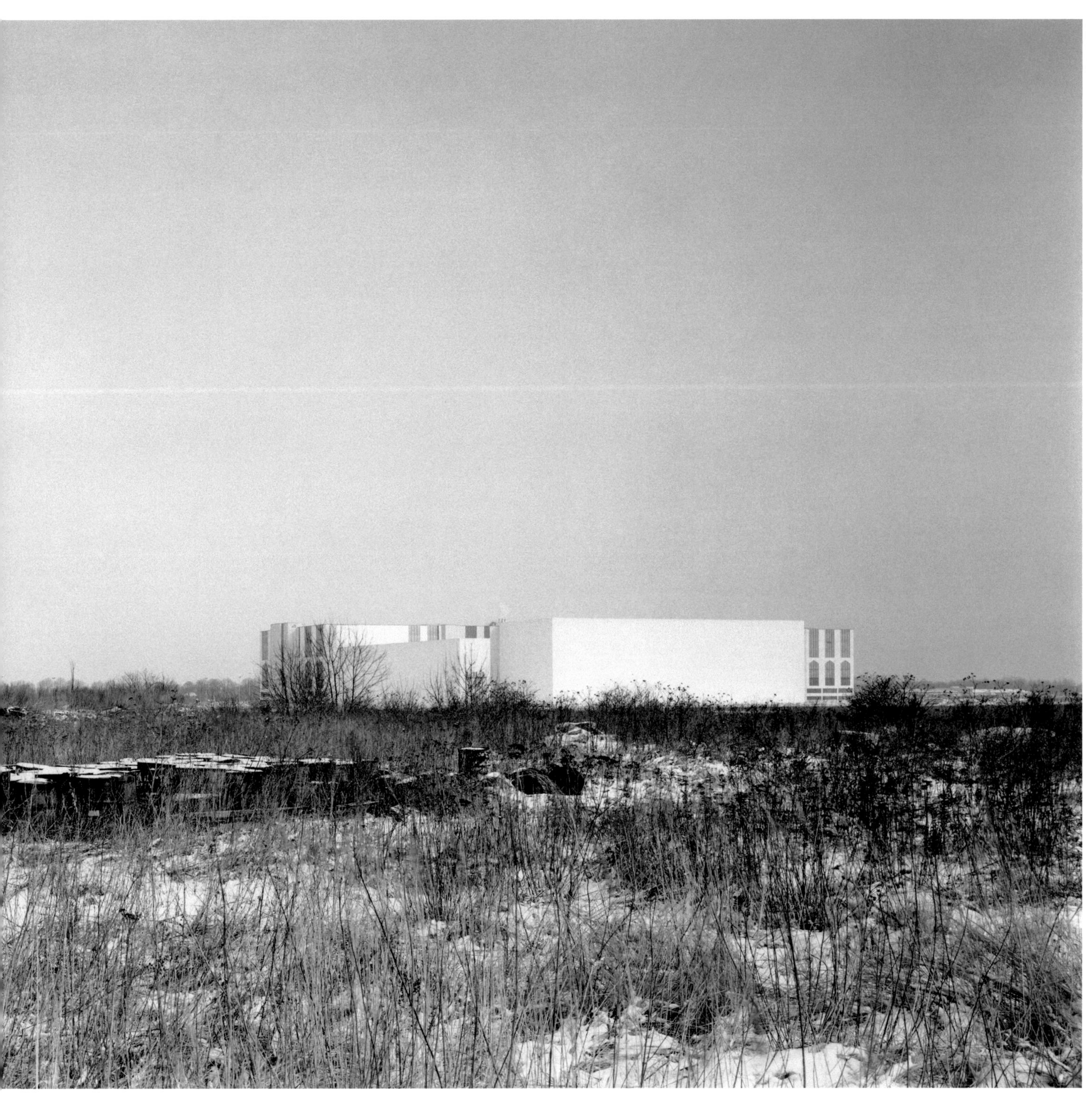

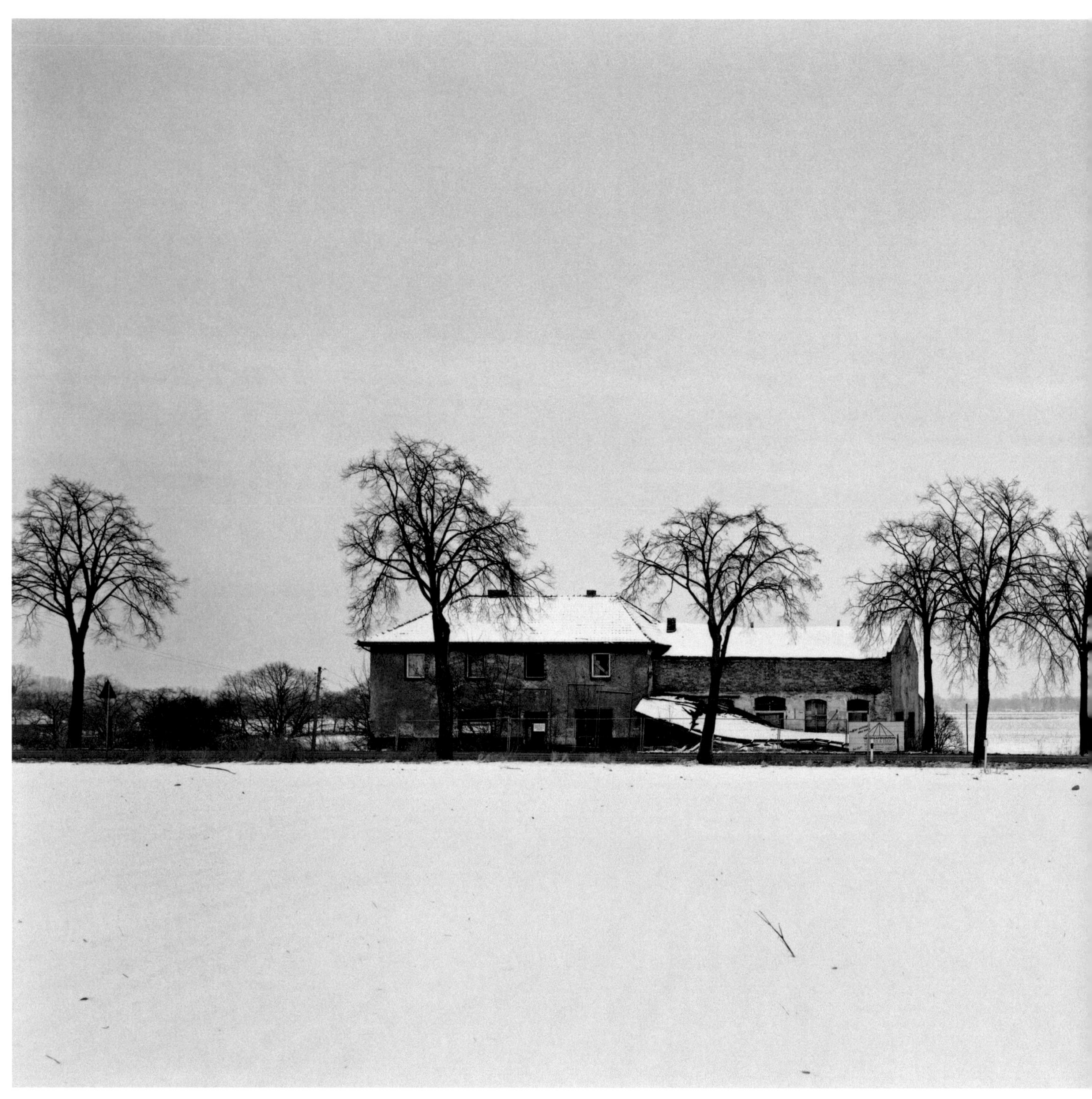

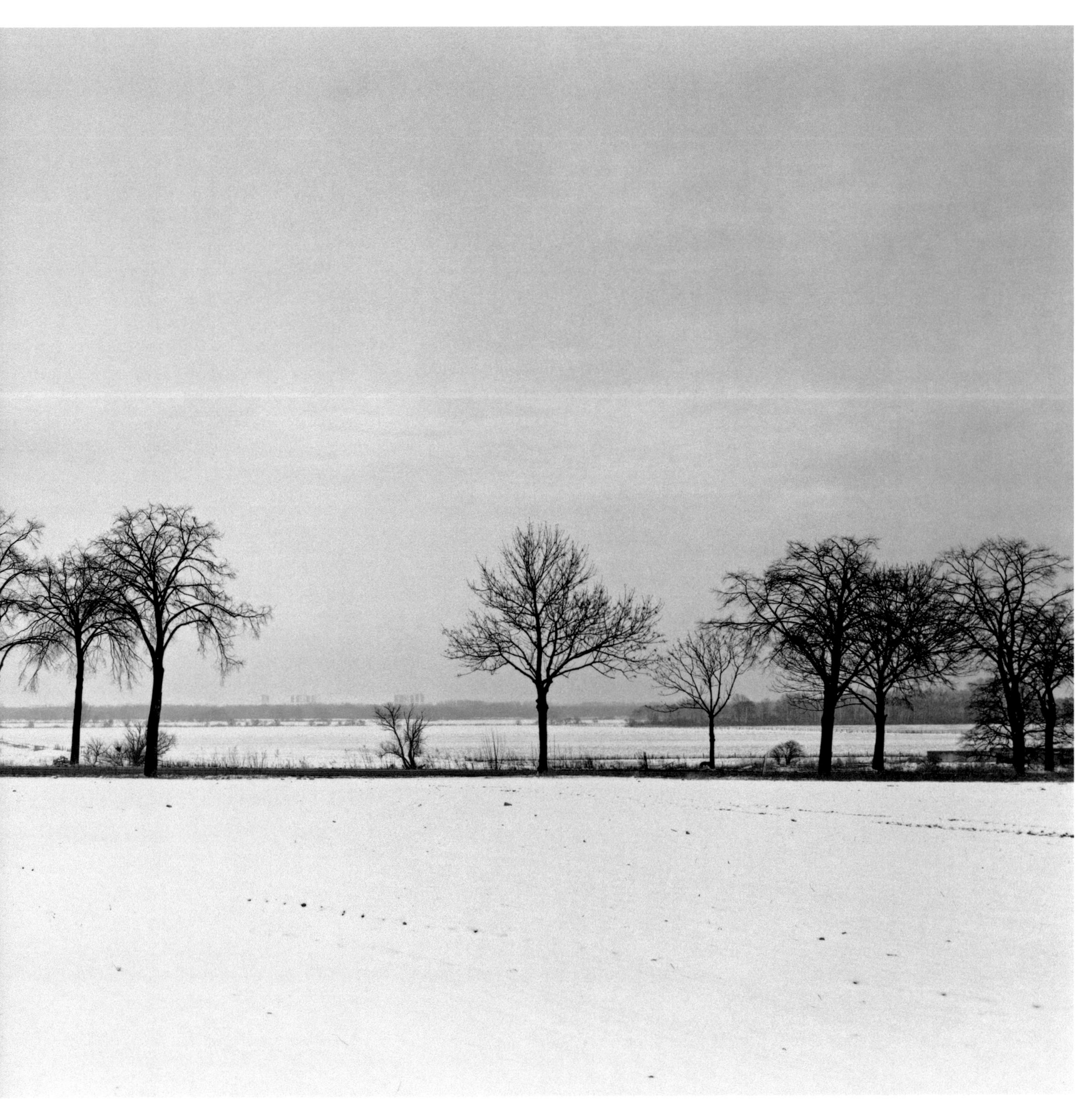

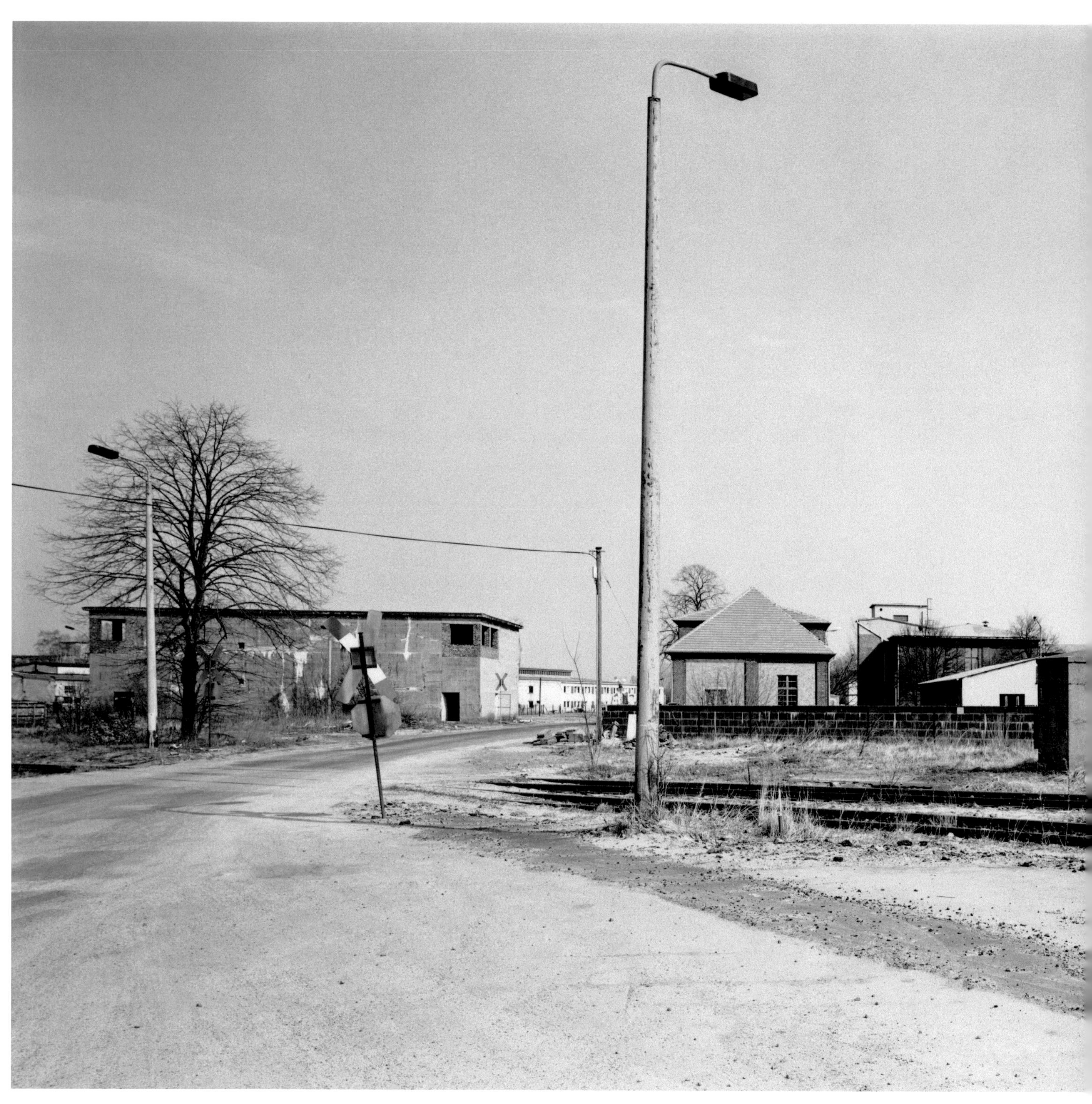

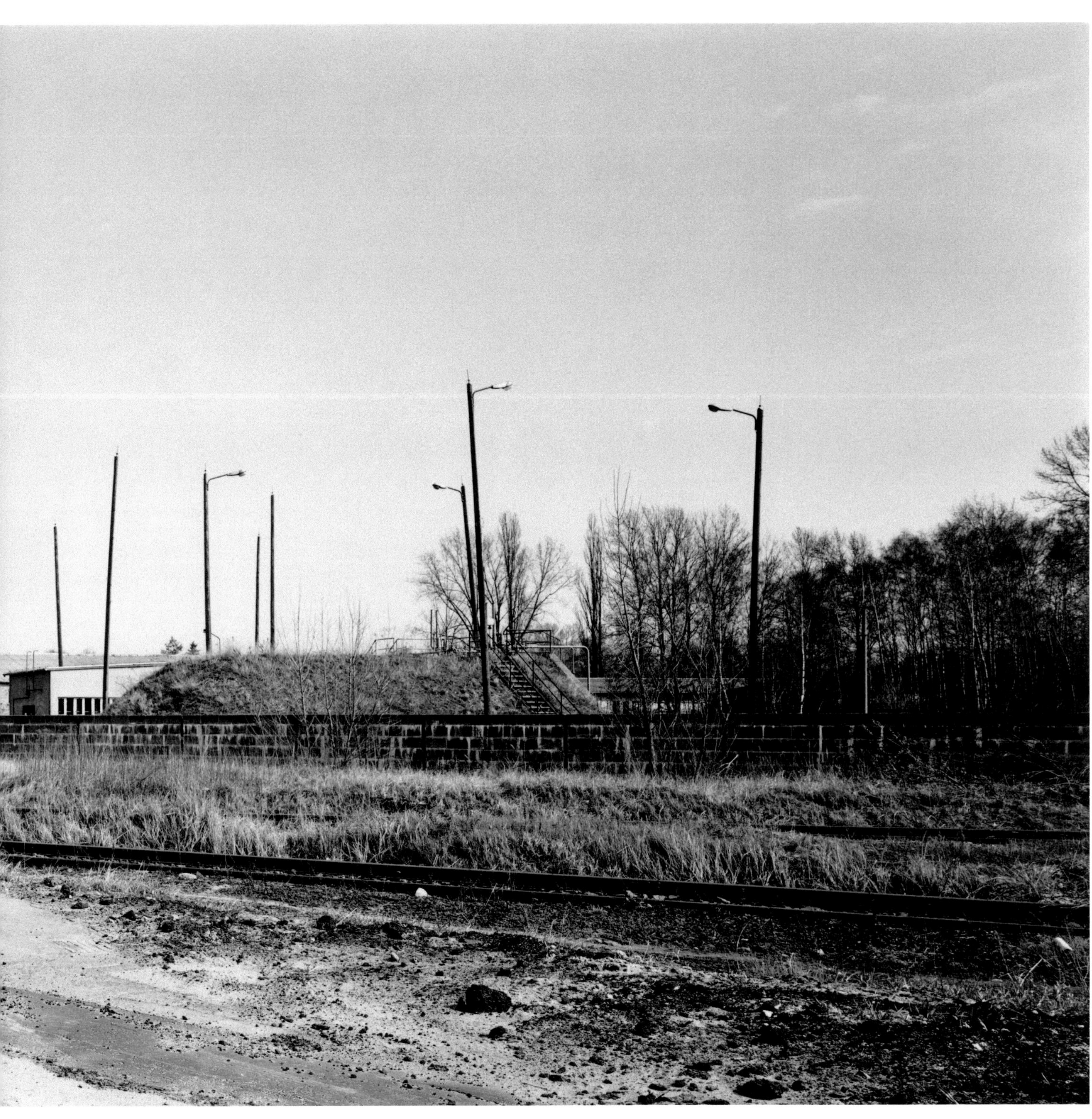

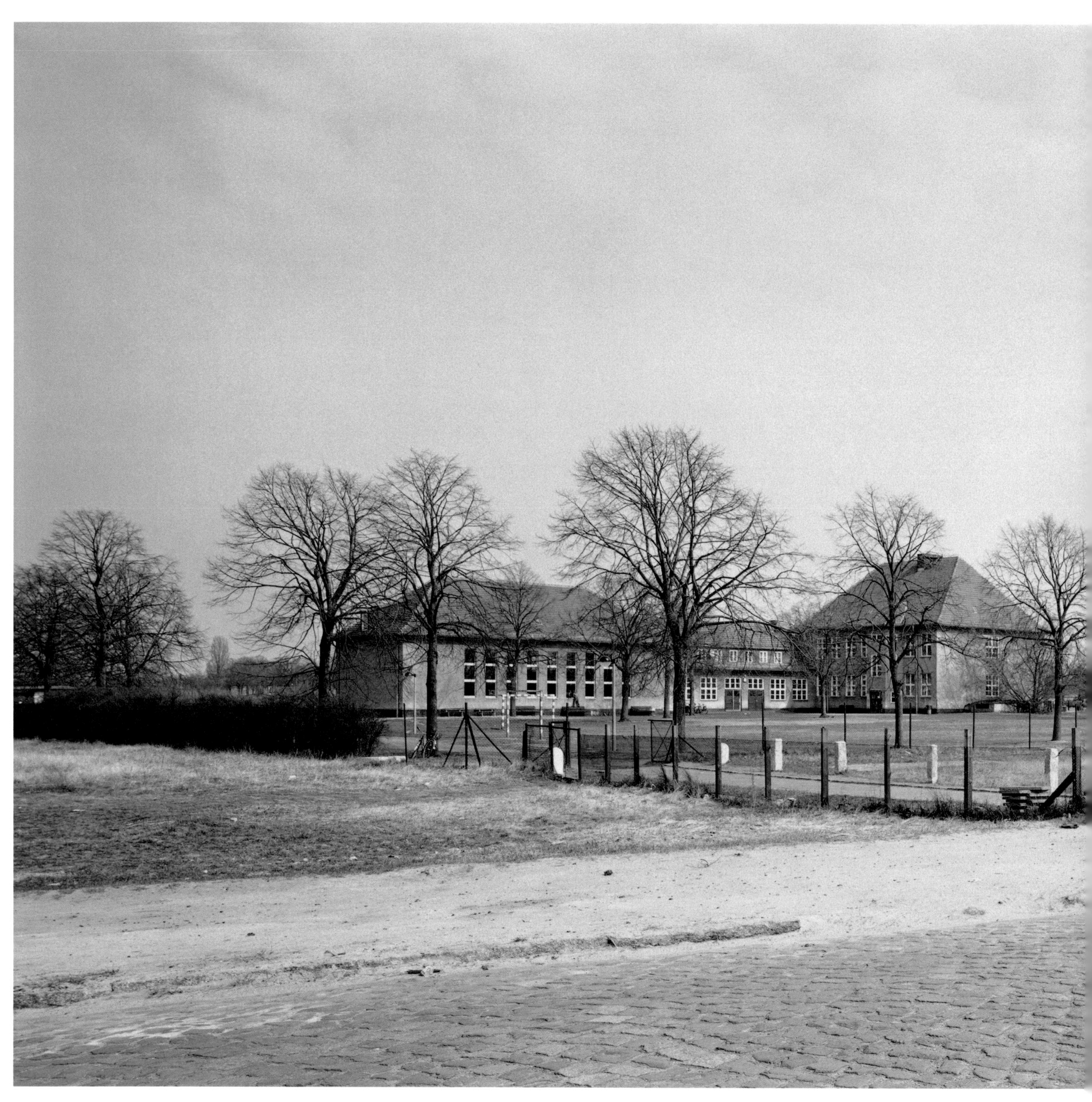

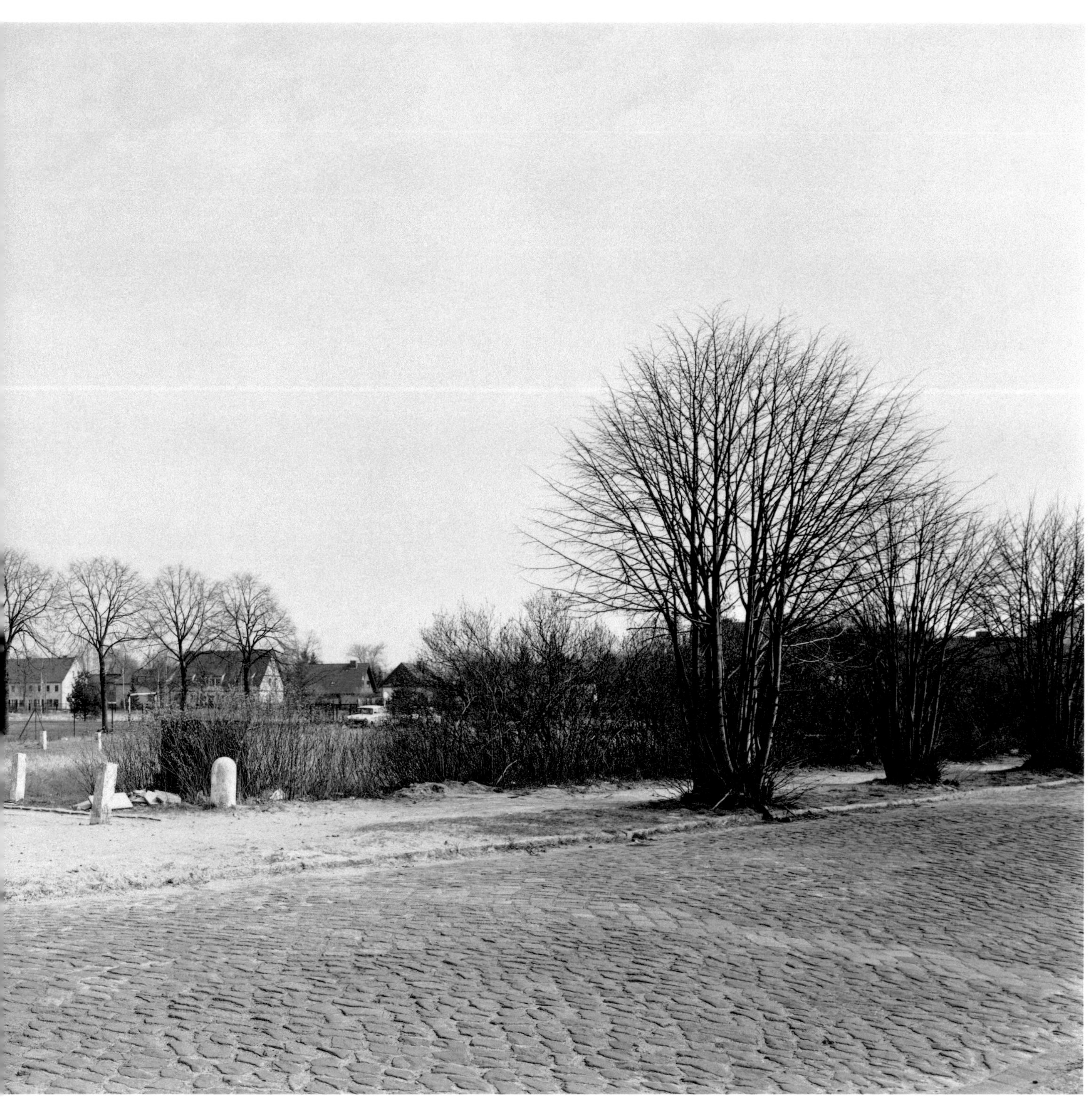

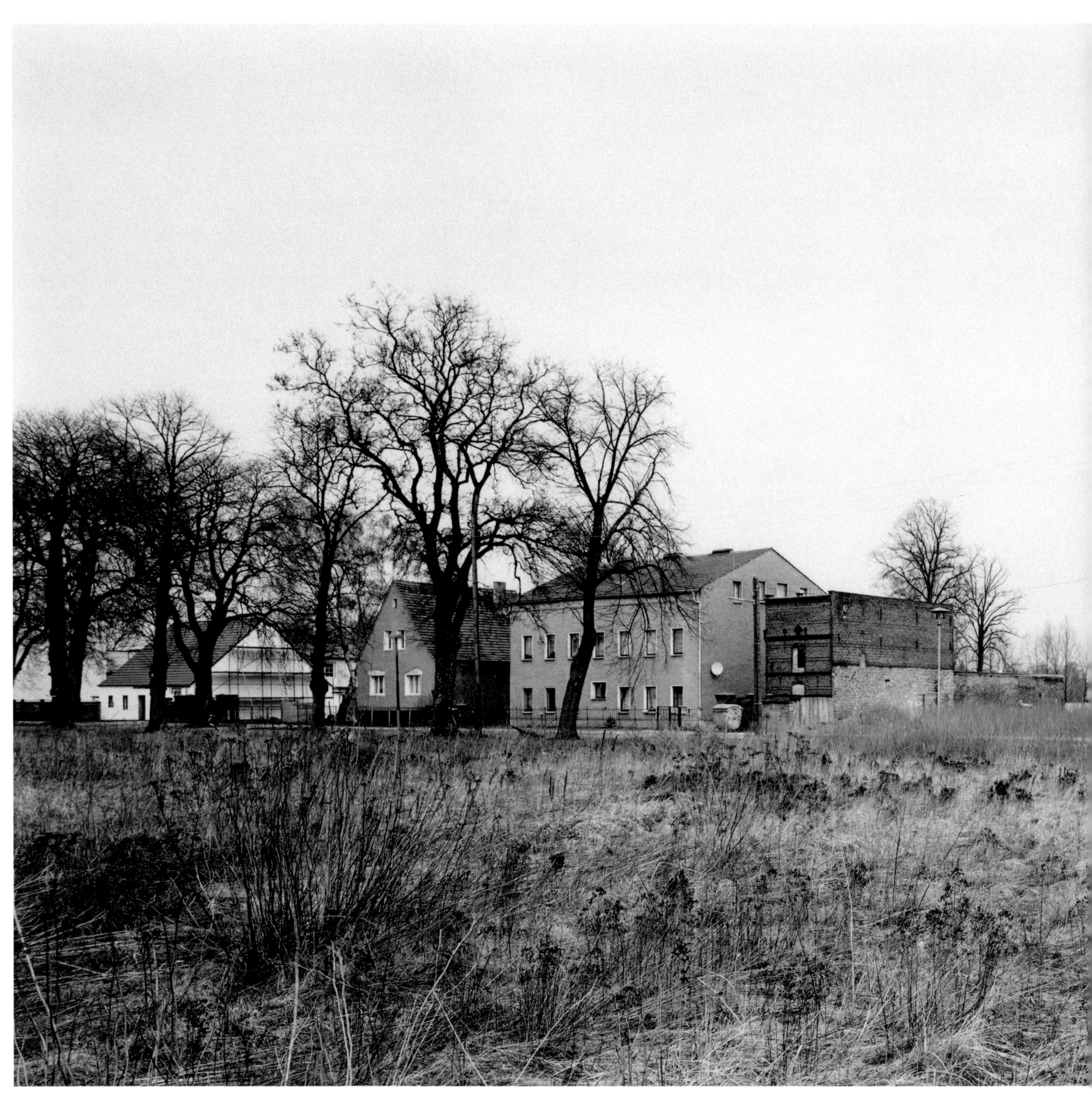

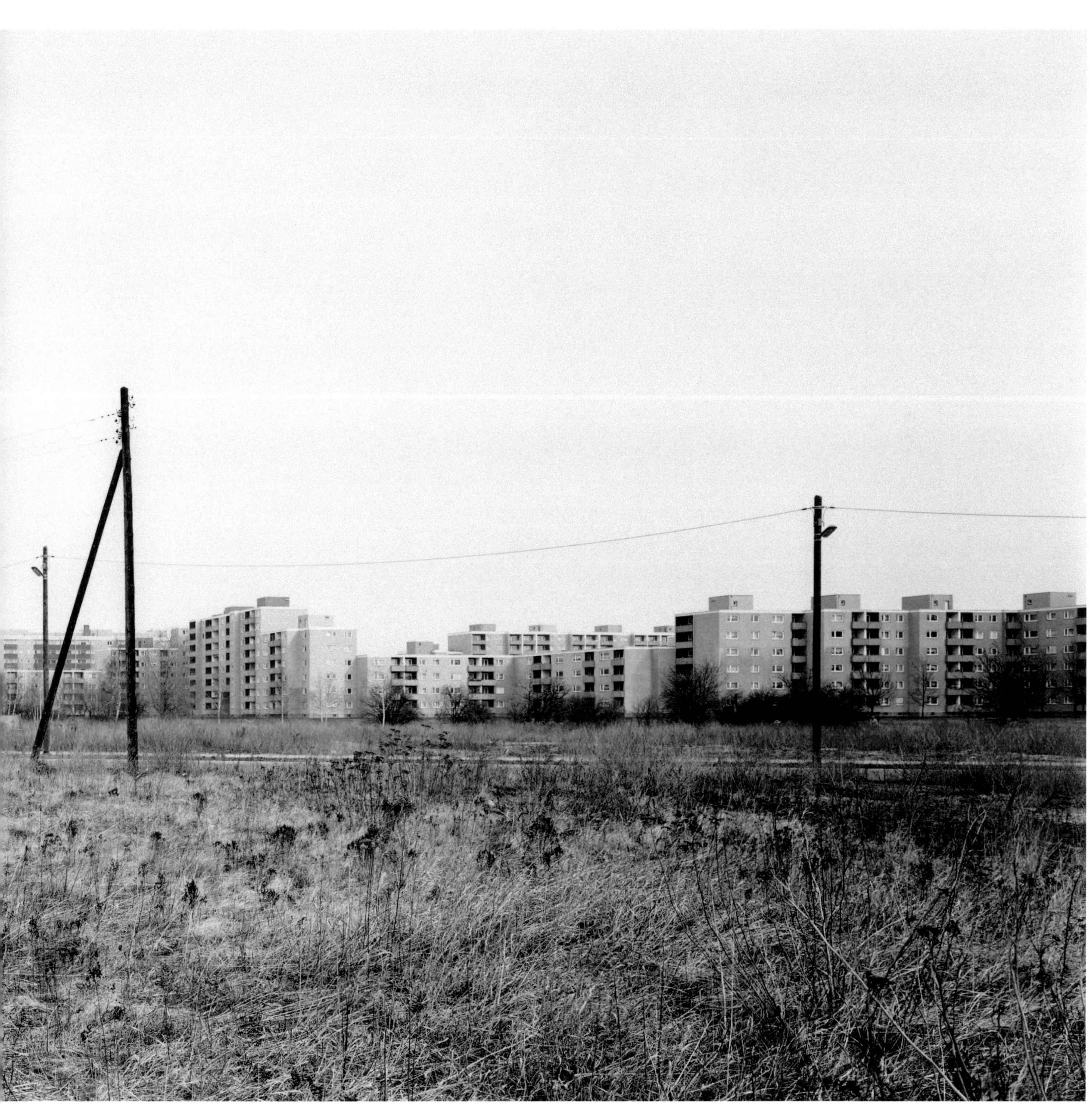

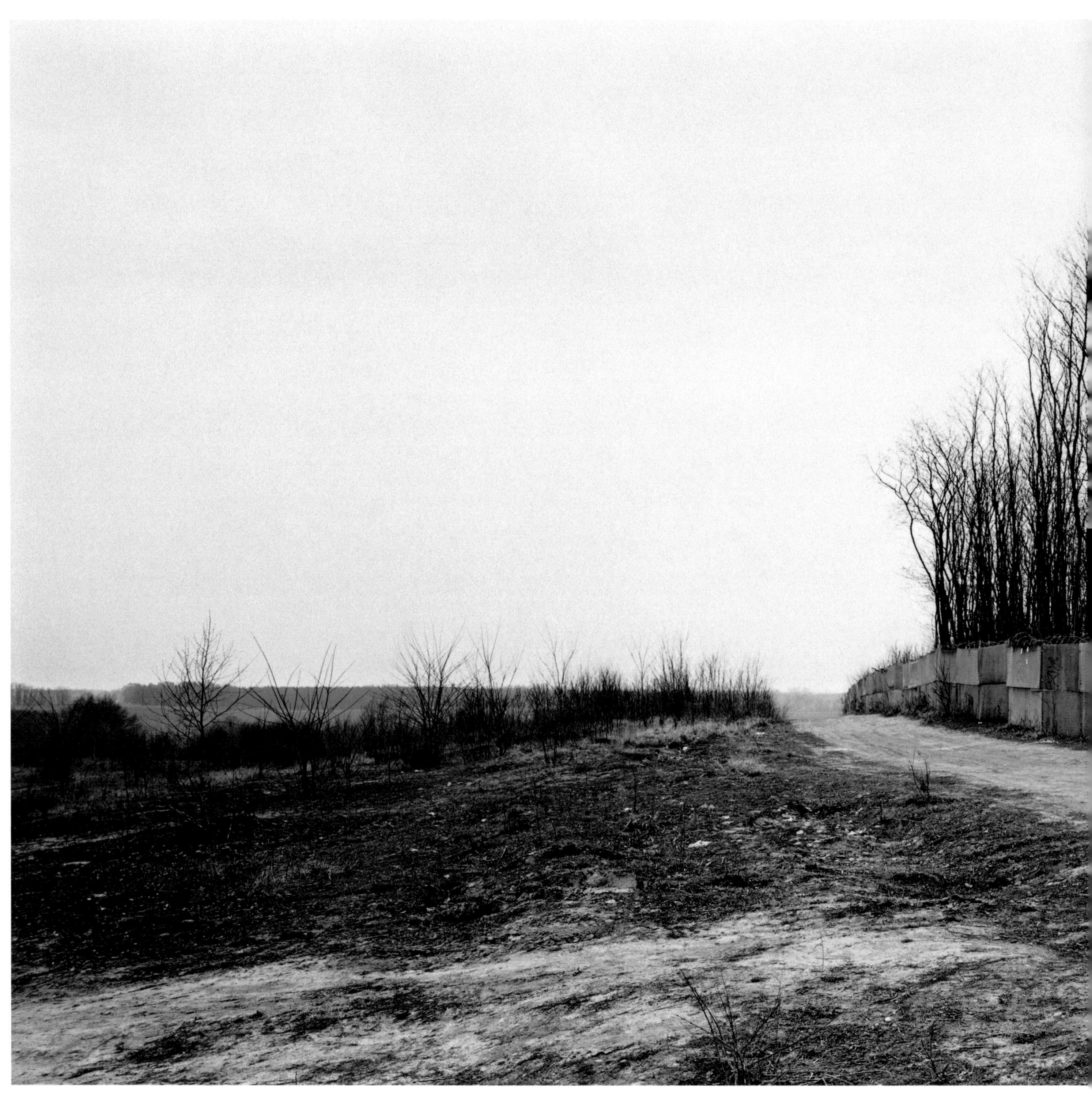

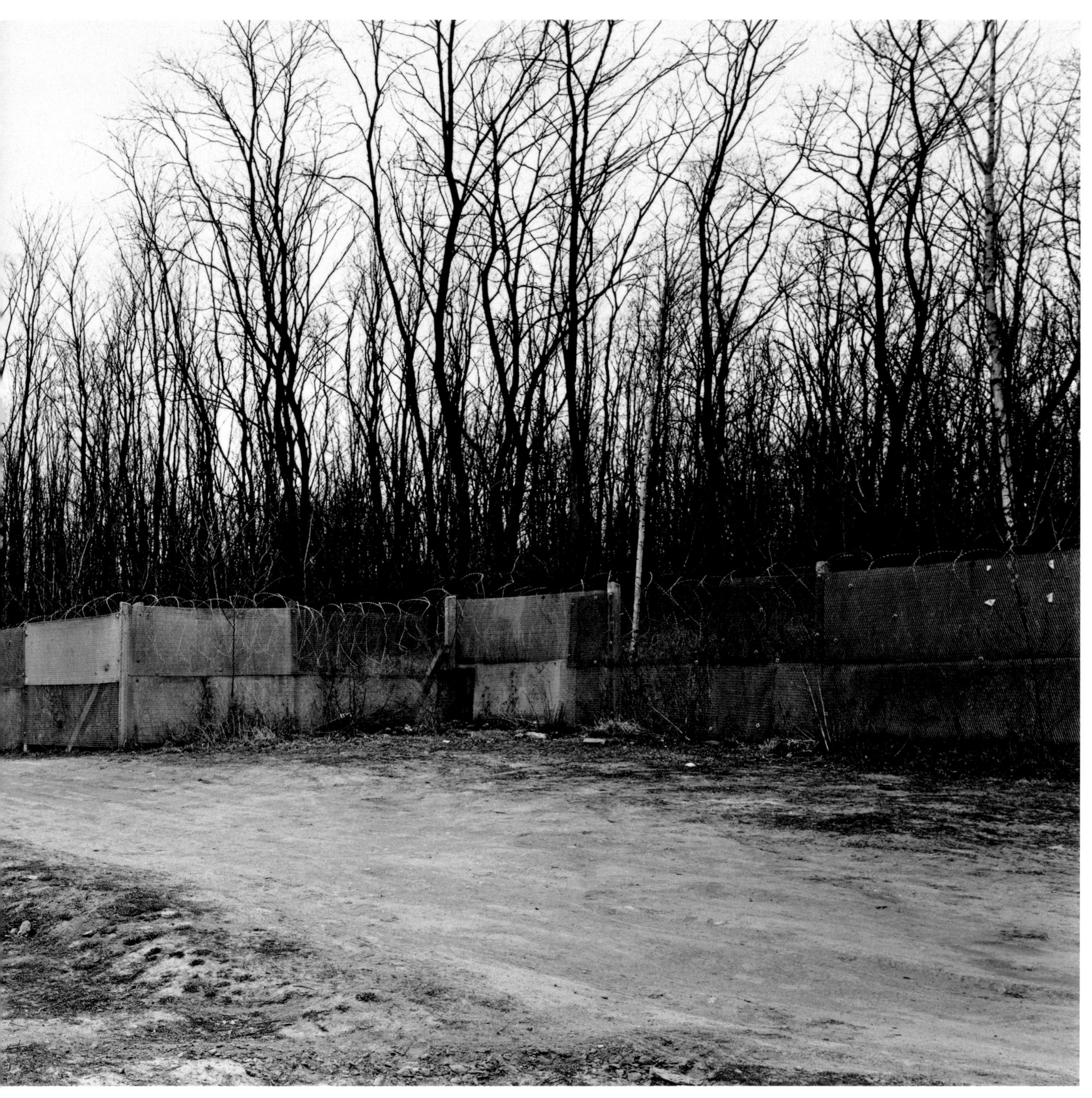

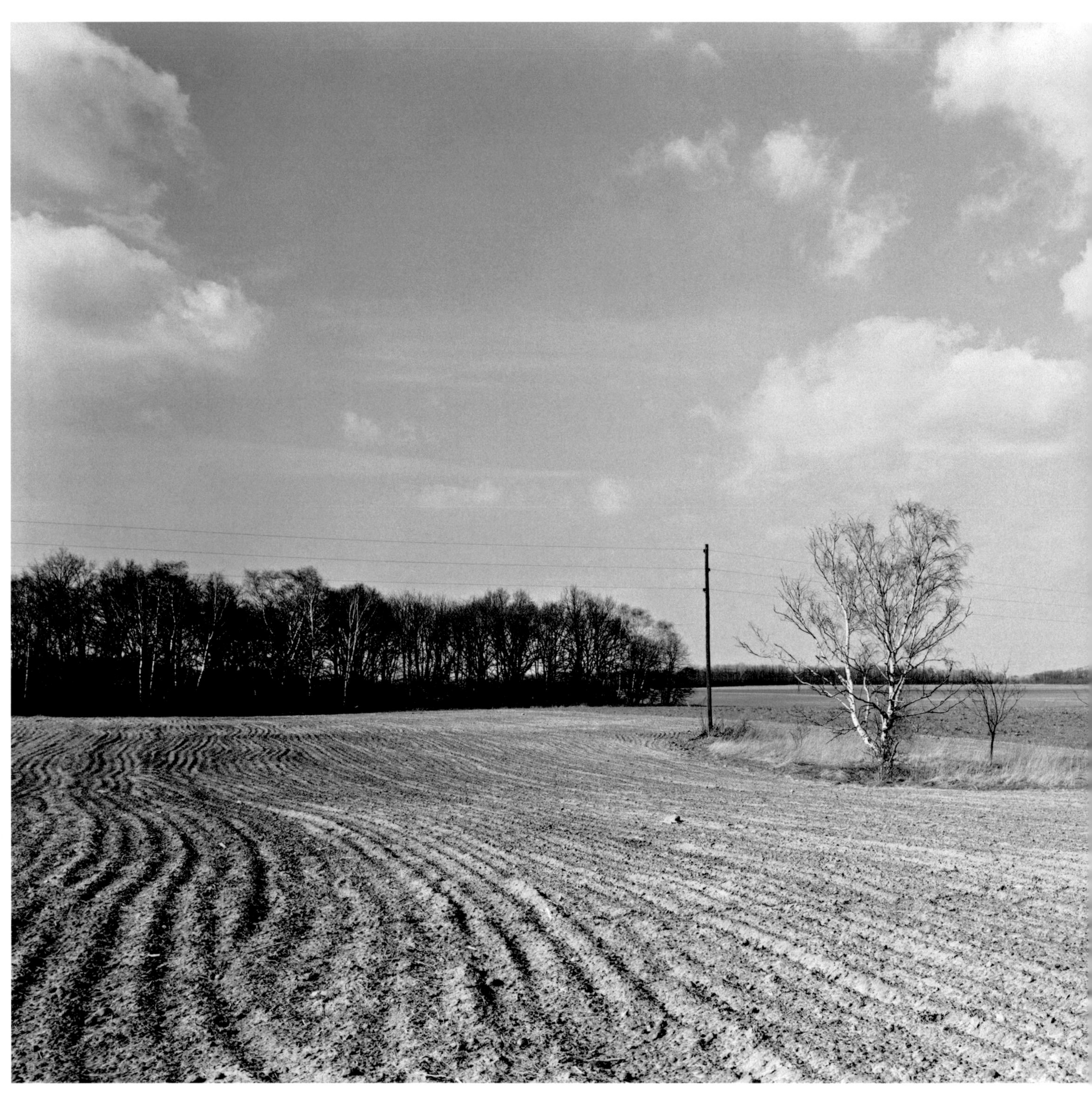

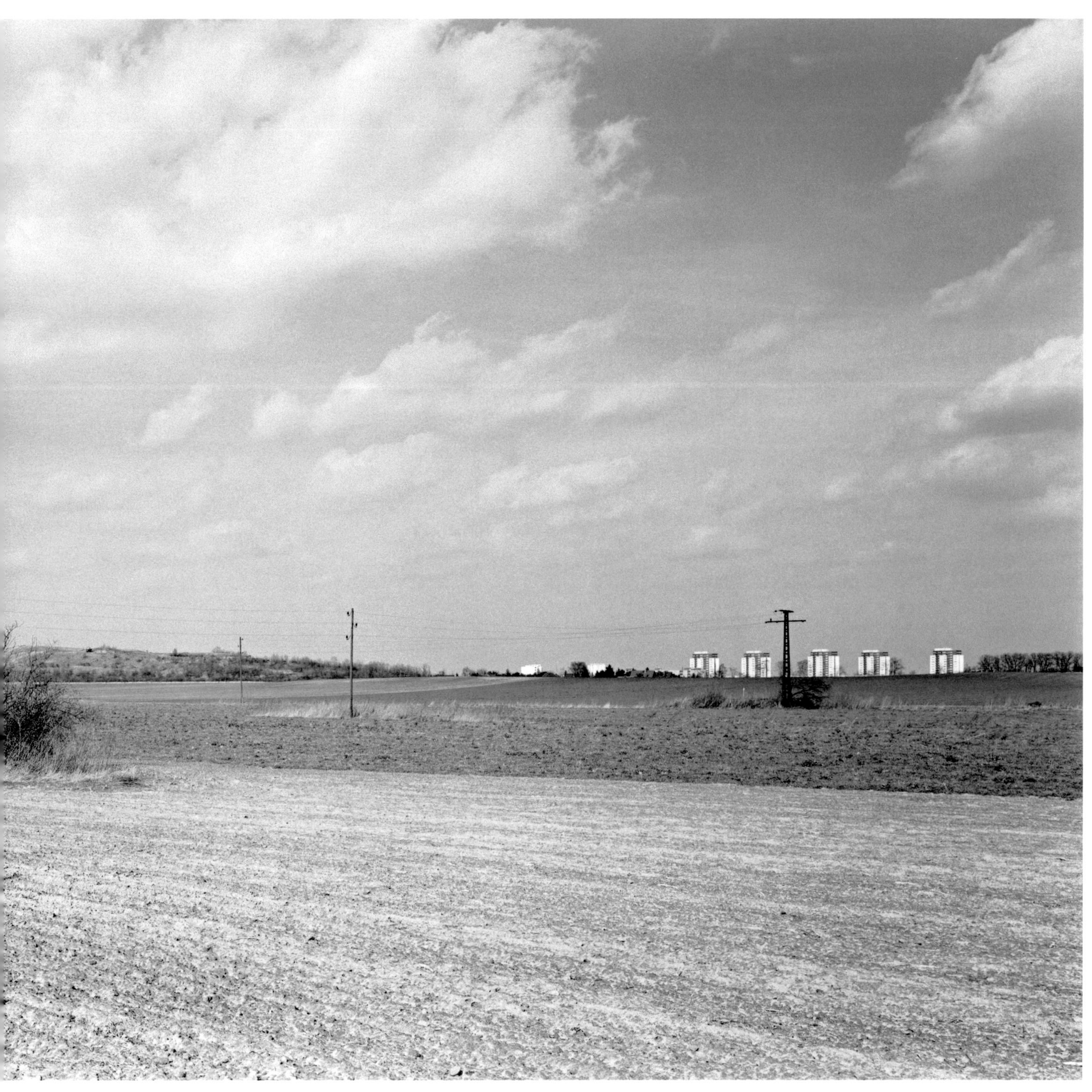

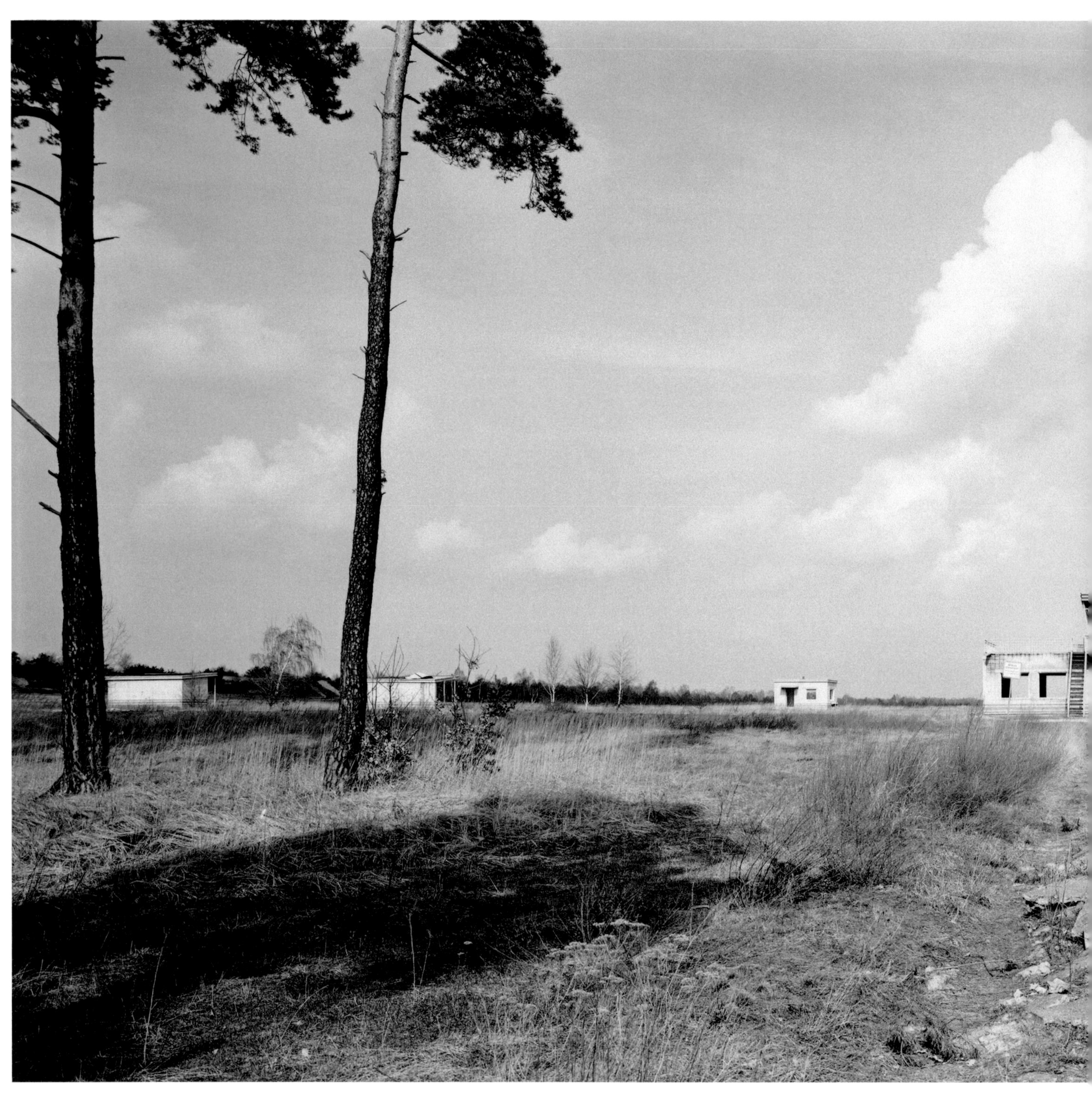

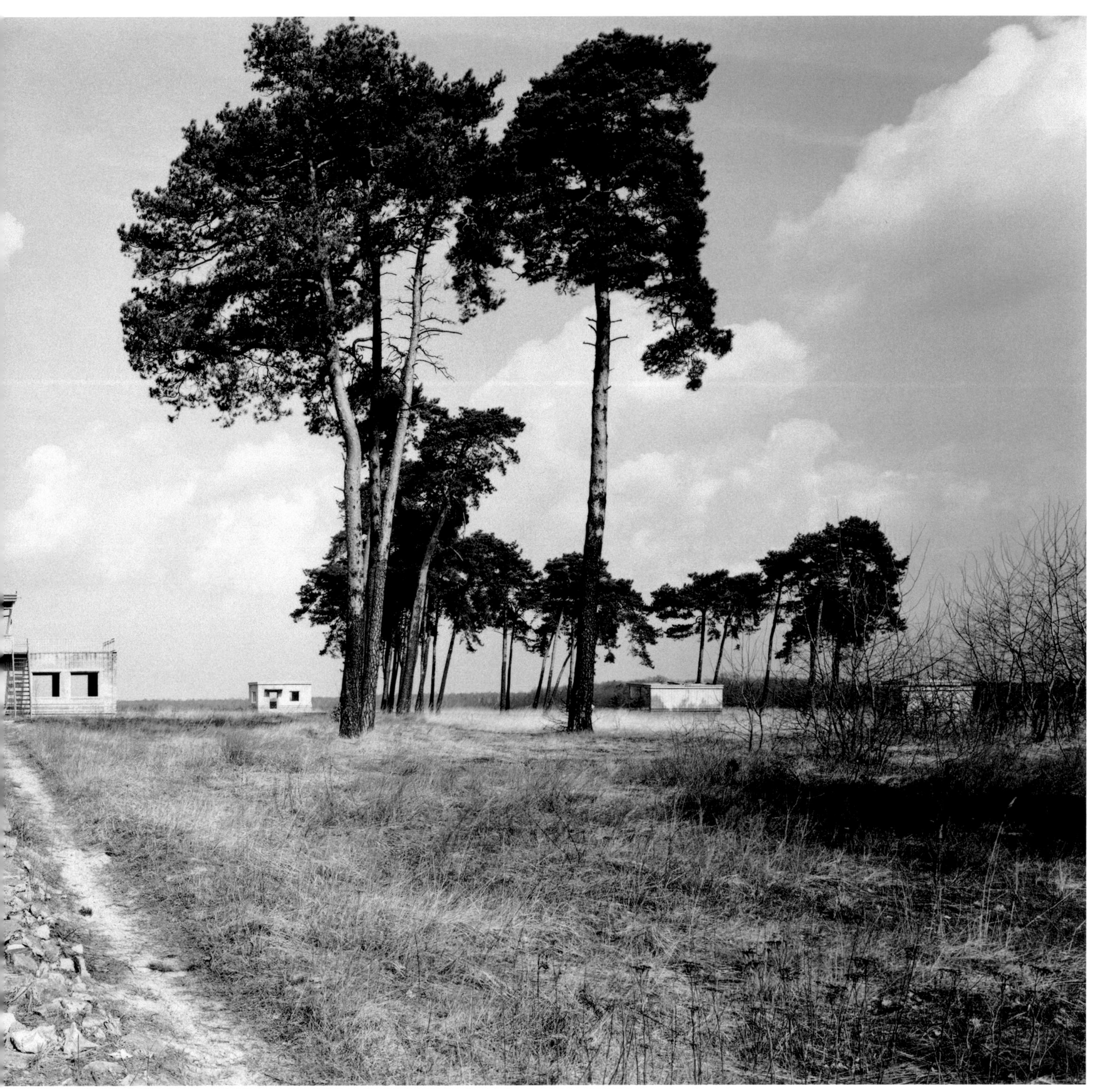

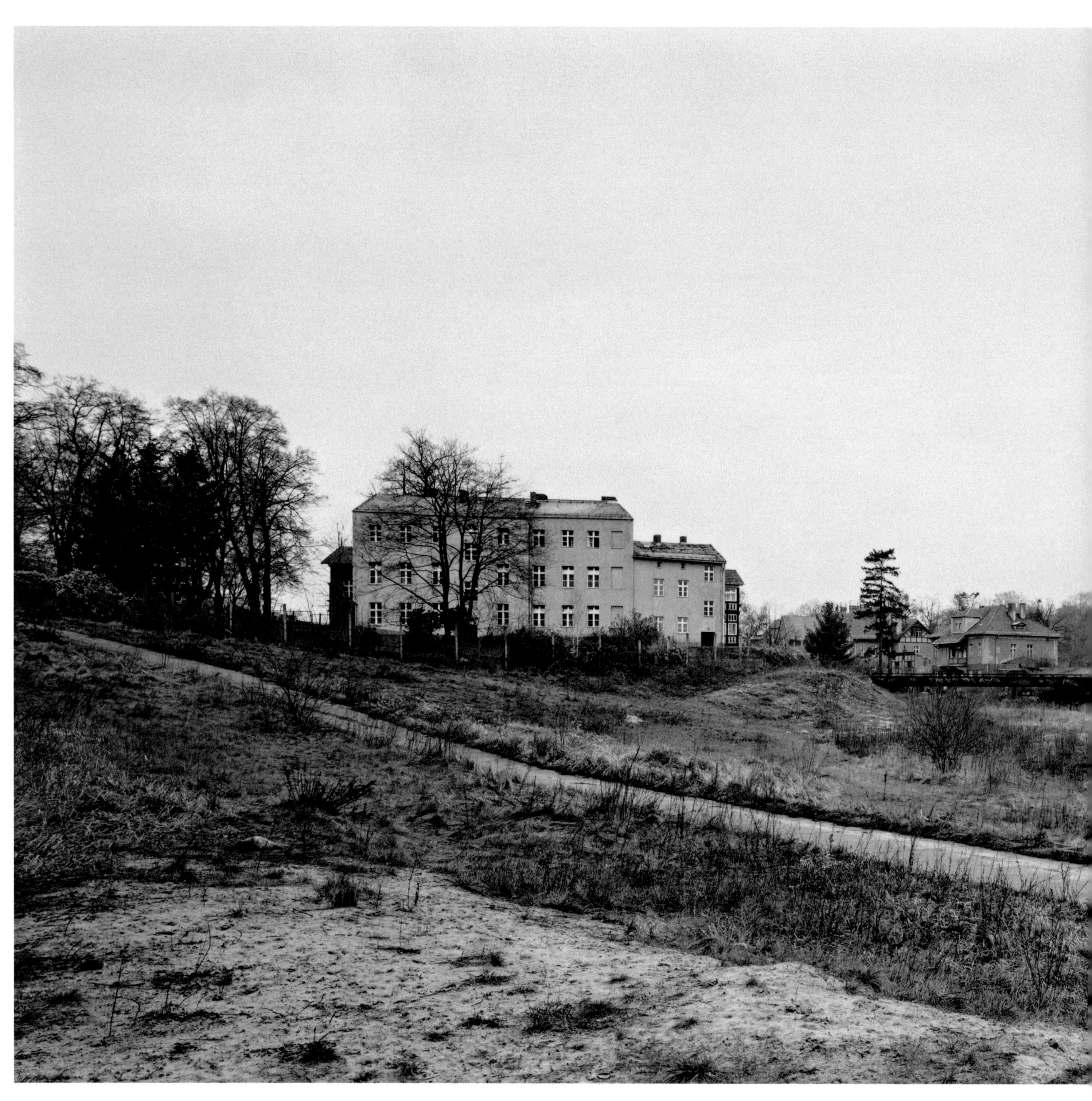

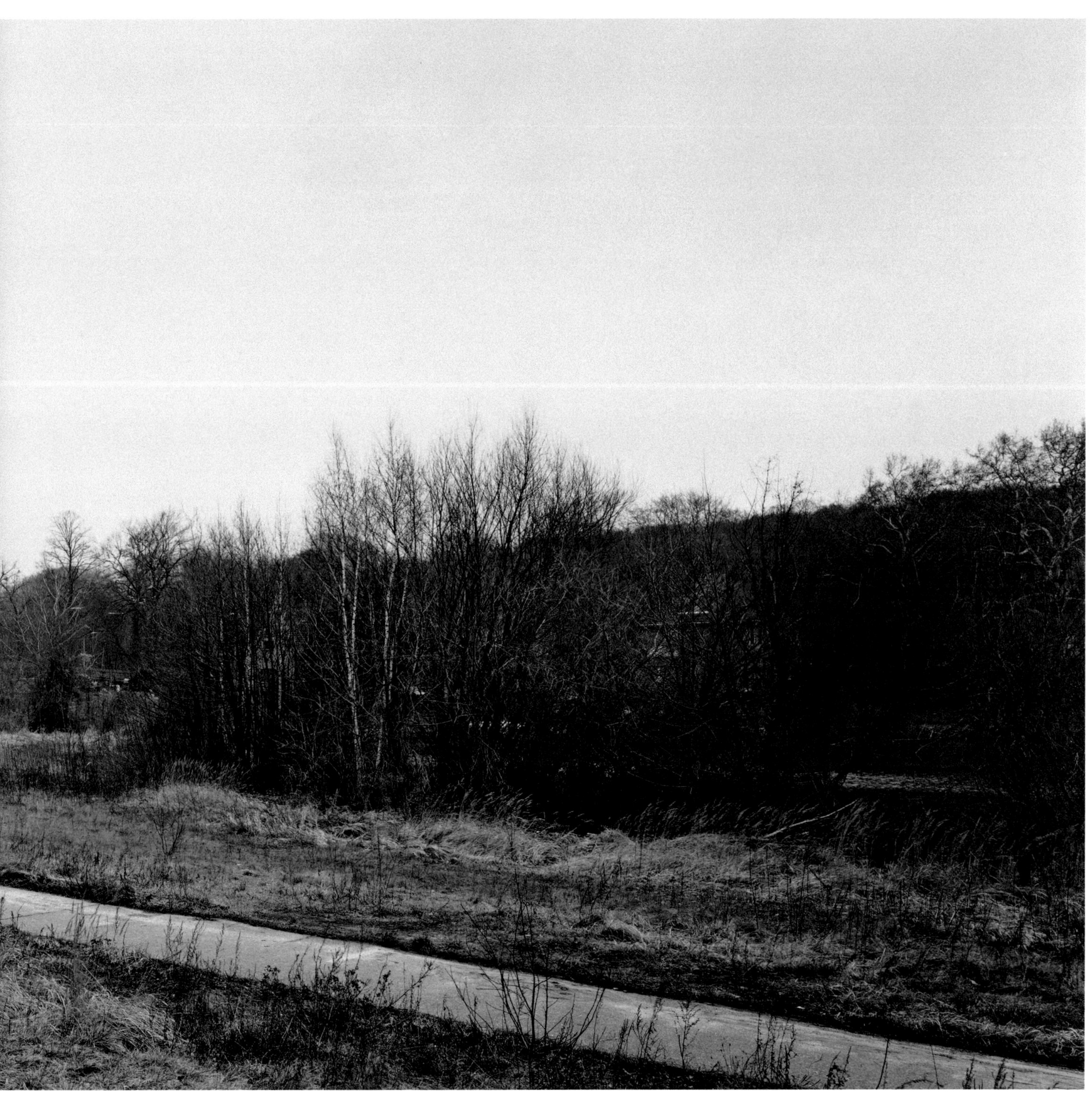

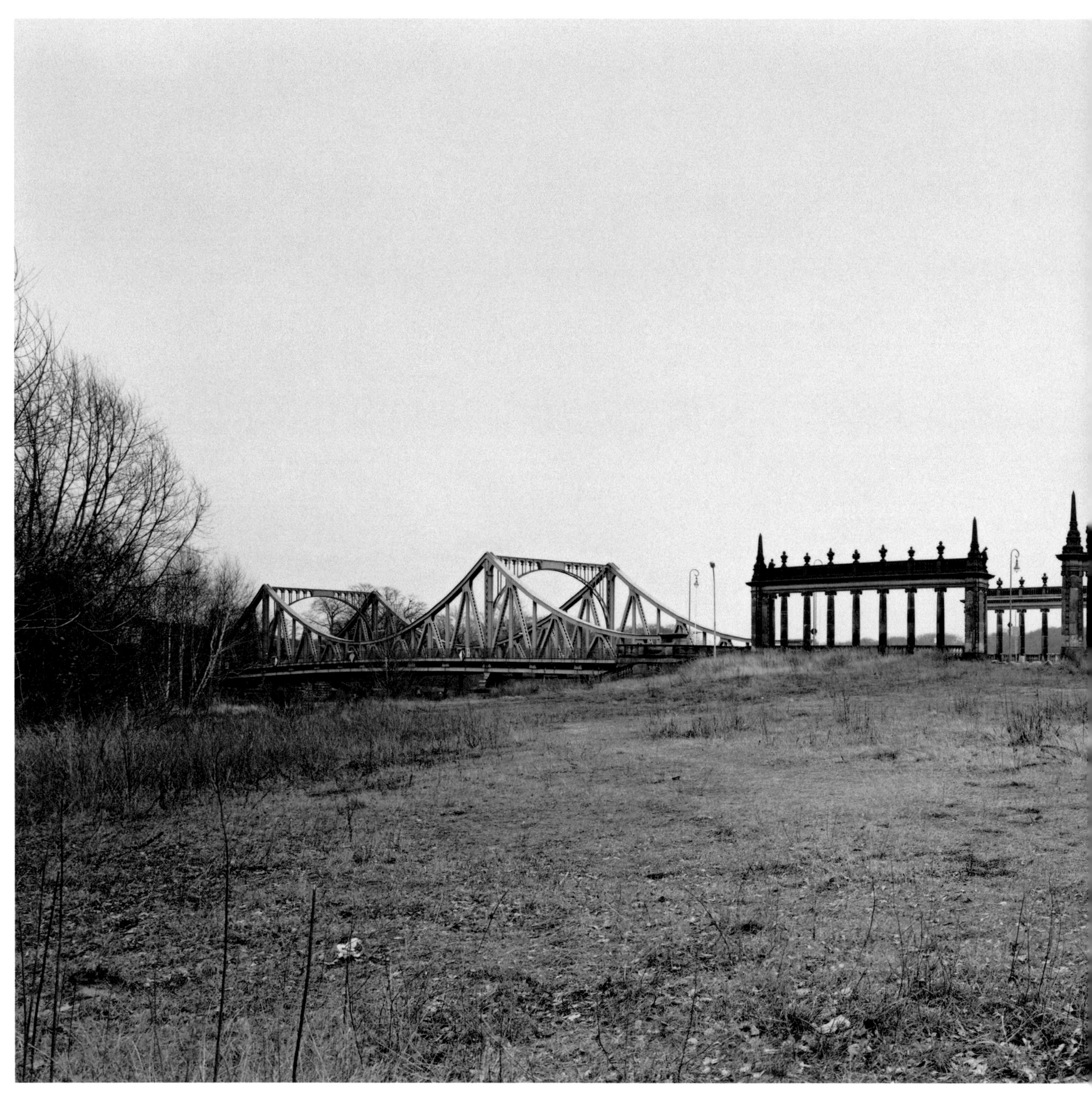

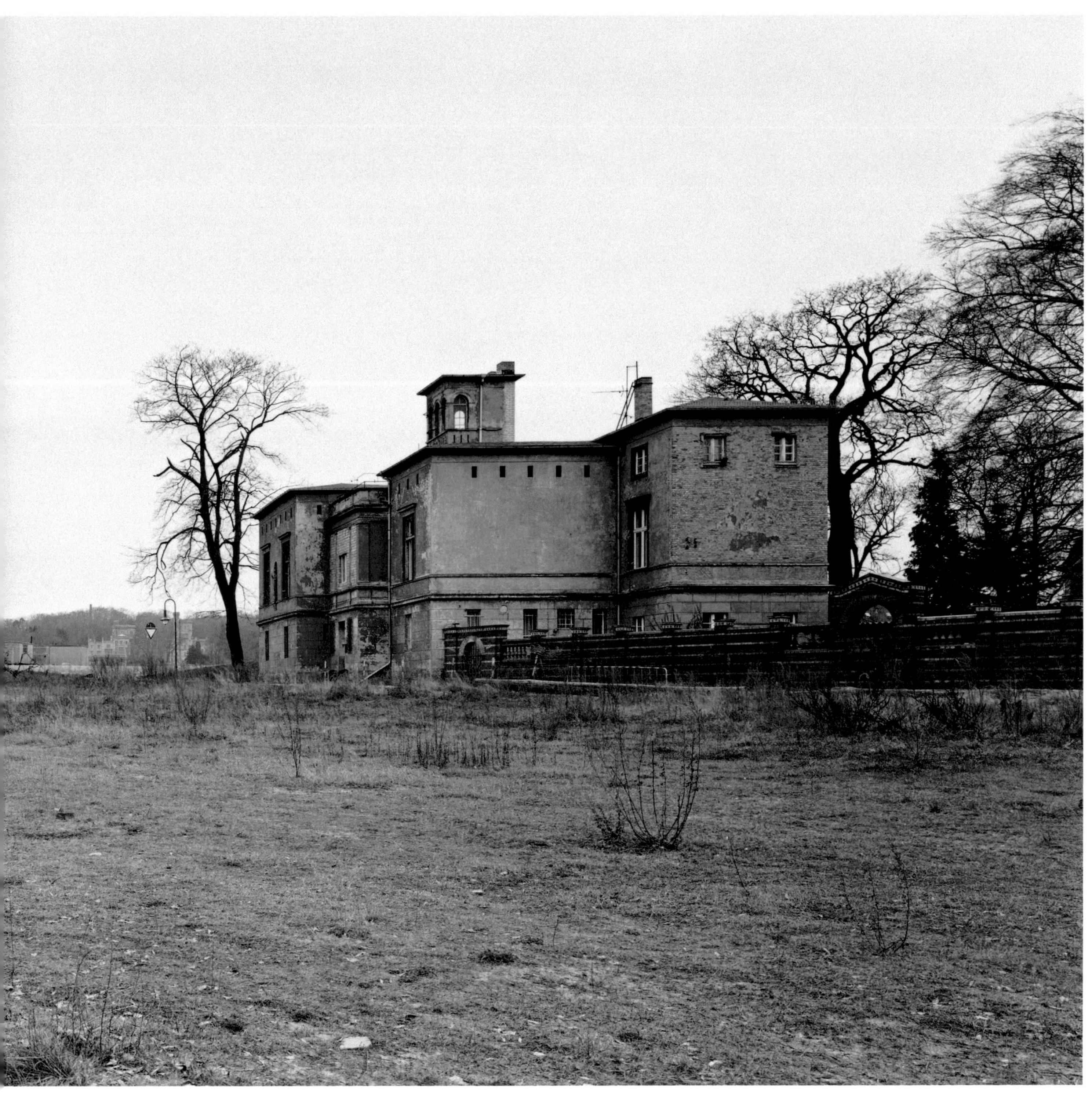

Kein Anfang und kein Ende

Ulrich Domröse

Stadtrand Berlin ist eine Arbeit über die Peripherie Berlins und die Spuren der jüngeren märkischen Geschichte. Vor allem aber ist es eine Arbeit über die Wirren der Umbruchszeit vier Jahre nach dem Fall der Mauer, also zu einem Zeitpunkt, als das Bauwerk selbst nur noch eine amorphe Masse war.

Als André Kirchner im *Tagesspiegel* vom 22.3.1993 las, dass auf dem Gelände des ehemaligen Grenzkontrollpunktes Dreilinden die Abfertigungshalle der DDR-Grenztruppen abgerissen werden solle, begann er am Tag darauf mit der Arbeit. Er nahm seine Linhof-Panoramakamera, fuhr nach Drewitz, schraubte sie auf das Stativ und machte von ebenjenem Grenzkontrollpunkt drei Aufnahmen.

Die Zeitungsmeldung war der Zündfunken für ein Projekt, das er seit längerem geplant hatte. Er wollte die Peripherie Berlins vor dem Hintergrund der jüngsten historischen Ereignisse von der Stadtgrenze aus fotografieren. Auf diese Weise könnte er eine Ahnung davon vermitteln, wie sich der Stadtrand mit der Geschichte Berlins verknüpft. Von der Stadtgrenze aus wollte er deshalb fotografieren, weil sich mit dem Fall der Mauer im Herbst 1989 auch für ihn, den West-Berliner, ein neues, befreiendes Gefühl der Weite eingestellt hatte. Und ihm damit eine veränderte Perspektive auf die Stadt möglich war.

Im Frühjahr 1993 war auf die Euphorie nach der Wiedervereinigung bereits die Ernüchterung gefolgt. Die Schnelligkeit der politischen und wirtschaftlichen Veränderungen hatte für den Osten so radikale Umbrüche gebracht, dass sich hier viele Menschen schlichtweg überfordert fühlten. Aber auch im Westen wuchs die Skepsis, denn es zeigte sich, dass nun alte Gewohnheiten und Ansprüche infrage gestellt wurden. Andererseits war mit der Beendigung des Ost-West-Konfliktes nicht nur auf der wirtschaftlichen, sondern auch auf der globalen politischen Ebene vieles möglich geworden, was seit dem 2. Weltkrieg als undenkbar gegolten hatte. Einen Beleg für die zerrissene Gefühls- und Interessenlage dieser Jahre lieferte der Parlamentsentscheid über die zukünftige Hauptstadt des wiedervereinigten Deutschlands, bei dem 1991 nur eine knappe Mehrheit der Bundestagsabgeordneten für Berlin votiert hatte.

Aber nach dieser Entscheidung konnte kein Zweifel mehr bestehen, dass sich die Stadt in kurzer Zeit verändern und wieder wachsen würde – Anzeichen dafür gab es 1993 bereits überall. Bis dahin allerdings hatte sich das Umland vier Jahrzehnte lang aufgrund der politischen Verhältnisse in der Nachkriegszeit und der damit verbundenen Teilung Berlins nur wenig verändert. West-Berlin fehlte es infolge der vielfältigen Beschränkungen, die mit seiner geografischen und politischen Insellage zusammenhingen, an größeren Wachstumsmöglichkeiten. In Ost-Berlin fehlte für ein prosperierendes Gemeinwesen die entsprechende Wirtschaftskraft. Neben dem Mauerstreifen selbst gab es im Weichbild der Stadt lediglich durch die großen kompakten Plattenbaugebiete – vor allem dem Märkischen Viertel im Westen und den riesigen Neubaugebieten Marzahn, Hellersdorf und Hohenschönhausen im Osten – bemerkenswerte Veränderungen.

Vor dem Herbst 1989 kannte André Kirchner den Osten Berlins nur im Rahmen von Tagesausflügen und das Umland vor allem aus der Perspektive des Zugreisenden. Er war Anfang 1981 von München nach West-Berlin gezogen und hatte sich in den folgenden Jahren selbst zum Architektur- und Stadtfotografen herangebildet. Die Mauer diktierte den Radius, in dem er sich bewegte. Am intensivsten setzte er sich mit den auffälligen und teilweise skurril wirkenden Relikten des vorangegangenen Krieges auseinander: den Brandmauern, Brachen und Rückbauten (Abb. 1). Dann, mit der neuen Bewegungsfreiheit nach 1989, zog es ihn zuerst in die alte Stadtmitte, wo er sich mit den drei Serien *Offener Himmel* (1990)[1], *Nacht Berlin Mitte* (1990) und *Berlin Mitte Zentrifugal* (1991/92) (Abb. 2) der östlichen Stadthälfte mit ihren nur schlecht vernarbten Spuren des Krieges und dem Verfall der letzten vier Jahrzehnte zuwandte.

Bis zu diesem Zeitpunkt war Kirchner also noch immer mit der Darstellung des Urbanen aus innerstädtischer Perspektive beschäftigt. Das Gefühl der Weite wurde zum ersten Mal 1992 in Dresden zum Thema seiner Arbeit, als er sich dem Stadtraum von außen zu nähern begann. Auf der Suche nach einer angemessenen ästhetischen Form, fing er an, parallel zu seiner gewohnten Großformatkamera mit einer Panoramakamera zu arbeiten. Ein glücklicher Zufall führte ihn während seiner Ausflüge in das Dresdner Umland in eine Ausstellung mit Panoramafotografien von Josef Sudek über das Nordwestböhmische Braunkohlerevier (Abb. 3). An diesen zwischen 1957 und 1962 entstanden Aufnahmen beeindruckte ihn vor allem, dass Sudek trotz der schonungslosen Darstellung, mit der er die Zerstörung einer Kulturlandschaft schilderte, statt eines vordergründig anklagenden einen poetischen Grundton wählte.[2] Obwohl Kirchner seine eigenen Panoramen als durchaus gelungen ansah, nahm er sie nicht in sein Buch *Dresdner Kampagne – Tagebuch des Fotografen* auf. Noch vertraute er der Ästhetik seiner Großformatkamera mehr.

Doch als der Beitrag im *Tagesspiegel* erschien und zum Auslöser für sein neues Berlin-Projekt wurde, entschied er sich sofort dafür – und reagierte damit indirekt und spontan auf die allgemeine Neugier und Aufregung in dieser von politischen, sozialen und kulturellen Um-

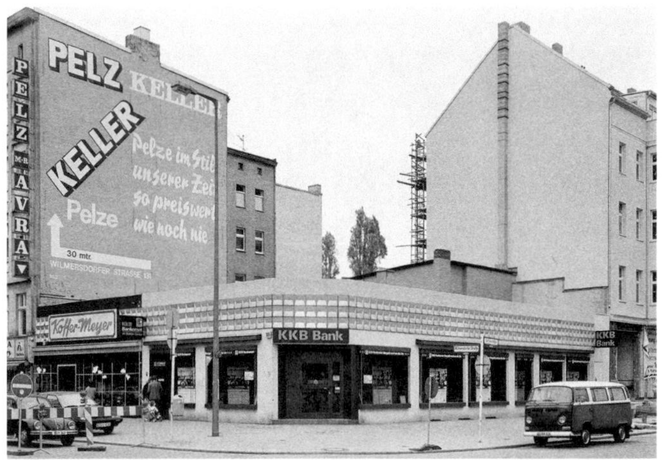

1

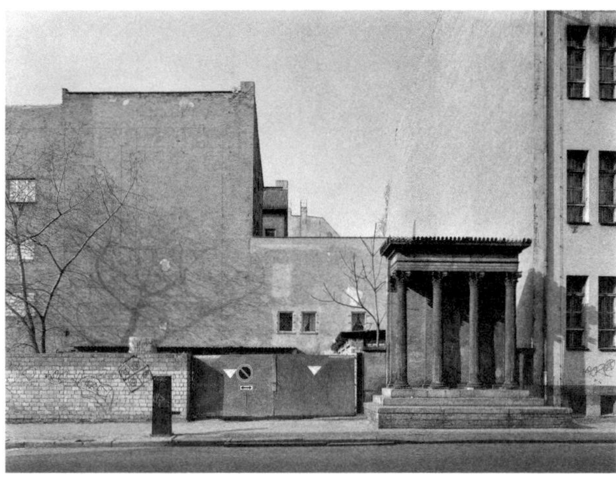

2

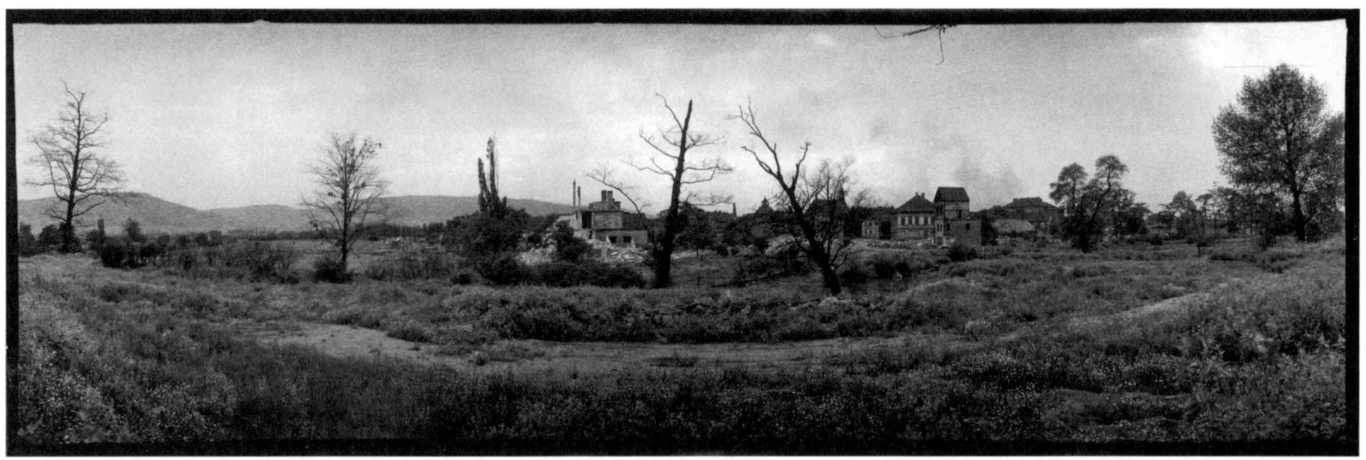

3

Abb. / **Fig.** 1
André Kirchner
Wilmersdorfer Straße, Ecke Schillerstraße, 1989
Silbergelatinepapier / **Silver gelatin print**
36 × 50 cm

Abb. / **Fig.** 2
André Kirchner
Berlin-Mitte, Koppenplatz, 1991
aus der Serie / **from the series**
KONSTRUKTION BERLIN
Silbergelatinepapier / **Silver gelatin print**
26,6 × 36,2 cm

Abb. / **Fig.** 3
Josef Sudek
Bílý dum na pokraji Souše (Weißes Haus am Rande von Souš / **White House on the Edge of Souš**), 1959, aus der Serie / **from the series**
Smutná krajina (Traurige Landschaft / **Sad Landscape**), 1957–1962
Silbergelatinepapier / **Silver gelatin print**
10 × 30 cm

Abb. / **Fig.** 4
John Knox
Glasgow, 1809
Öl auf Leinwand, Halbrund-Panorama / **Oil on canvas, semicircular panorama**
31 × 120 cm, Original umfasst 280 m² / **original measures 280 m²**

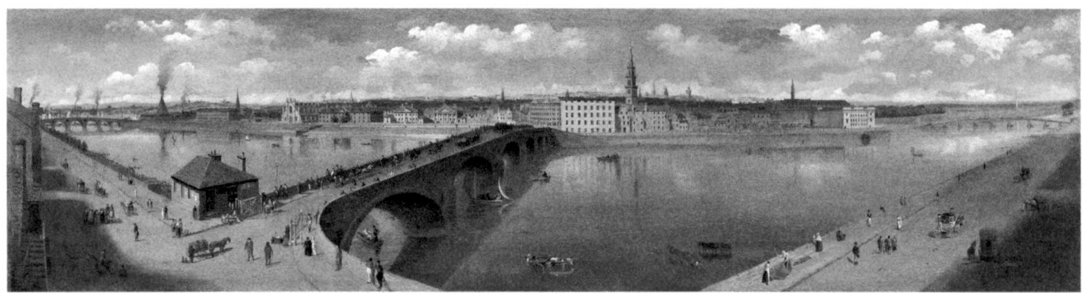

4

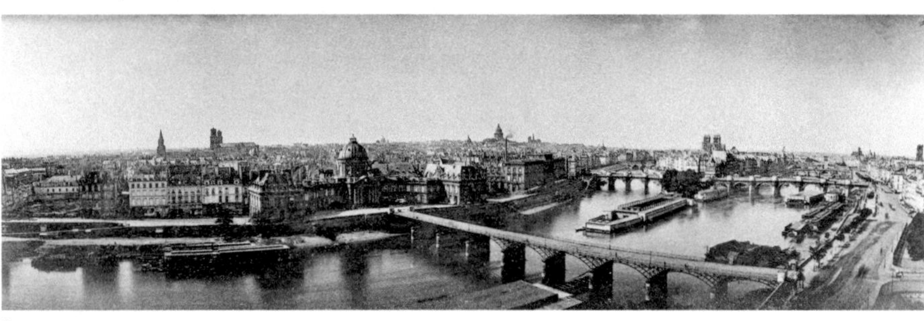

5

Abb. / **Fig.** 5
Friedrich von Martens (zugeschrieben / **attributed**)
La Seine, la rive gauche et l'île de la Cité à Paris (France), ca. 1845
Panoramadaguerreotypie / **Panorama daguerreotype**
11 × 38,8 cm

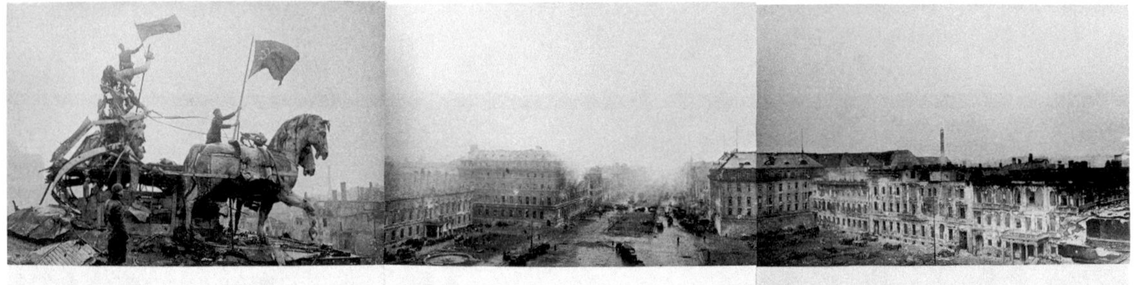

6

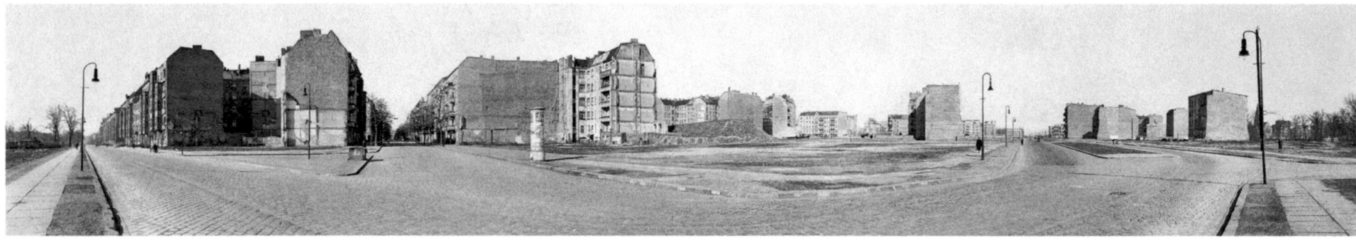

7

Abb. / **Fig.** 6
Jewgeni Chaldej
Panorama Pariser Platz, 2. Mai 1945
Silbergelatinepapier / **Silver gelatin print**
26,5 × 118 cm

Abb. / **Fig.** 7
Fritz Tiedemann [rekonstruiert und interpretiert von / **reconstructed and interpreted by** Arwed Messmer, 2008]
Am Friedrichshain, 5. März 1952
Inkjetprint / **Inkjet print**
127 × 762 cm

brüchen beherrschten Zeit.[3] Denn die besondere Qualität und der Erfolg panoramatischer Bilder – die es bereits ab 1787 in gemalter Form (Abb. 4) und ab 1845 auch als Daguerreotypien gab (Abb. 5) – war von Beginn an mit der Sehnsucht nach mehr Information und einer spannenden Unterhaltung durch die Erweiterung des Seh- und Erlebnisfeldes verknüpft.[4]

Panoramen zeigten seit ihren Anfangstagen besondere Orte oder Attraktionen. Wohl deshalb wurde auch das zerstörte Berlin nach dem Ende des Zweiten Weltkrieges ungewöhnlich häufig auf diese Weise fotografiert. Hier nutzten sowohl Sieger wie Besiegte die Ästhetik für ihre Zwecke. Die einen, um möglichst wirkmächtig ihren Triumph zu demonstrieren (Abb. 6), die anderen, um damit einen Denk-Raum für die städtebauliche Zukunftsplanung zu schaffen (Abb. 7).[5]

Die Kamera, für die sich André Kirchner entschied, umfasst einen Wirklichkeitsausschnitt von 91°. Im Gegensatz zu den technischen Möglichkeiten solcher Apparate, die schon in der Frühzeit der Fotografie einen Ausschnitt von mehr als 150° abdecken konnten, entsteht damit ein gemäßigtes Panorama.[6] Das garantiert, dass die jeweilige Fotografie noch immer als EIN Bild wahrgenommen werden kann und dennoch genug Informationen bereithält, um die vielen Details »lesend« zusammenzufügen. Außerdem schließt dieses Objektiv auffällige Verzerrungen am Bildrand und Verzeichnungen im horizontalen Bereich aus, was bei größeren Panoramen nicht zu verhindern ist und zu unangenehmen Irritationen und damit zu Glaubwürdigkeitsverlusten im Sinne des Dokumentarischen führt[7] – wie es bei der Vorstellung des ersten gemalten Panoramas 1787 in London geschah, wo die fehlende perspektivische Exaktheit der Grund dafür war, dass sich das neue Bildmedium im ersten Anlauf nicht durchsetzen konnte.

Doch Kirchner ist ein Dokumentarfotograf, der dem Wirklichkeitsgehalt seiner Bilder vertraut und sie deshalb auch als Beweismittel für den Zustand der Stadt verstanden wissen will. Damit sein Projekt auch auf eine andere Weise mit der Wirklichkeit in einem überprüfbaren Zusammenhang gebracht werden kann, orientierte er sich an der Stadtgrenze von Groß-Berlin, wie sie 1920 im Zuge einer Gebietsreform durch Eingemeindungen festgelegt worden war und mit ihrer Länge von 234 Kilometern nahezu noch immer der heutigen Ausdehnung Berlins entspricht. Von hier aus richtete er seine Kamera konsequent auf die Stadt, – wobei er die dörflichen Strukturen als Teil des Stadtgebietes aufgefasst hat – und machte sich so auf die Suche nach den Spuren, die die Menschen am Stadtrand hinterließen.[8] Da sich der Grenzstreifen von 1961 zwischen West-Berlin und dem heutigen Land Brandenburg mit der Grenzziehung von 1920 deckte, bewegte er sich etwa zu gleichen Teilen entlang der ehemaligen Territorien von Ost- und West-Berlin.

Diese Art des Dokumentarismus, der das Eindringen der Zivilisation in die Landschaft, vor allem aber in die Ränder der Städte untersucht, wurde Mitte der 1970er-Jahre von den »New Topographics« in den USA vertreten und entwickelte sich schon kurze Zeit danach zu einer Stilrichtung, die weltweit ihre Anhänger fand. Kirchner sympathisiert mit dieser Auffassung und dem zumeist konzeptuellen Ansatz, seit er Mitte der 1980er-Jahre in Kreuzberg mit der »Werkstatt für Photographie« in Kontakt gekommen war. Aber er gehört offensichtlich nicht zu den Apologeten eines unerbittlichen Regelwerks, mit dem die strengen Verfechter der topografischen Fotografie jede emotionale Beeinflussung ihrer nüchternen Zustandsbeschreibung zu verhindern suchen.[9]

Kirchner zeigt unterschiedlich weit gefasste landschaftliche Räume mit Wohngebieten, Wäldern, Feldern, Gewässern, Industrie- bzw. Militäranlagen, und alle möglichen Arten von wirtschaftlich genutzten Objekten. Wo sich das Gesichtsfeld verdichtet, vorrangig bei Gebäuden und Gebäudekomplexen, sind sie in die Halbtotale gerückt. Häufig befindet sich im Zentrum der Aufnahmen – doch fast nie genau in der Bildmitte – Bäume oder Baumgruppen, Gebüsch, Stromleitungsmasten, Laternen und allerlei technische und architektonische Gebilde. Sie werden als vertikale Kompositionselemente und auch zur rhythmischen Gliederung in der abwechslungsarmen märkischen Landschaft eingesetzt – wobei manche dieser Gegenstände und Dinge durch ihre scheinbaren Funktionslosigkeit geradezu absurd erscheinen. Daneben führen Wege, Straßen, Baum- und Strauchreihen, Elektroleitungen, aber auch in sich gestaffelte Gebäudekomplexe, Betonplatten, Flüsse, Bäche und Felder in die Tiefe des Bildraums und unterstützen damit nachdrücklich die Illusion des als »Naturraum«[10] wahrgenommenen Panoramablicks. Flächig wirkende Aufnahmen, meist mit starker Horizontalreihung (9, 20, 21, 25, 26, 51), dagegen sind selten. Da, wo im ersten Augenblick scheinbar pure Landschaften erscheinen (6, 8, 13, 44, 57), sind bei genauerem Hinsehen dennoch kleinste Relikte von dörflicher oder urbaner Zivilisation am Horizont zu sehen. Um den panoramatischen Grundgedanken dieser Arbeit wirkungsvoll zu unterstützen, hat Kirchner die Horizontlinie, im Sinne eines typologischen Gestaltungsmittels, stets auf das untere Drittel des Bildes gelegt.

All diese Strukturelemente führen zu einer komplexen und harmonisch ausgewogenen Bildkomposition. In der ungebremst erscheinenden Weite der Landschaft führt das dazu, dass der Blick sich nicht festsaugt an den Schuttbergen und Autowracks, den verwilderten Pflanzungen und verkrüppelten Bäumen. All die Spuren des Verfalls, des Vandalismus und der Verwahrlosung bekommen so in einem spürbaren größeren Ganzen ein menschliches Maß – in dem sie allerdings auf subkutane Art dennoch ihre Wirkung tun. Auf diese Weise beschreiben die Bilder die Melancholie einer gesellschaftlichen Zwischenzeit.

Während die dingliche Welt auf diesen Bildern etwas über die zivilisatorische Geschichte dieser Region in den zurückliegenden 150 Jahren erzählt – also von der gründerzeitlichen Architektur und den damaligen technischen Errungenschaften bis zu den kleinen und großen Zeichen der Umbruchszeit am Beginn der 1990er-Jahre –, lässt die Kargheit der märkischen Landschaft ein Gefühl für den Zustand des Lebensraumes entstehen, der Berlin trotz aller Globalisierungstendenzen noch immer grundiert.

Stadtrand Berlin ist zwischen März 1993 und Februar 1994 fotografiert worden (Abb. 8), wobei es zwischen den einzelnen Aufnahmen Pausen bis zu mehreren Wochen gab. André Kirchner entschied sich ohne besonderen Anlass, die Stadt gegen den Uhrzeigersinn zu umkreisen. Aufgrund der voraussehbaren Dauer des Projekts waren die unterschiedlichen Jahreszeiten von vornherein einkalkuliert. Aus den 150 Aufnahmen, die in dieser Zeit entstanden, wählte er die 60 abgebildeten Motive aus, die heute zu *Stadtrand Berlin* gehören. Mit Rücksicht auf die Gesamtwirkung des Projekts war er um einen proportional ausgewogenen Bildanteil aus allen Gebieten entlang der Stadtgrenze bemüht. Die 24 × 50 cm großen Ausstellungsbilder entsprechen den technischen Möglichkeiten in seinem Labor, in dem er alle Motive selbst entwickelte, bearbeitete und vergrößerte. Das relativ kleine Format zwingt zu einem nahen Herantreten und damit zu einem intimen genauen Schauen.

Stadtrand Berlin ist mit seinem inhaltlichen Anspruch und der ästhetischen Umsetzung so angelegt, dass es nach einer 360°-Inszenierung verlangt. Solch eine Präsentation würde, wenn auch entfernt, an die Idee der großen gemalten Panoramen und Dioramen des 19. Jahrhunderts erinnern. Die überraschende Wirkung solcher Bilder, die die Betrachter schon um 1800 angezogen und zu Begeisterungsstürmen veranlasst hatte, verfängt auch heute noch, denn »mit der bildhaften Übersetzung des horizontal bewegten Blicks [hing] eine Wiedergabe des unmittelbar wahrgenommenen ›Naturraums‹ und damit eine räumliche Wirkung zusammen«[11] mit der »das Streben nach möglichst vollkommener Illusion der Wirklichkeit mit dem Streben nach größtmöglicher Exaktheit der Abbildung« erreicht werden sollte[12] – ein Beweis für die Verführungskraft dieser Art von Bildern sind die heutigen IMAX-Kinos und die vielerorts neu entstandenen Panoramabauten, die sich großer Beliebtheit erfreuen.

Was nun die abgebildete Realität auf den Bildern betrifft, so ist diese vor- und außerstädtische Landschaft heute zu großen Teilen verschwunden. An ihrer Stelle sind Straßen, Wohnsiedlungen und Einkaufszentren entstanden.

1 Hier experimentierte er erstmals mit dem »segmentierten Panorama«, indem er zwei durch einen leichten horizontalen Schwenk der Kamera entstandene Bilder aneinanderfügte. Diese Technik schien ihm letztlich ungeeignet, weil damit lediglich Unikate entstehen konnten.

2 Anregend wurden für ihn auch die Panoramaaufnahmen Klaus Kinolds, dessen Katalog *Panorama-Klaus Kinold*, Köln 1990, er sich zur selben Zeit kaufte.

3 Später entstanden noch weitere Panoramaarbeiten. Dazu gehören: *Innerstädtische Grenze* (1992–97), *Gutsanlagen in der Mecklenburgischen Schweiz* (1994), *Spreeufer in Schöneweide* (1998), *Baufeld Biesdorf-Süd* (2000), *City Tour Berlin* (2009) und *B 1* (2016).

4 Heinz Buddemeier, *Panorama, Diorama, Photographie*, München 1970, und *Sehsucht, das Panorama als Massenunterhaltung des 19. Jahrhunderts*, Frankfurt am Main 1993.

5 Florian Ebner, »Entgrenzte Blicke – Das Panorama, das digitale Bild und Arwed Messmer als der Neue Fotograf«, in: *So weit kein Auge reicht – Berliner Panoramafotografien aus den Jahren 1949–1952*, Berlin 2008.

6 Dabei besteht zwischen der Bildhöhe und -breite ein Verhältnis von 2:1. Dagegen beträgt der menschliche Sehsinn von zwei unbeweglichen Augen 200°, ist aber nur in einem Winkeldurchmesser von zwei Grad scharf. Deshalb gleiten die Augen ständig über das Sichtfeld und erst im Gehirn entsteht daraus ein Bild. Siehe dazu Buddemeier 1993 (wie Anm. 4), S. 301. Außerdem ist Kirchners Kamera mit einem »Hochversatz« ausgerüstet, der das Objektiv um acht Millimeter hoch verstellt, wodurch eine leicht erhöhte Perspektive möglich wird. Auf diese Weise entfällt das Kippen der Kamera, um stürzende Linien zu vermeiden. Außerdem ermöglicht der Hochversatz, dass die untere horizontale Ebene des Bildes herabgesenkt werden kann und so die darüber befindlichen Dinge, z.B. hohe Gebäude, in ihrer Ganzheit erscheinen. Eine weitere äußerst nützliche Hilfe bei dieser Kamera ist der abnehmbare Sucher, der es gestattet, den genauen Standort festzulegen, ohne die Kamera jedes Mal aufwendig aufzubauen zu müssen.

7 Die Verzeichnungen und Verzerrungen werden beeinflusst von der Qualität des Objektivs und davon, ob es sich um ein schwenkbares oder starres Objektiv handelt.

8 Aus der entgegengesetzten Blickrichtung, dem Inneren der Stadt nach außen, fotografierte Hans W. Mende 1978/79 für sein Projekt *Grenzbegehung*. Er orientierte sich an der 161 Kilometer langen West-Berlin umschließenden Mauer. Aus der gleichen Perspektive entstand bereits zwischen 1969–72 *The Berlin Wall* von Shinkichi Tajiri, der sich dafür entlang der 43 Kilometer langen innerstädtischen Grenze bewegte. Neben diesen beiden großen topografischen orientierten Arbeiten zur Situation West-Berlins im Schatten der Mauer, sei auch an *Waffenruhe* (1985–87) von Michael Schmidt und *Topografie der Berliner Mauer: 1973–1990* von Karl-Ludwig Lange erinnert.

9 Für sie wäre ein unterschiedlich bewölkter Himmel, üppige Vegetation und Schnee ein Tabu. Für André Kirchner hat die Großformat-Fotografie, die Schwarz-Weiß-Technik und die Verweigerung des Anekdotischen eine weit größere Bedeutung.

10 Christiane Stahl, »Friedrich von Martens (1806–1885) – Panoramadaguerreotypie und fotografischer Verismus in der Frühzeit der Fotografie«, in: *Fotogeschichte*, 72, 1999, S. 3–14.

11 Ebd., S. 11.

12 Buddemeier 1970 (wie Anm. 4), S. 18.

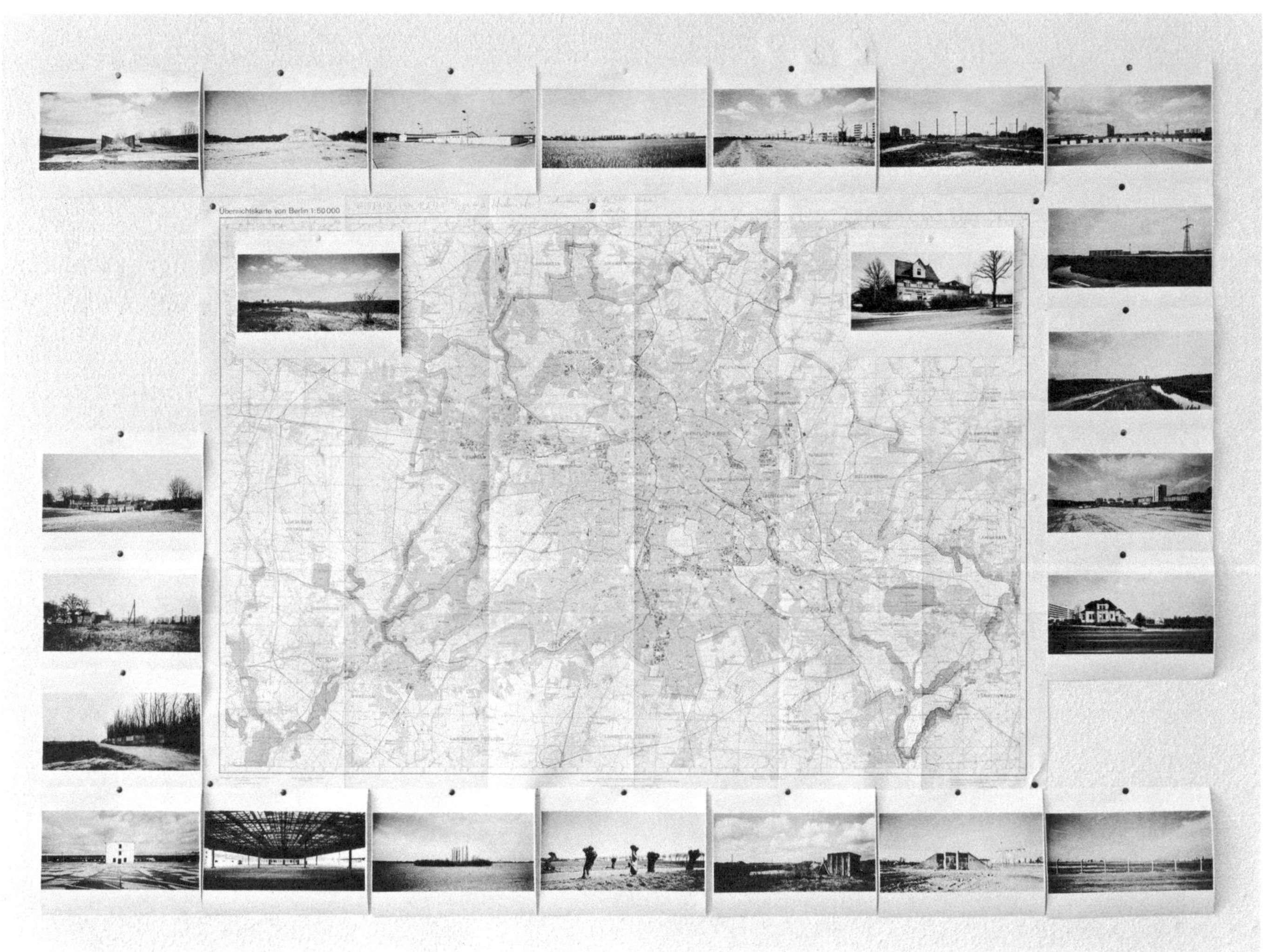

8

Abb. / **Fig.** 8
André Kirchner
Übersichtskarte mit Fotografien aus der Serie *Stadtrand Berlin*.
Aufgenommen im damaligen Studio Kirchners in Berlin-Neukölln, 1993 /
Area map with photographs from the series *Stadtrand Berlin*, taken in Kirchner's former studio in Neukölln in Berlin, 1993
Silbergelatinepapier / **Silver gelatin print**
24 × 30 cm

No Beginning and No End

Ulrich Domröse

Stadtrand Berlin, as the title suggests, is a work about Berlin's urban edge. It tracks the city's periphery and vestiges of recent history in the surrounding March of Brandenburg. But most of all it is a work about upheaval in a period of change, marking a time, four years after the Wall came down, when the structure itself had disintegrated into an amorphous mass.

On March 22, 1993, André Kirchner read in the *Tagesspiegel* that the former checkpoint building operated by East German border guards at Dreilinden was about to be demolished. He started work the next day. He picked up his Linhof Panoramic, drove over to Drewitz, fixed the camera to the tripod, and took three photographs of said checkpoint.

The newspaper report ignited a project that he had actually been planning for a while. He wanted to photograph the periphery of Berlin from the city boundary against the backdrop of recent historical events. He hoped to convey some idea of how the urban edge linked into Berlin's history. The reason for taking these pictures from the boundary was that he too, as a West Berliner, had experienced that new, liberating feeling of open skies when the Wall fell in fall 1989. Besides, it allowed him to explore a different perspective on the city.

By the spring of 1993, post-unification euphoria had given way to more sober sentiments. The speed of political and economic change had brought such radical upheaval to the East that many of its inhabitants simply felt overwhelmed. Meanwhile, skepticism was growing in the West, as it turned out that old habits and entitlements were being challenged. On the other hand, the end of East-West conflict had made a lot of things possible, not only in the economic sphere but also in global politics, which had seemed unthinkable since World War II. One indication that emotions were ambivalent and interests divided during those years came in 1991, when the German parliament was asked to decide where the future capital of the united country should lie. Only a slim majority voted for Berlin.

Once that decision had been made, there was no longer any doubt that the city would soon undergo a transformation and begin to grow again—and in 1993 the signs were everywhere. Until that point, however, the edgelands had altered very little in the previous four decades because of the postwar political situation and, as part of that grander picture, the division of Berlin. There was little leeway for West Berlin to expand due to various restrictions associated with its geographical and political status as an island. East Berlin had lacked the economic clout to create a prosperous community. Apart from the Wall itself, the only notable changes to the urban footprint had come from big, compact housing developments of prefabricated concrete—in particular Märkisches Viertel in the West and the enormous complexes in Marzahn, Hellersdorf, and Hohenschönhausen in the East.

Before fall 1989, André Kirchner's acquaintance with East Berlin had been confined to day trips, while his knowledge of the hinterland derived above all from the perspective of a train passenger. He had moved to West Berlin from Munich in early 1981 and in the ensuing years had trained himself in architectural and urban photography. The Wall dictated the radius of his movements. His attention was caught primarily by conspicuous, often bizarre relics of the previous war: the exposed fire walls, the wastelands, the missing buildings (fig. 1). Then, with his new freedom of mobility after 1989, he was drawn first into the old center, devoting three series—*Offener Himmel* (Open Sky, 1990),[1] *Nacht Berlin Mitte* (Night in the Center of Berlin, 1990), and *Berlin Mitte Zentrifugal* (Centrifugal Center of Berlin, 1991–92) (fig. 2)—to the eastern half of the city with its barely healed scars of war and the deterioration of the past forty years.

Thus far Kirchner was still busy portraying the urban fabric from an inner-city viewpoint. The sense of expanse first became a theme in his work in 1992 in Dresden, when he began to approach the urban space from the outside. In his quest for an appropriate aesthetic form, he had started using a panorama camera alongside his customary large-format camera. A stroke of fortune during an excursion into the surroundings of Dresden led him to an exhibition of panoramic photographs by Josef Sudek on the theme of lignite mining in northwestern Bohemia (fig. 3). What impressed him most about these images taken between 1957 and 1962 was that Sudek, despite mercilessly exposing the destruction of a cultural landscape, had chosen a lyrical tone in preference to a loud indictment.[2] Although Kirchner was pleased with his own panoramas, he did not include them in his photographic travel log *Dresdner Kampagne—Tagebuch des Fotografen* (Dresden Campaign—The Photographer's Diary). He still had greater faith in the aesthetic generated by his large-format camera.

But when that report appeared in the *Tagesspiegel* and triggered his next Berlin venture, he immediately opted to take the plunge—responding indirectly and spontaneously to the universal curiosity and excitement of the time, motivated by political, social, and cultural turbulence.[3] After all, the particular quality and success of panoramic images—which had been around since 1787 in painted form (fig. 4) and since 1845 as daguerreotypes (fig. 5)—had always been associated with a desire for more information and for the delightful entertainment afforded by widening the field of vision and experience.[4]

Ever since their incipience, panoramas had chosen special places or attractions as their subject matter. That is probably why the ruins of Berlin had been photographed in this way with uncommon frequency after World War II. Both victors and vanquished employed this aesthetic for purposes of their own: the former to signal their triumph with maximum impact (fig. 6), the latter to generate a conceptual space for future urban design (fig. 7).[5]

The camera selected by André Kirchner has an angle of capture of ninety-one degrees. Compared with the technical potential of such cameras, which even in the early days of photography were able to cover an angle greater than 150 degrees, the panorama this creates is a moderate one.[6] It ensures that each single photograph can be perceived as ONE picture and yet still provide enough information for the "reader" to put together. Moreover, this lens avoids obvious distortions around the edges and horizontal warping, effects which larger panoramas cannot prevent and which cause unpleasant disorientation in the viewer, damaging the credibility of a documentary project.[7] This is what happened to the first painted panorama when it was shown in London in 1787: erratic perspective accounted for the failure of this new visual medium to establish its credentials at the first attempt.

But Kirchner is a documentary photographer who trusts that his pictures contain reality and consequently wants people to see them as evidence for the condition of the city. To place his project within a verifiable framework of reality in a different sense, he took his bearings from the urban boundary of Greater Berlin as defined in 1920 in the wake of territorial reforms that incorporated a number of outlying villages. This 234-kilometer boundary is almost totally congruent with Berlin's present footprint. From this line he consistently turned his camera on the city, interpreting village structures as part of the urban fabric, as he set off to track human activity along the city's edge.[8] Because the border strip created in 1961 between West Berlin and today's State of Brandenburg matched the boundary drawn in 1920, his itinerary took him in almost equal parts around the former territories of East and West Berlin.

This kind of documentarism that examines how civilization encroaches into the landscape, but above all into the margins of cities, was advocated in the mid-1970s by New Topographics in the United

States and evolved soon afterwards into a style with an international following. Kirchner has displayed an affinity with this view and its largely conceptual approach ever since the mid-1980s, when he came into contact with the Photography Workshop in Kreuzberg. Evidently, however, he is no apologist for inflexible rulebooks like the one wielded by strict proponents of topographic photography at pains to banish all emotional influence from the sober description of facts.[9]

Kirchner presents landscapes of varying magnitude with housing, forest, fields, water bodies, industrial installations, military sites, and all kinds of economically useful objects. Wherever the range of vision is compressed, primarily in the case of buildings and built complexes, these are coalesced into a full-figure shot. In the middle of the image—although almost never precisely centered—there will be a lone tree or a clump, some bushes, electricity pylons, street lamps, or some other technical or architectural construct. They insert themselves into the unchanging Brandenburg landscape as vertical elements in the composition or rhythmic markers—although many of these objects come across as absurd in their apparent lack of function. Alongside them paths, roads, rows of trees and shrubs, power lines, but also tiered buildings, concrete paving, rivers, streams, and arable strips, carve a way into the depths of the picture space, emphatically reinforcing the illusion created by the panoramic framing that this is a "natural space."[10] Flatter impressions are rare, and even these tend to figure a pronounced horizontal pattern (9, 20, 21, 25, 26, 51). What seems at first glance to be a landscape pure and simple (6, 8, 13, 44, 57) turns out on closer scrutiny to reveal tiny relics of rural or urban civilization on the horizon. Effectively reinforcing the panoramic idea behind the work, Kirchner always sets his line of horizon over the bottom third of the picture like a typographical design feature.

These structural elements all give rise to a complex, harmoniously balanced composition. Within the seemingly rampant enormity of the landscape, this prevents the gaze being sucked in by a mound of war rubble or an abandoned vehicle, by a stretch of vegetation run wild or a cluster of stunted trees. In this manner, all these traces of decay, vandalism, and neglect acquire a human scale within the palpably broader whole—and yet subcutaneously they maintain their impact. And so these images describe the melancholy of a social interregnum.

While the world of things in these photographs tells a history of civilization in this region over the last 150 years, from the architecture born of Germany's first unification in the late nineteenth century and the technical achievements of that era to major and minor hints of transformation in the early 1990s, the austere landscape of the March conveys a sense of the habitat on which Berlin still remains founded, for all the global trends.

Stadtrand Berlin was photographed between March 1993 and February 1994 (fig. 8), but with breaks of several weeks between the pictures. André Kirchner decided for no particular reason to circle the city counterclockwise. Given the foreseeable duration of the project, the seasons were factored in from the outset. From the 150 photographs taken over this period, he selected the sixty motifs reproduced here to constitute *Stadtrand Berlin*. Conscious of the overall effect, he was concerned to strike balanced proportions between different areas along the city boundary. The twenty-four-by-fifty-centimeter exhibition prints reflect the technical capabilities of his own laboratory, where he developed, processed, and enlarged all the motifs himself. The relatively small format forces the viewer to step closer and to take a careful, intimate look.

In terms of both the substance it seeks to convey and its aesthetic implementation, *Stadtrand Berlin* invites arrangement as a 360-degree spectacle. Such a presentation would be reminiscent, albeit remotely, of the large panorama paintings and dioramas of the nineteenth century. The surprising impact of those works, which were already pulling in the crowds around 1800 and prompted storms of enthusiasm, still has the power to fascinate today. The aim, after all, was to achieve "the desire for the most perfect illusion of reality possible through the desire for the greatest accuracy of depiction possible,"[11] bearing in mind that "the pictorial translation of the sideways gaze was associated with a reproduction of the directly perceived 'natural space' and hence with a spatial impact."[12] Today, evidence of the seductive force of such pictures can be found in IMAX cinemas and in the popular panoramic buildings appearing in so many places.

As to the reality in these landscapes, much of what we see here in the suburbs and hinterland of Berlin has already vanished, displaced by roads, housing developments, and retail outlets.

1 Here he experimented for the first time with the "segmented panorama" by juxtaposing two images taken with a slight horizontal turn of the camera. In the end he decided that this technique was untenable as it would only produce one-off results.

2 He was also inspired by the panoramas taken by Klaus Kinold, whose catalogue *Panorama-Klaus Kinold* (Cologne, 1990), he purchased at the same time.

3 Other panoramic works followed. They include: *Innerstädtische Grenze* (1992–97), *Gutsanlagen in der Mecklenburgischen Schweiz* (1994), *Spreeufer in Schöneweide* (1998), *Baufeld Biesdorf-Süd* (2000), *City Tour Berlin* (2009), and *B 1* (2016).

4 Heinz Buddemeier, *Panorama, Diorama, Photographie* (Munich, 1970), and *Sehsucht, das Panorama als Massenunterhaltung des 19. Jahrhunderts* (Frankfurt am Main, 1993).

5 Florian Ebner, "Entgrenzte Blicke—Das Panorama, das digitale Bild und Arwed Messmer als der Neue Fotograf," in *So weit kein Auge reicht—Berliner Panoramafotografien aus den Jahren 1949–1952* (Berlin, 2008).

6 The ratio between the height and width of the photograph is 2:1. By contrast, human vision based on two unmoving eyes scans two hundred degrees, but the angle of sharp focus is only two degrees. Hence the eyes constantly glide across the field of vision and the image itself is created in the brain. See Buddemeier, *Sehsucht*, 301. Besides, Kirchner's camera is equipped with a "height offset" to adjust the lens upwards by eight millimeters, permitting a slightly raised perspective. This means the camera does not have to be tilted and stops the lines from converging. Moreover, the offset shifts the lower horizontal plane of the image further down, and so the things above it, like tall buildings, are shown in their entirety. Another extremely useful feature of this camera is the removable viewfinder, as the location can be precisely defined without requiring a complex operation to set up the camera again every time.

7 Distortion and warp are influenced by the quality of the lens and whether it swivels or is rigid.

8 In 1978–79 Hans W. Mende took pictures from the opposite direction, from inside the city to outside, for his project *Grenzbegehung*. His orientation was defined by the 161-kilometer wall enclosing West Berlin. Shinkichi Tajiri had adopted the same perspective in 1969–72 for *The Berlin Wall*, working his way along the forty-three-kilometer border between the two halves of the city. Apart from these two major works with a topographical approach to the situation of West Berlin in the shadow of the Wall, mention should be made of *Waffenruhe* (Ceasefire) (1985–87) by Michael Schmidt and *Topografie der Berliner Mauer: 1973–1990* by Karl-Ludwig Lange.

9 A sky of variegated cloud, lavish vegetation or snow would have been anathema to them. For André Kirchner, large-format photography, black-and-white technique, and the denial of anecdote have a far broader significance.

10 Christiane Stahl, "Friedrich von Martens (1806–1885)—Panoramadaguerreotypie und fotografischer Verismus in der Frühzeit der Fotografie," *Fotogeschichte* 72 (1999): 3–14.

11 Buddemeier, *Panorama, Diorama, Photographie*, 18.

12 Stahl, "Friedrich von Martens," 11.

Werkliste / List of Works

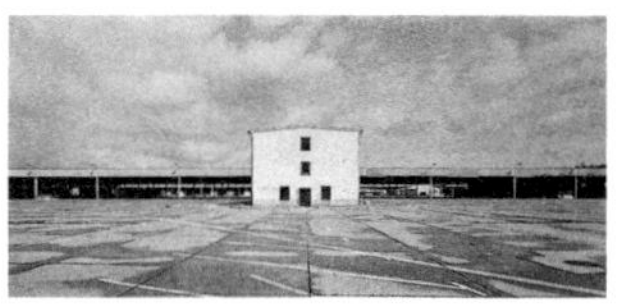

01
Im Süden Berlins (kurz: Süd), Dreilinden, ehem. Grenzkontrollpunkt Drewitz, 13,5 ha Betonfläche über früherer Müllkippe, Blick nach Nordost (kurz: → NO)
In the south of Berlin (abbreviated: south), Dreilinden, former Checkpoint Drewitz, 13.5 hectares of concrete over a former garbage dump, facing north-east (abbreviated: → NE)

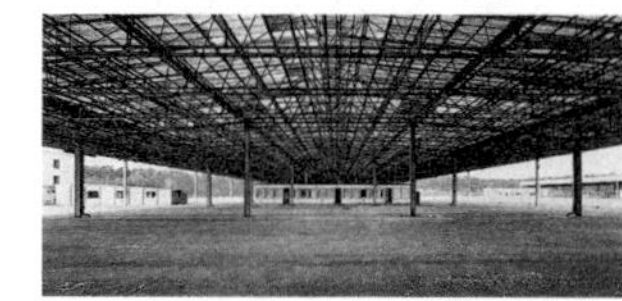

02
Süd, Dreilinden, südliche Abfertigungshalle vor dem Abriss für die Errichtung eines Büro- und Technologieparks, »Europarc Dreilinden«
South, Dreilinden, south transit hall before demolition to make way for the office and technology zone Europarc Dreilinden
→ NW

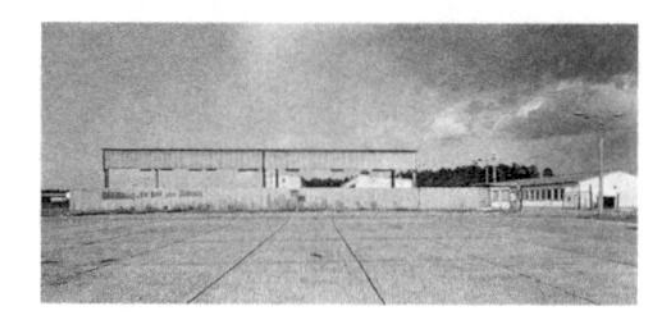

03
Süd, Dreilinden, Kontrollpunktsgebäude östlich der Autobahn
South, Dreilinden, checkpoint complex east of the highway
→ NO / **NE**

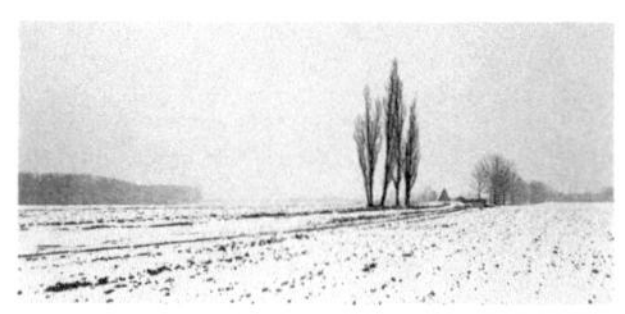

04
Süd, Großbeeren, Schlachtfeld mit Denkmal westlich des Orts
South, Grossbeeren, battle site and monument west of the town
→ N

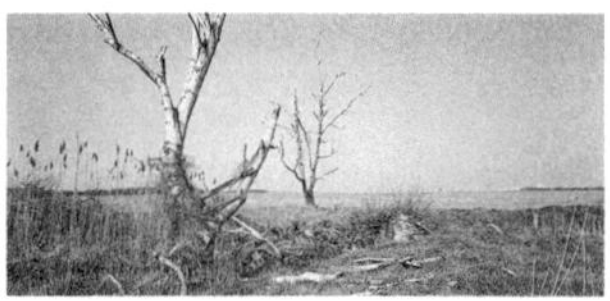

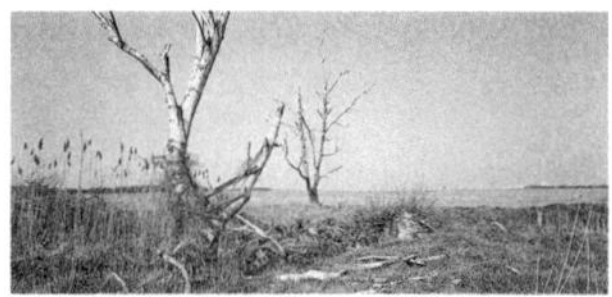

05
Süd, Birkholz, Rieselfelder vor Lichtenrade
South, Birkholz, sewage farm near Lichtenrade
→ NW

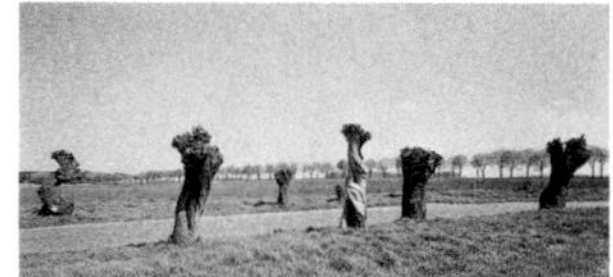

06
Süd, Chaussee von Rangsdorf nach Großmachnow
South, road from Rangsdorf to Grossmachnow
→ NO zur B96 / **NE towards B96**

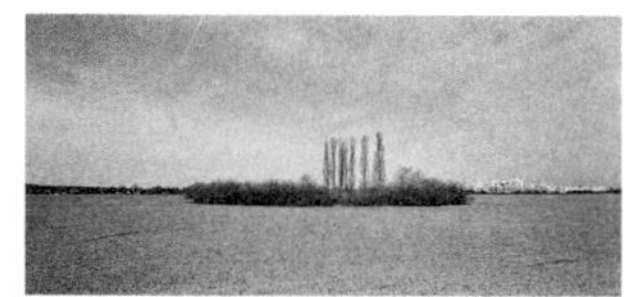

07
Süd, Kleinziethen, Felder östlich von Lichtenrade
South, Kleinziethen, fields east of Lichtenrade
→ NW

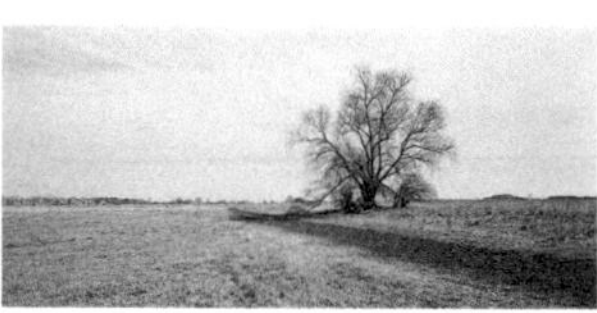

08
Süd, Großziethen, Luchwiesen, Blick nach Rudow
South, Grossziethen, moor, towards Rudow
→ NW

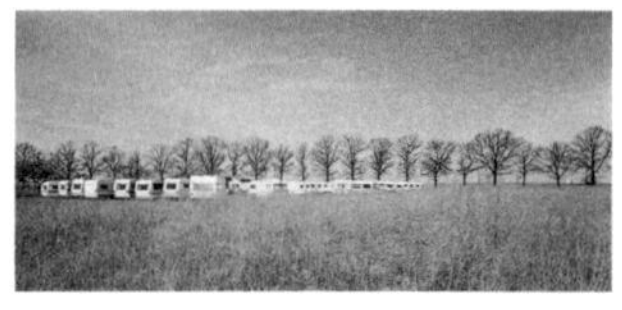

09
Süd, Großziethen, an der Rudower Chaussee
South, Grossziethen, Rudower Chaussee
→ N

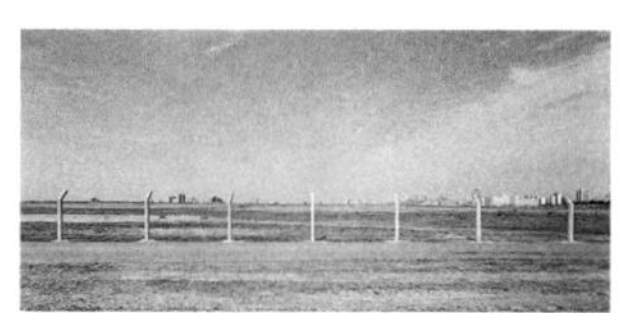

10
Süd, Großziethen, Bauerwartungsland vor Buckow
South, Grossziethen, development land near Buckow
→ N

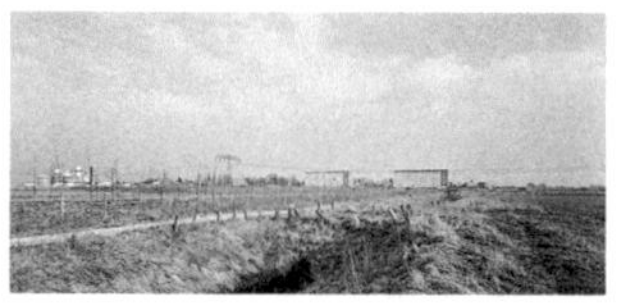

11
Süd, Waßmannsdorf, Klärwerk, Siedlung und Rieselfelder südlich von Großziethen
South, Wassmannsdorf, sewage works, settlement, and sewage farm south of Grossziethen
→ NO / **NE**

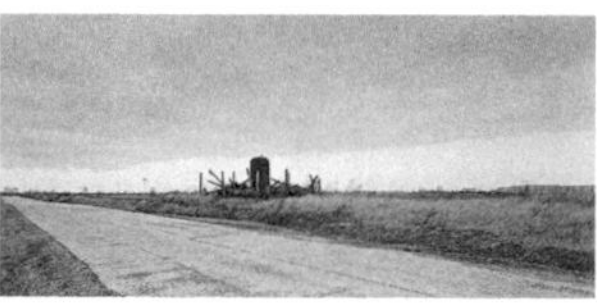

12
Süd, Schönefeld, erschlossenes und wieder aufgegebenes Bauland vor Rudow
South, Schönefeld, abandoned building land near Rudow
→ NO / **NE**

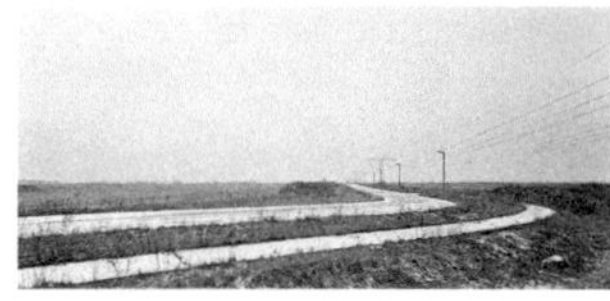

13
Süd, Schönefeld, nicht kartierte Grenzstraße vor Rudow
South, Schönefeld, unmapped border road near Rudow
→ NW

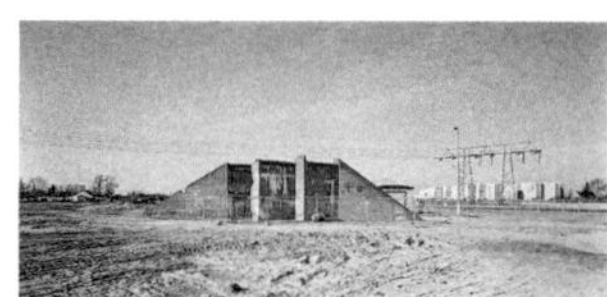

14
Süd, Schönefeld, Brückenfundament im Bereich des ehem. Grenzkontrollpunkts vor Rudow
South, Schönefeld, bridge foundations by the former checkpoint near Rudow
→ NO / **NE**

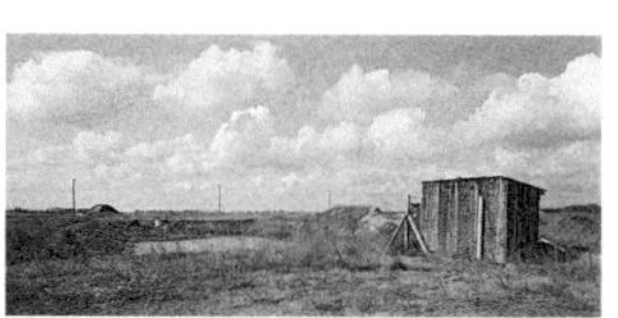

15
Süd, Schönefeld, Teich nördlich des Bahnhofs
South, Schönefeld, pond north of the station
→ NW

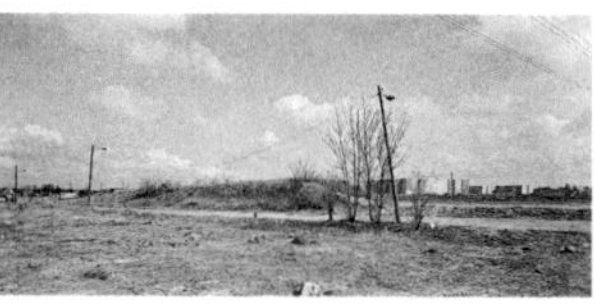

16
Süd, Schönefeld, ehem. Grenzkontrollpunkt an der Waltersdorfer Chaussee, Blick nach Altglienicke
South, Schönefeld, former checkpoint on Waltersdorfer Chaussee, toward Altglienicke
→ NO / **NE**

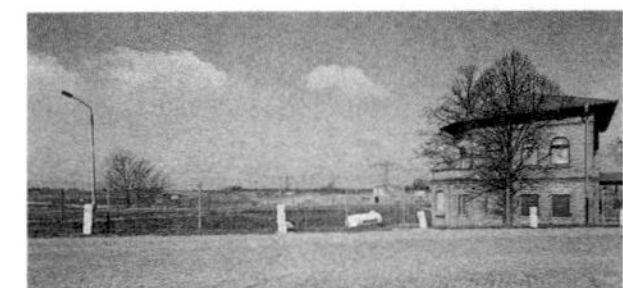

17
Süd, Schönefelder Chaussee
South, Schönefelder Chaussee
→ NW

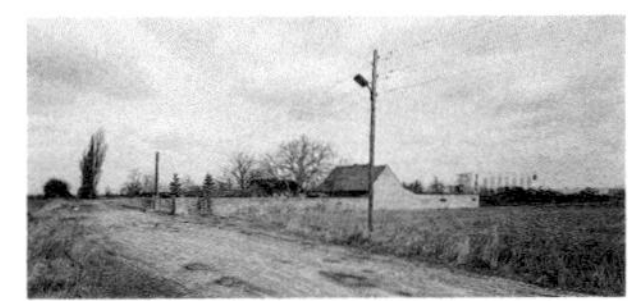

18
Süd, Waltersdorf, Bohnsdorfer Weg westlich der Autobahn nach Dresden, Blick zum Einkaufszentrum am Nordrand des Dorfs
South, Waltersdorf, Bohnsdorfer Weg west of the Dresden highway, toward the shopping center at the north end of the village
→ NO / **NE**

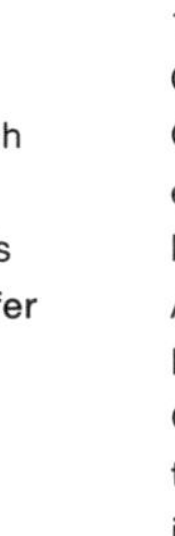

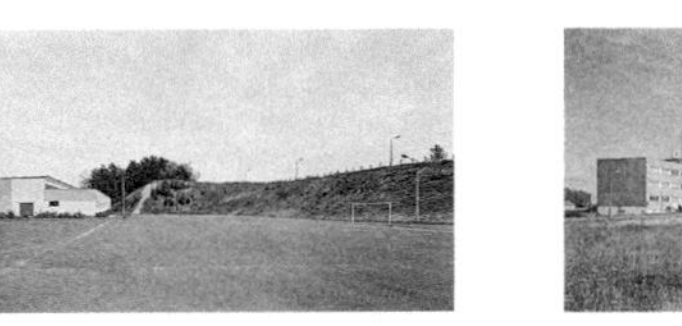

19
Ost, »Berliner Schweiz« in den Gosener Bergen am Seddinsee, ehem. Ausbildungs- und Schulungszentrum der Hauptabteilung Aufklärung des MfS (»Stasi«)
East, "Berlin's Switzerland" in the Gosen Hills on Seddinsee, former training center for the foreign intelligence arm of the Ministry of State Security ("Stasi")
→ O / **E**

20
Ost, Gosen, ehem. Stasi-Funkzentrale vor Umwandlung in Gewerbezentrum »Müggelpark«
East, Gosen, former Stasi radio headquarters later converted into Müggelpark commercial center
→ O / **E**

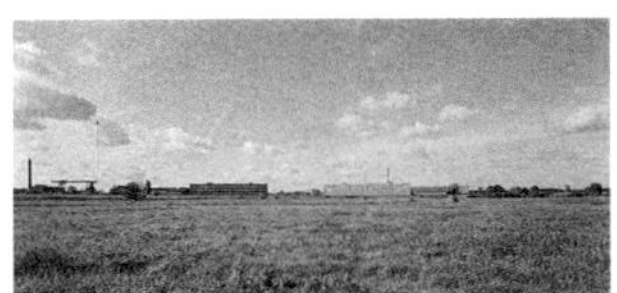

21
Ost, Gosen, ehem. Stasi-Funkzentrale an der Storkower Straße, Landschaftsschutzgebiet Spreewiesen
East, Gosen, former Stasi radio headquarters on Storkower Strasse, conservation area in the floodplain of the river Spree
→ W

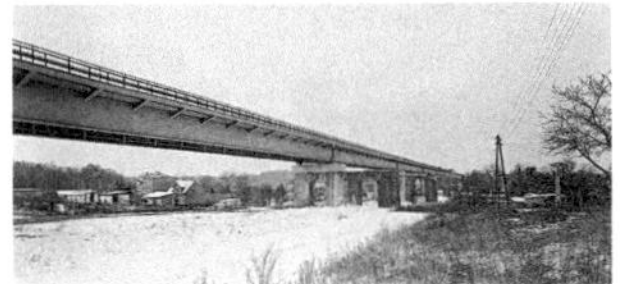

22
Ost, Rüdersdorf, Viadukt des Berliner Rings
East, Rüdersdorf, viaduct for Berlin's beltway
→ NW

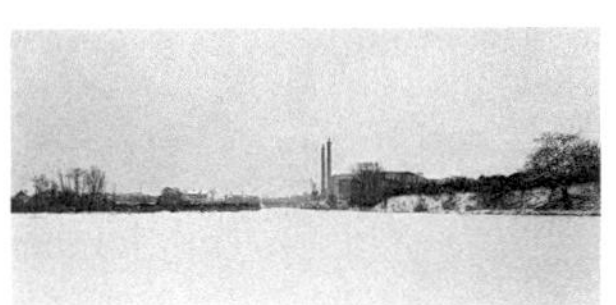

23
Ost, Rüdersdorf, Blick von der Straße nach Tasdorf auf Kanalhafen der Rükana Futtermittelwerke und den ruinierten Gasthof »Zum Schwarzen Adler«
East, Rüdersdorf, view from the road toward Tasdorf with the canal port used by feed phosphate producer Rükana and ruins of the restaurant "Zum Schwarzen Adler"
→ O / **E**

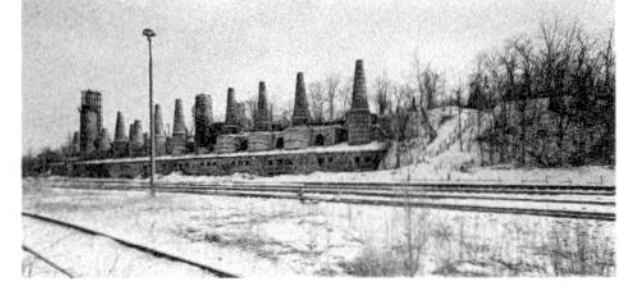

24
Ost, Rüdersdorf, Nordseite der Schachtofenbatterie der Kalkwerke
East, Rüdersdorf, north side of the shaft furnaces for the lime works
→ SO / **SE**

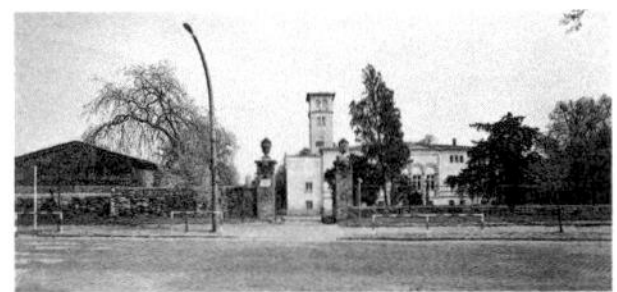

25
Ost, Dahlwitz, »Speise-Treffpunkt und Freizeit-Objekt« im Schloß der von Tresckow
East, Dahlwitz, "dining and leisure venue" in a stately home once built for the Von Tresckow family
→ SO / **SE**

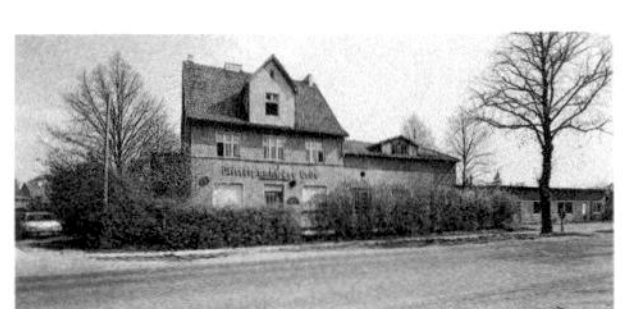

26
Ost, Hellersdorf, leerstehender Gasthof an der Mahlsdorfer Straße vor Hönow
East, Hellersdorf, empty guesthouse on Mahlsdorfer Strasse near Hönow
→ SO / **SE**

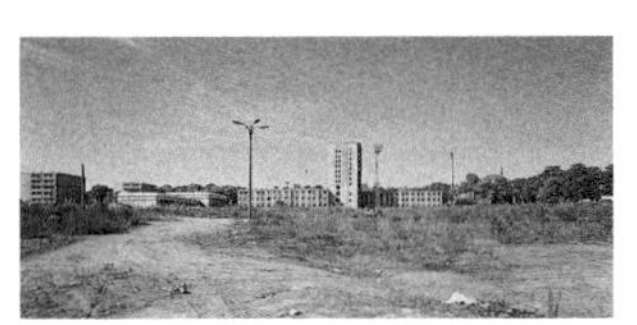

27
Ost, Biesdorf-Nord, im Wuhletal, Neubauruine der Krankenhauserweiterung
East, Biesdorf-Nord, on the River Wuhle, derelict remains of a new hospital extension
→ W

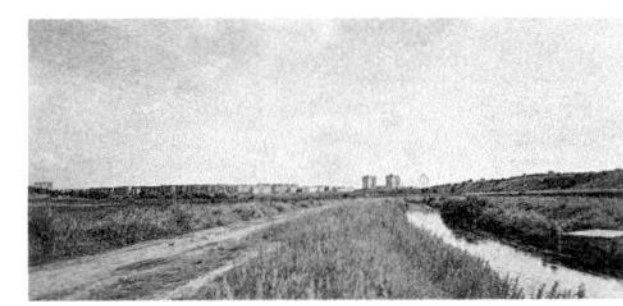

28
Ost, Marzahn, die Wuhle vor Hellersdorfer Neubaugebiet
East, Marzahn, the river Wuhle passes new housing in Hellersdorf
→ N

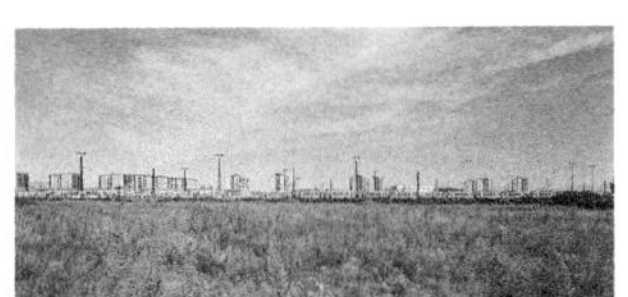

29
Ost, Marzahn, Straßenbahndepot an der Landsberger Allee
East, Marzahn, tram depot on Landsberger Allee
→ N

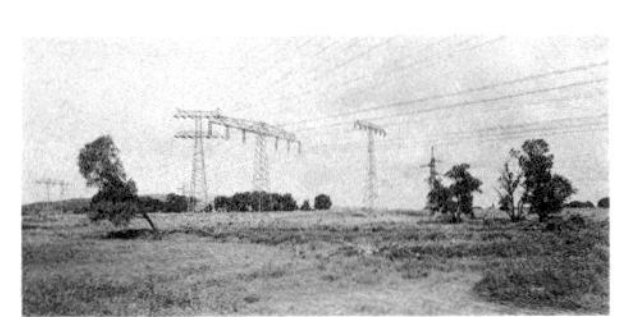

30
Ost, Eiche Süd A, Bauland, Blick nach Marzahn-Falkenberg
East, Eiche Süd A, building land, toward Falkenberg (Marzahn)
→ NW

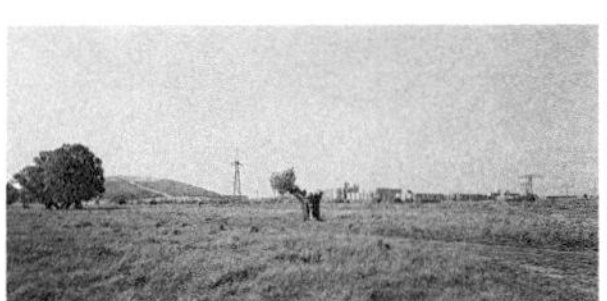

31
Ost, Eiche, Stadtgrenze und Schuttberg vor Marzahn an der Wuhle
East, Eiche, city boundary and hill of rubble near Marzahn on the river Wuhle
→ W

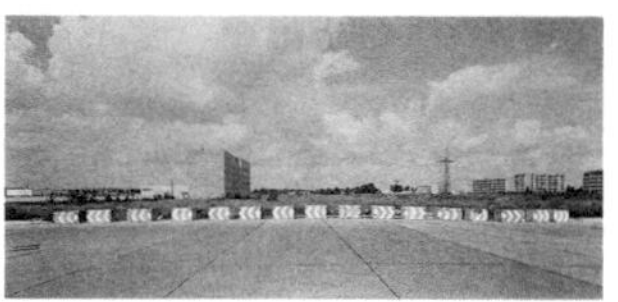

32
Ost, Marzahn, Ende der Wuhletal-straße
East, Marzahn, the end of Wuhle-talstrasse
→ W

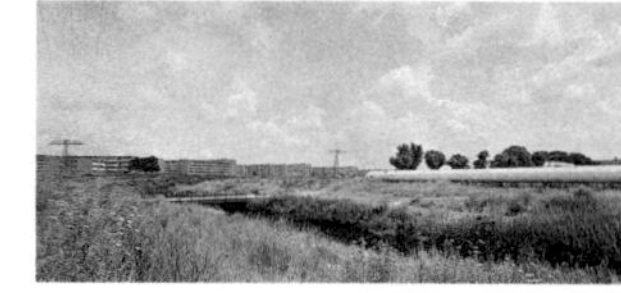

33
Ost, Marzahn, Falkenberg, Wuhle und Hellersdorfer Weg
East, Marzahn, Falkenberg, river Wuhle and Hellersdorfer Weg
→ NO / **NE**

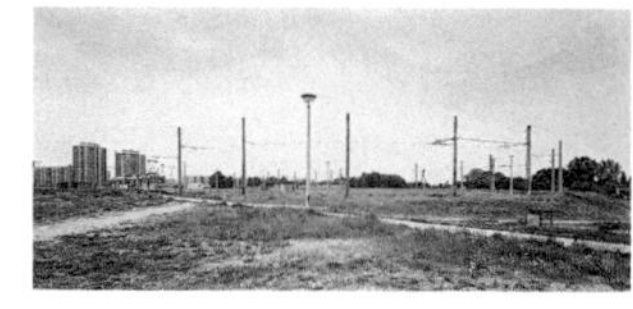

34
Ost, Hohenschönhausen, Straßen-bahnwendeschleife Wartenberg
East, Hohenschönhausen, tram loop, Wartenberg
→ NW

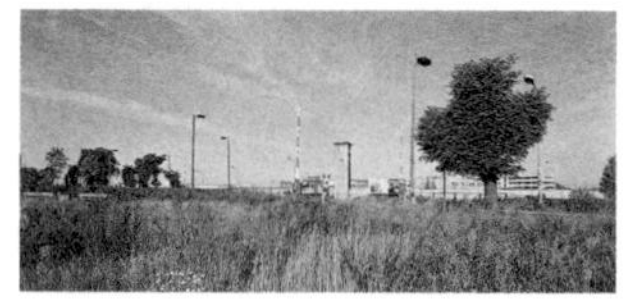

35
Ost, Hohenschönhausen, Stadt-grenze Ahrensfelde
East, Hohenschönhausen, city boundary at Ahrensfelde
→ NW

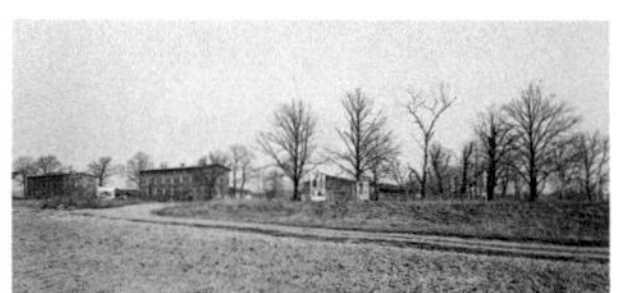

36
Nord, Karow, ehem. Gutshof an der Bucher Straße
North, Karow, former manor estate on Bucher Strasse
→ SO / **SE**

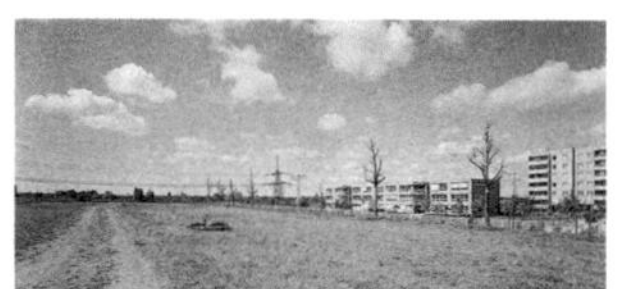

37
Nord, Buch, Siedlung an der Karower Chaussee außerhalb des Berliner Rings
North, Buch, housing develop-ment on Karower Chaussee outside the beltway
→ SW

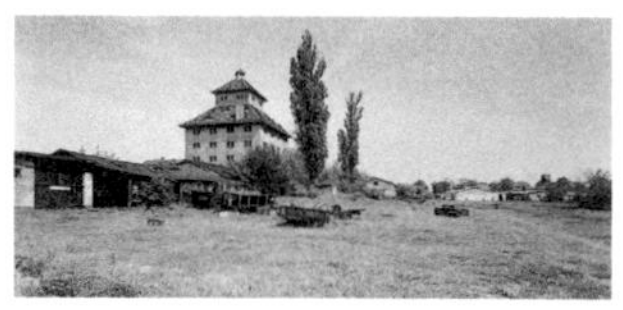

38
Nord, Speicher des ehem. Stadt-guts Hobrechtsfelde an der Stadtgrenze
North, granary on the former municipal farm at Hobrechtsfelde by the city boundary
→ NO / **NE**

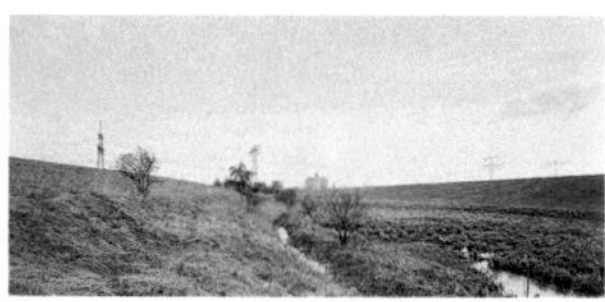

39
Nord, Mühlenbeck, Rieselfelder und Klärwerk Schönerlinde am Berliner Ring
North, Mühlenbeck, sewage farm and treatment unit at Schöner-linde on the beltway
→ O / **E**

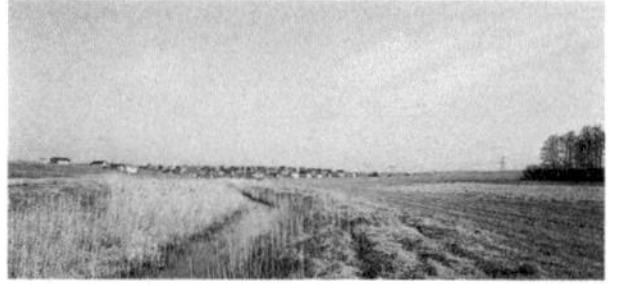

40
Nord, Mühlenbeck, Lauben-kolonie am östl. Ortsrand vor Berliner Ring
North, Mühlenbeck, garden allotments at the east end of town by the beltway
→ NW

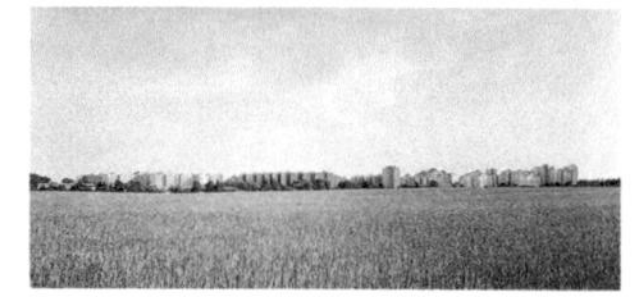

41
Nord, Lübars, Am Alten Bernauer Heerweg vor dem Märkischen Viertel
North, Lübars, the Prussian army road by the housing development Märkisches Viertel
→ S

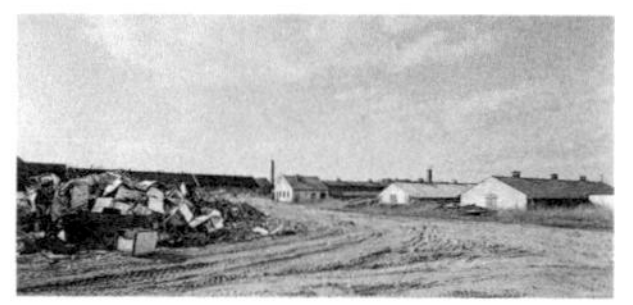

42
Nord, Stolpe-Dorf, früher Rittergut, dann Stadtgut an der Hohen-Neuendorfer Straße, ruinierte Schweinemastanlagen
North, Stolpe village, former feudal manor on the road to Hohen-Neuendorf, later a municipal farm, ruins of the pig-breeding unit
→ W

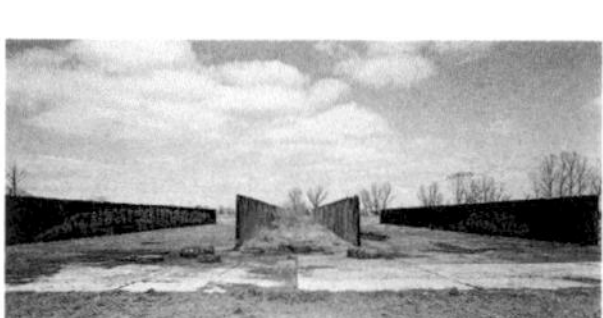

43
Nord, Stolpe-Dorf, Silage-Stütz-mauer des aufgegebenen Stadt-guts am Tegeler Weg, errichtet aus den gleichen Betonsegmenten wie die Berliner Mauer, die hier einen Kilometer entfernt war
North, Stolpe village, retaining walls for silage on the abandoned municipal farm on Tegeler Weg, built from the same concrete segments as the Berlin Wall, which once stood a few hundred yards from here
→ N

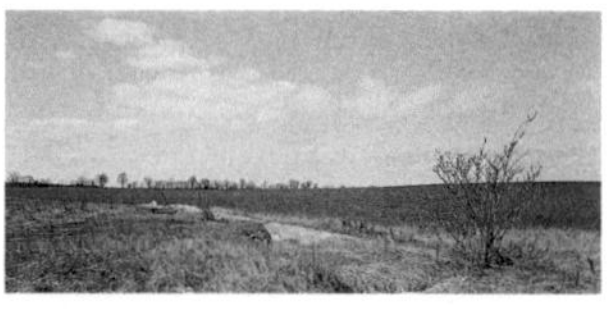

44
Nord, Stolpe-Dorf, Hausstelle im ehem. Grenzstreifen vor Frohnau
North, Stolpe village, traces of a building in the former border strip near Frohnau
→ NW

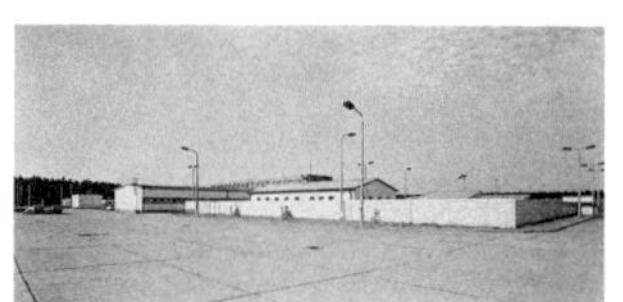

45
Nord, Stolpe, ehem. Kontroll-punkt östlich der Autobahn nach Hamburg
North, Stolpe, former checkpoint on the east side of the Hamburg highway
→ SW

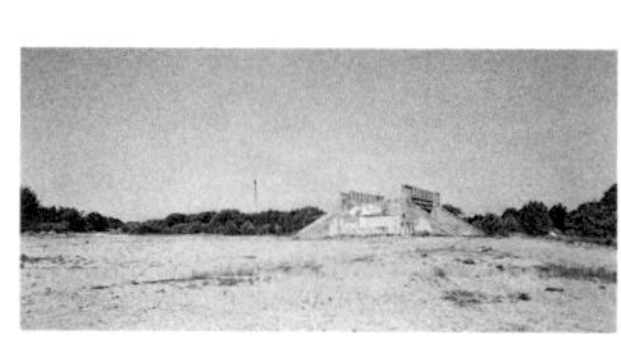

46
Nord, Stolpe-Süd, S-Bahn-Brückenfundament im ehem. Grenzstreifen vor Heiligensee
North, Stolpe-Süd, foundations of a suburban rail bridge in the former border strip near Heiligensee
→ NW

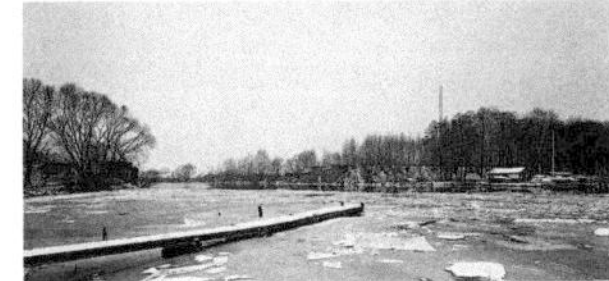

47
Nord, Hennigsdorfer Havelufer, zerstörte S-Bahnbrücke
North, banks of the River Havel in Hennigsdorf, damaged suburban rail bridge
→ SW

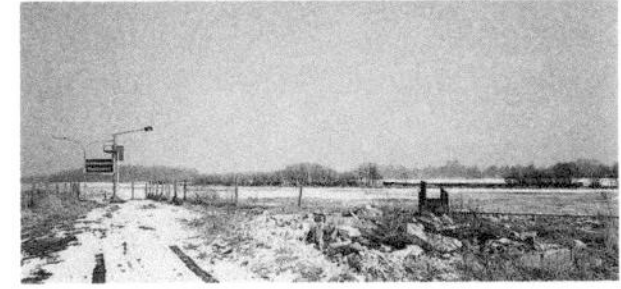

48
West, Hennigsdorf, Landspitze zwischen Havelkanal und Nieder-Neuendorfer See, ehem. Kontrollpunkt für die Schiffahrt
West, Hennigsdorf, land spit between the Havel Canal and Nieder-Neuendorfer See, former waterway checkpoint
→ NO / **NE**

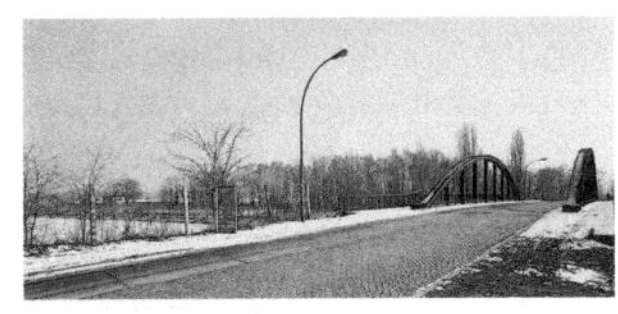

49
West, Hennigsdorf, Spandauer Allee, Brücke über den Havelkanal
West, Hennigsdorf, Spandauer Allee, bridge over the Havel Canal
→ SO / **SE**

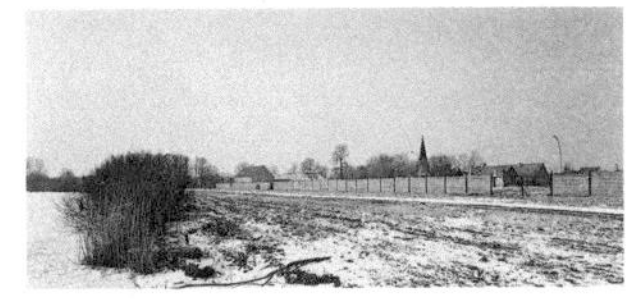

50
West, Nieder-Neuendorf, Grenzstreifen und Mauerrest am Havelufer vor Heiligensee
West, Nieder-Neuendorf, border strip and traces of the Berlin Wall on the bank of the river Havel near Heiligensee
→ SW

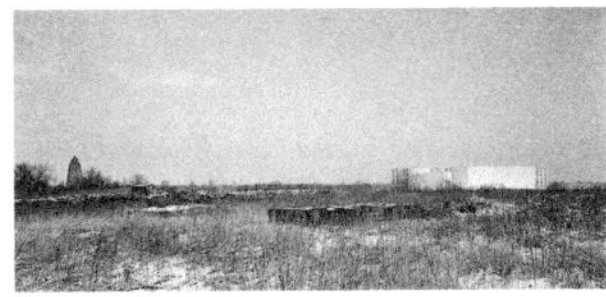

51
West, Falkensee, Munitionsbunker, Müllkippe und neue Herlitz-Zentrale vor Albrechtshof
West, Falkensee, ammunition bunker, garbage dump, and new Herlitz offices near Albrechtshof
→ NO / **NE**

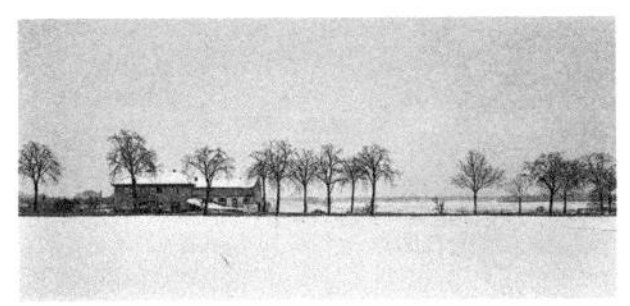

52
West, Dallgow, ruinierter Gasthof an der B5
West, Dallgow, derelict inn on highway B5
→ NO / **NE**

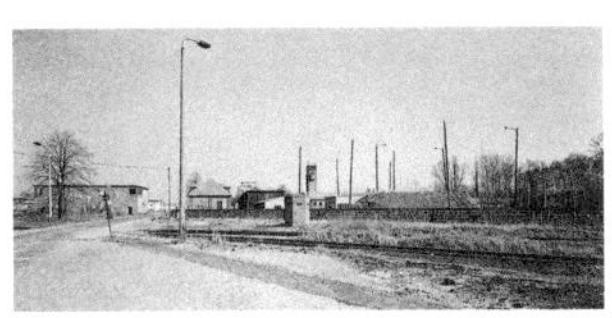

53
West, Staaken, Industriegebiet am ehem. Flugplatz
West, Staaken, industrial zone on the former airfield
→ NW

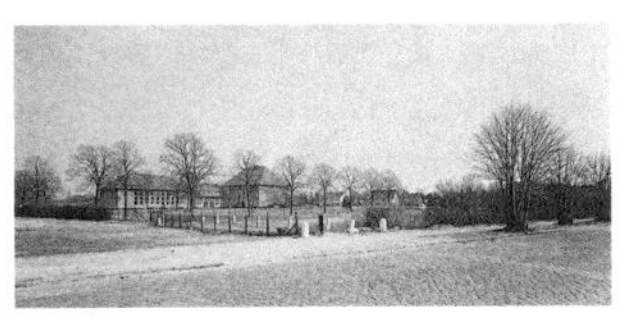

54
West, Staaken, Schule an der Feldstraße im ehem. Grenzstreifen vor dem Nennhauser Damm
West, Staaken, school on Feldstrasse in the former border strip off Nennhauser Damm
→ NO / **NE**

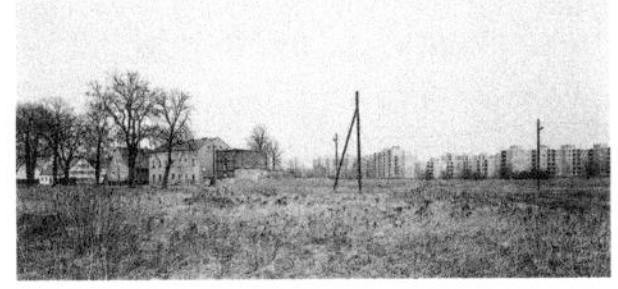

55
West, Staaken, ehem. Grenzstreifen an der Hauptstraße
West, Staaken, former border strip on Hauptstrasse
→ NO / **NE**

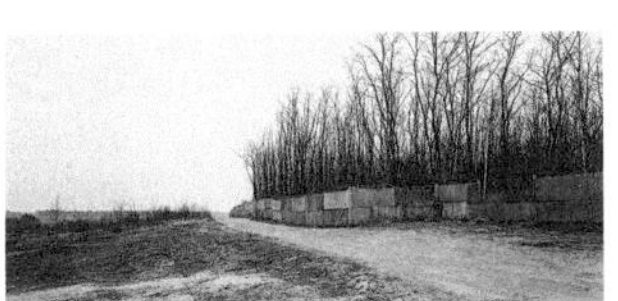

56
West, Staaken, Fort Hahneberg, das jetzt mit Teilen der ehem. Grenzbefestigung vor weiterer Zerstörung gesichert wird
West, Staaken, Fort Hahneberg, now secured against further destruction along with sections of the former border fortifications
→ S

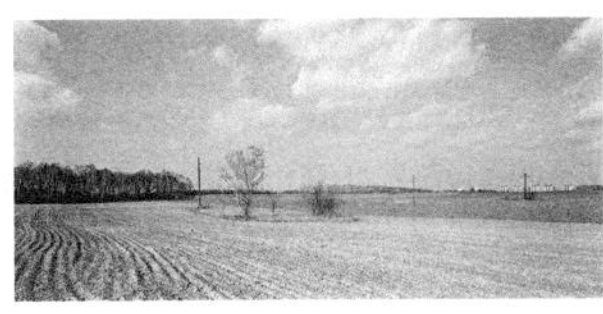

57
West, Engelsfelde, Grünanlage Hahneberg (Trümmerberg) und Siedlung Weinbergshöhe an der Stadtgrenze
West, Engelsfelde, park on the rubble hill Hahneberg and Weinbergshöhe estate on the city boundary
→ N

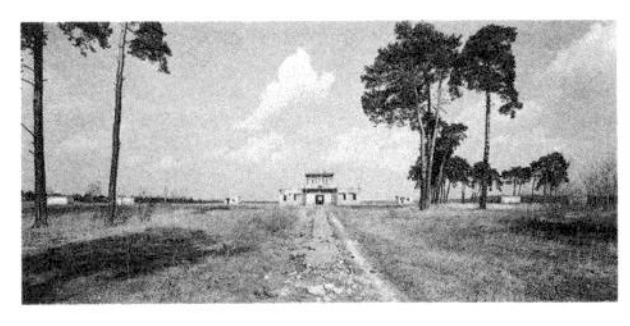

58
West, Groß-Glienicke, ehem. sowjetisches Militärgelände in der Döberitzer Heide, nördlich von Krampnitz an der Potsdamer Chaussee
West, Gross-Glienicke, former Soviet military site on Döberitzer Heide, north of Krampnitz on Potsdamer Chaussee
→ N

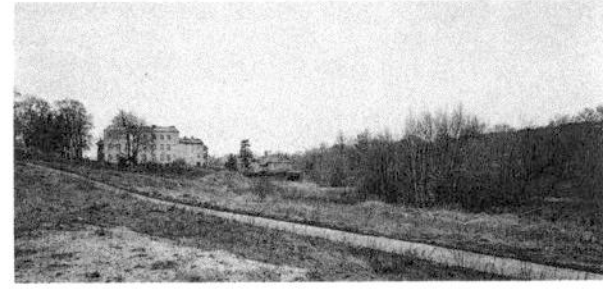

59
West, Babelsberg, Klein-Glienicke, ehem. Grenzstreifen am Griebnitzsee
West, Babelsberg, Klein-Glienicke, former border strip on Griebnitzsee
→ NW

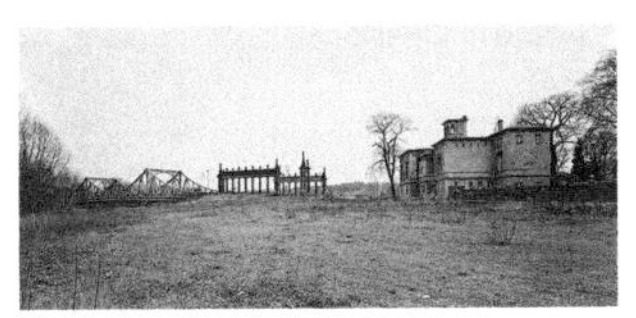

60
West, Potsdam, Berliner Vorstadt, Glienicker Brücke, ehem. Kontrollpunkt »Brücke der Einheit«
West, Potsdam, Berliner Vorstadt, Glienicke Bridge, former "Bridge of Unity" checkpoint
→ NO / **NE**

André Kirchner

Geboren 1958 in Erlangen. Studium der Klassischen Philologie und Geschichte in München und Berlin. 1981 Umzug nach Berlin und Beginn der Stadtfotografie. 1984/85 Besuch der Werkstatt für Fotografie in Kreuzberg. Selbständig als Fotograf und Autor seit 1986, Schwerpunkt Stadtdokumentation und Architekturfotografie; eigenes Schwarzweiß-Labor und Projektraum für Ausstellungen. Lebt und arbeitet in Berlin-Schöneberg.

Born in Erlangen in 1958. Studied classical philology and history in Munich and Berlin. Moved to Berlin in 1981 and began urban photography. Attended the Photography Workshop in Kreuzberg in 1984–85. Has been a freelance photographer and writer since 1986 with a focus on city documentation and architectural photography; has his own black-and-white laboratory and a project space for exhibitions. Lives and works in Schöneberg in Berlin.

Öffentliche Sammlungen (Auswahl) / Public collections (selection)

Albertina, Wien / **Vienna**; Berlinische Galerie, Berlin; Kupferstich-Kabinett, Dresden; Lenbachhaus, München / **Munich**; Museen der Stadt Bamberg; Museum für Fotografie, Berlin; Die Neue Sammlung, München / **Munich**; Staatliche Galerie Moritzburg, Halle; Staatsgalerie Stuttgart; Stadtmuseum Berlin; Städtische Sammlung und Kunstmuseum Erlangen

Ausstellungen, Veröffentlichungen und Förderungen (Auswahl) / Selected Exhibitions, Publications, and Funding

2019
STADTRAND BERLIN 1993/94
Einzelausstellung / **Solo exhibition**; Berlinische Galerie, Berlin.

2018
Die West-Berliner Jahre – 1981 bis 1990
Einzelausstellung zum 8. Europäischen Monat der Fotografie / **Solo exhibition during the 8th European Month of Photography**; Haus am Kleistpark, Berlin.

2017
Bahnbogen 22 bis 79, Gleisdreieck Berlin 1964 und 2014
Ausstellung mit / **Exhibition with** Janos Frecot; Haus am Kleistpark, Berlin.

2015
Atelier Kirchner
Ausstellung; Eröffnung als Projektraum für Fotografie-Ausstellungen, Berlin.
Exhibition; Kirchner's studio in Berlin opens as a project space for photography exhibitions.

2013
Mitteilungen aus der Dunkelkammer
Textbeitrag zu Janos Frecot / **Essay for Janos Frecot's book** *Die Jahre mit der Kamera – Berlin 1964 bis 1966*, Nicolai Verlag, Berlin.

2012
30 Jahre Stadtfotografie Berlin – 1981 bis 2011
Einzelausstellung / **Solo exhibition**; Galerie im Rathaus Tempelhof & Tempelhof Museum, Berlin.

2009
OFFENER HIMMEL BERLIN 1990
Zum zwanzigjährigen Jubiläum des Mauerfalls 1989. Ausstellungsbeteiligung / **Contribution to an exhibition on the twentieth anniversary of the fall of the Berlin Wall**; Max Liebermann Haus, Berlin.
Katalog / **Catalogue**: *Szenen und Spuren eines Falls*.

East – Zu Protokoll
Ausstellungsbeteiligung / **Group exhibition**; Museum der Bildenden Künste, Leipzig.
Katalog / **Catalogue**; Steidl Verlag, Göttingen.

2007
BAUKÖRPER
Ausstellung / **Exhibition**: *Blicke, Passanten. 1930 bis Heute*; Albertina, Wien / **Vienna**.

2004
ERFRISCHUNGEN
Einzelausstellung / **Solo exhibition**; Galerie Pernkopf, Berlin.

2002
BERLINER MEISTERWERKE
Einzelausstellung / **Solo exhibition**; Galerie Pernkopf, Berlin.

1997
SCHWEBENDE LASTEN
Einzelausstellung / **Solo exhibition**; Städtische Galerie [Palais Stutterheim], Erlangen.

1995
BERLIN MITTE ZENTRIFUGAL
Ausstellung / **Exhibition**: *Über die Großen Städte*; Akademiegalerie im Marstall, Berlin.
Projekt und Katalog / **Project and catalogue**; NGBK [Neue Gesellschaft für bildende Kunst], Berlin.

1992
NACHT BERLIN-MITTE 1990
Ausstellung / **exhibition**: *Jahreslabor*; Berlin [Berlinische Galerie, Martin-Gropius-Bau].
Katalog der Photographie-Stipendiaten Berlins / **Catalogue of Berlin photographers on public grants.**

1990
RÜCKBAUTEN (Berliner Ecken 1988/89)
Fotografische Erörterung zum Phänomen der fehlenden Eckhäuser in West-Berlin / **Photographic notes on the phenomenon of missing corner buildings in West Berlin.**
Teil-Ausstellung / **Exhibition section**; Haus am Kleistpark, Berlin.

1986
HIER UND DORT
Erste Einzelausstellung / **First solo exhibition**; Galerie im Körnerpark, Berlin.

Monografien / Monographs

2019
Stadtrand Berlin / Berlin: The City's Edge 1993/94. Ausstellungskatalog / **Exhibition catalogue**; Berlinische Galerie, Hartmann Projects, Stuttgart.

2018
Die West-Berliner Jahre – Fotografien von 1981 bis 1990. Ausstellungskatalog / **Exhibition catalogue**; Edition Braus, Berlin. [Mit Unterstützung der Senatsverwaltung für Kultur, Berlin] / **[Funded by the Senate Department of Culture, Berlin]**

2012
Schauplatz Berlin – Der Aufbau der Neuen Mitte. Nicolai Verlag, Berlin.

2000
Dresdner Kampagne – Tagebuch des Fotografen. Verlag der Kunst, Dresden & Amsterdam.

1986
Hier und Dort. Europäische Stadtlandschaften und gesammelte Materialien zur Geschichte der modernen Fotografie. Ausstellungskatalog; Selbstverlag / **Exhibition catalogue; self-published.**